THOMAS HODGKIN
Letters from Palestine 1932–36

EDITED BY E.C. HODGKIN

Quartet Books
London   New York

First published by Quartet Books Limited 1986
A member of the Namara Group
27/29 Goodge Street, London W1P 1FD

Copyright © estate of Thomas Hodgkin 1986

British Library Cataloguing in Publication Data

Hodgkin, Thomas
Thomas Hodgkin: letters from Palestine
1932–36.
1. Palestine—History—1929–48
I. Title II. Hodgkin, E.C.
956.94'04'0924   DS126

ISBN 0–7043–2595–0

Typeset by M C Typeset Limited, Chatham, Kent
Printed and bound by Nene Litho
and Woolnough Bookbinding,
both of Wellingborough, Northants

Contents

Introduction

My brother Thomas was an unusual person and a most unusual colonial servant, as these letters will demonstrate. I believe his letters have the additional advantage of throwing a narrow but bright light on some aspects of the political and social life of Palestine between 1932 and 1936 – years which, with the great increase in Jewish immigration caused by the rise of Nazism, and the violent Arab reaction to it, were critical for the British mandate – and in particular on the character of the then High Commissioner, General Sir Arthur Wauchope. The letters also illumine the political development of an intelligent young man in the gloomy thirties.

Thomas Hodgkin was born in 1910 into what Noel Annan has called the 'intellectual aristocracy'. One grandfather, after whom he was named, was the banker and historian, author of *Italy and her Invaders*; the other was A. L. Smith, Master of Balliol. His father was a Fellow, later Provost, of Queen's College, Oxford. Cohorts of uncles, aunts and cousins (his father could claim eighty-four first cousins; he himself thirty-five) appeared on the horizon for shorter or longer periods, welcome or unwelcome, achieving usually some degree of success in their chosen occupation, or, less often, the clicked tongue and silence which betokened failure. But the privilege Thomas could count on was one of puritan tradition, not of wealth.

Thomas was sent to the Dragon School, Oxford, which he enjoyed, to Winchester, which at first he hated but later tolerated, and then with a scholarship to Balliol, which he loved. For four years, 1928–32, he played a leading part in the life of the college, in its societies and in games where enthusiasm rather than skill was demanded. He spoke at the Union, acted with the OUDS, and wrote frequently for the *Isis*. In the vacations he paid several visits to Greece, where, with friends, he walked great distances, slept rough, grew a beard, and was bitten by a supposedly mad dog on the Albanian border. He also managed to work hard, getting, to his intense chagrin, only a second in Mods, but eventually a good first in Greats.

This summary perhaps gives the impression of someone taking

advantage of a favoured childhood and youth to prepare for a conventional career, but such an impression would be misleading. Thomas's outstanding characteristic was an incurable romanticism, and this could blossom into eccentric behaviour which charmed or irritated according to the mood of the beholder. He had no use for moderation. He admired and cultivated a certain flamboyance, whether of action, dress or thought. He fell in love easily, and out of love painfully. He saw people as he thought they ought to be, rather than as they really were, and so judged them in superlatives. Opinions change, but characters do not, and the reader who finds Thomas writing that he has put aside romantic ideas and is now a realist should not be deceived. He never did.

When Thomas left Oxford the question had to be faced – what was to happen next? Everyone agreed that he had exceptional qualities of mind and character, and that any institution ought to count itself lucky to command them. But what institution? Magdalen was prepared to give him a Senior Demyship for a year so that he could write a thesis on the Roman government of Palestine, which was a part of the eastern Mediterranean he had long wanted to visit, and as Palestine came under the Colonial Office he thought he might as well apply for a job there. He was duly interviewed by the Director of Recruitment, Sir Ralph Furse, who, by one of those happy accidents which were more common in those days than they are now, was a friend of his parents – indeed, Furse's wife Celia, a daughter of Sir Henry Newbolt (another family friend), had been a bridesmaid at their wedding. No doubt this had nothing to do with the fact that shortly afterwards Thomas was, at the end of August 1932, called for a second interview at which he was offered a job – in the Gold Coast administration.

I well recall the emotions this offer aroused. It came at a time when we were as usual spending the summer holidays in Bamburgh Castle, and the Captain's Lodging was full of relations and friends. Their verdict was unanimous – for Thomas to bury himself in darkest Africa would be an appalling waste. It would mean his disappearing from civilization for who knows how long – that is, if he survived, for we had all read *The Unbearable Bassington* and knew about the short expectation of life on the Fever Coast.

As Thomas was later to achieve an international reputation as a historian of Africa, to play a not unimportant part in the Gold Coast's transition to an independent Ghana, and to enjoy the friendship of the apostle of independence, Kwame Nkrumah, there is a bizarre quality about a letter which he wrote at this time to one of the Balliol Fellows. 'Sligger' Urquhart, described by Harold Nicolson as 'most subtle of dons', watched carefully over the destinies of the more presentable of the College's undergraduates, and it is clear from Thomas's opening sentence, 'It was beautiful of you to write to dissuade me from Africa: I am dissuaded', that his advice had been the same as everyone else's. After explaining how he reached this decision, Thomas concludes: 'All my interests are here or in the Near East: the more I read history the more I am certain that it would be impossible to give up friends and sociabilities unless one could continue learning and forming relationships in that way – and one couldn't do that in the Gold Coast – a country with no past and no history – and no present either – only perhaps a promising future – and that at kindergarten level.' Thomas did not destroy this letter, but filed it away with the rest, probably amused at the contrast between his years of ignorance and years of enlightenment.

So the Gold Coast job was turned down, and Thomas was left to get to Palestine by the only way which seemed to offer itself – as unpaid assistant to Professor Garstang of Liverpool University for the next season at the excavations which he was then conducting at Jericho.

Extracts from some of the letters which Thomas wrote from Jericho start off the collection, and show how soon it became apparent that archaeology was not his métier. He had none of the skills which that profession requires. Bronze Age pots bored him. He considered Garstang fussy and narrow-minded and his French wife a terror. But there were compensations. He fell in love with the country, with the play of light over the mountains of Transjordan, with the flowers that shot up everywhere after the winter rains, and with the mysterious *wadis* leading up into the Judaean hills. He liked trying to organize gangs of labourers. He began to make friends and to learn Arabic.

After the Jericho dig closed down Thomas wandered for some weeks through Syria, nominally for the cause of his thesis but more for the pure pleasure of travel. When, at the end of July, he left to return to England, it was with a conviction that this was the part of the world which, somehow or other, he must come back to.

He had already while in Jericho made tentative enquiries about getting a job in the Palestine administration, though it seemed unlikely that after his cavalier rejection of the Colonial Office's first offer he would be given a second chance. But he was. In April 1934 a cadetship in the administration of the Government of Palestine became vacant. It was offered to Thomas, and he accepted rejoicing.

Britain had been awarded the Palestine mandate (a form of trusteeship under the League of Nations) at the San Remo Conference in 1920, and the first High Commissioner (equivalent of Governor in other territories administered, as Palestine was, by the

Colonial Office) was appointed in July of the same year. This was Sir Herbert Samuel, the Liberal politician. He was succeeded by Field-Marshal Lord Plumer and Sir John Chancellor, and in 1931 by Major-General Sir Arthur Wauchope.

Britain was required, by the terms of the mandate, to carry out the policy of the Balfour Declaration, which encouraged the idea of a 'national home' for the Jews in Palestine, but also to develop self-governing institutions and to safeguard 'the civil and religious rights of all the inhabitants of Palestine, irrespective of race or religion'. By 1934 there had been considerable progress as far as the first obligation was concerned, the Jewish population having risen from 55,000 in 1918 to about 250,000. No progress could be seen on the second obligation, and not much on the third.

Arab opposition to the 'national home' had been manifested from the outset. There had been bloody clashes in 1920 and 1921, and a far more serious outbreak in 1929 in which 133 Jews and nearly a hundred Arabs had been killed. 'There can, in our view, be no doubt,' the Shaw Commission, appointed to investigate the disturbances, reported 'that racial animosity on the part of the Arabs, consequent upon the disappointment of their political and national aspirations and fear for their economic future, was the fundamental cause of the outbreak.' Racial animosity, and consequent tension between the two communities, persisted.

Thomas must have known, when he landed in Palestine for a second time, that he was to be part of an embattled and unpopular government. Why then did he two years later repudiate with bitter indignation this government and all its works and declare himself a Communist? I used to think the explanation was that he had undergone a process of conversion by remote control. Just as Saint Ignatius, lying wounded in the castle of Loyola with nothing to read but the lives of the saints, saw with absolute clarity the obligation to devote himself to the service of Christ, so Thomas, alone in his small house in Ain Karim, reading Lenin on imperialism or Stalin on the colonial problem, came to the inescapable conclusion that empires were wicked and doomed and he himself was an actual cog in an evil machine. It is true that, as Thomas said in his Antonius Lecture, 'During the eight months I had spent in England I had been mildly exposed to Marxist ideas, mainly through the influence of a dear friend, Derek Kahn'[1], who kept him supplied with suitable literature

---

[1] Derek Kahn (he changed his name to Blaikie in 1933) had been head of the school at Rugby and came up to Balliol two years after Thomas. He was an excellent scholar, a good linguist, dark, neat and good-looking, urbane, amusing, and, appropriately

once he was back in Palestine, but the transition remains rather puzzling all the s me.

At Oxford Thomas had shown no particular interest in politics; they were not what undergraduates bothered about in the twenties. Certainly he would not have called himself a Socialist, though out of family tradition he might have admitted to being a Liberal. Socialism was a good subject for undergraduate argument, like free will or the existence of a Supreme Being, but only for a few, like Hugh Gaitskell, an element in the choice of a career.

The letters that Thomas wrote from Jericho are the sort which any bright graduate of his time and background might have written – admiring the scenery, finding the 'natives' picturesque and alternately charming or tiresome, making jokes about his fellow English men and women. There is little of the embryo revolutionary here. Of course, it has to be remembered that he was writing to entertain his parents, and devoted though he was to them he would, when writing, try to keep off serious subjects like politics and love affairs.

There is another consideration. Hitler became German Chancellor while Thomas was in Jericho. There is no reference to that event in his letters, and as there was no wireless set in Jericho, and no English-language papers except the *Palestine Post*, I don't suppose he gave it much thought. But by the time he came back to Palestine, in May 1934, the slide towards war was well under way. In October 1933 Germany walked out of the Disarmament Conference and left the League of Nations. In August 1934 Hindenburg died and Hitler became President as well as Chancellor. The churches were persecuted and 'people's courts' set up. In September 1934 the Nazis murdered Dollfuss, the Austrian Chancellor. The year 1935 saw Italy's invasion of Abyssinia, the failure of the League of Nations, and the Nuremburg laws against the Jews. Everything, and everyone, became willy-nilly politicized.

I think that what Thomas missed most was real friends with whom to talk things over. During the nine months he spent in England he had plenty of opportunities for discussions, in Oxford and London, in Manchester where he had a temporary job as lecturer on philosophy at the university, and then in Cleator Moor in Cumberland, where he worked as education officer with the unemployed. But in Jerusalem his colleagues were civil servants concerned with their families and their work. A lot of time was spent alone in his Ain Karim house,

---

enough, destined for the diplomatic service. After attending a Mosley meeting in Oxford Town Hall his interests switched to politics. He edited *Left Review*, but by the time war came had moved towards Christianity. He was killed in Burma in 1944 while serving with the North West Frontier Rifles.

reading and brooding. So there may have been some truth in my earlier theory about his conversion.

In a long letter to his father (pp. 50–1), trying to justify to his parents his decision to give up an academic career, he admits that his political ideas are undeveloped, but that working as a government servant ought to develop them, and at any rate prevent him from becoming a reactionary – both of which hopes were abundantly fulfilled. He goes on to explain that, although he supposes 'one can't be actively a socialist or even I suppose actively a pacifist as a government servant', one might be able 'to alter things' a bit.[1] 'It is not the glamour of the East particularly that makes me want this job, but the glamour of trying to put beliefs into practice, and of modifying beliefs by experience of what happens in practice.'

It was, in fact, experience rather than theory, emotion rather than logic, that modified his beliefs. No doubt he ought to have realized what he was letting himself in for before he signed on as a colonial servant. This would have saved him a lot of misery and his colleagues a lot of exasperation and extra work. But he didn't, and perhaps his excuse could be that, as Orwell has written, 'in order to hate imperialism you have got to be part of it'.

It took Thomas rather longer – nearly a year instead of a week – to find that he was no more cut out to be a government servant than an archaeologist. It was not that he was a bad administrator; in fact he was a very good one, as his years running the Delegacy for Extra-mural Studies at Oxford and as Director of the Institute of African Studies at Ghana University were to show, but that he found the routine of work in the Secretariat almost as boring as digging in Jericho. He buoyed himself up with the thought that it would all be different when he 'got into a district', and so it might have been (although he would have found plenty of bureaucracy there too), but unfortunately when he did get sent to Haifa it was too late. His mind had been made up and the Arab rebellion had started.

The fact of the matter is that Thomas was one of those people who instinctively take the part of the ruled against the rulers, and who are therefore made uncomfortable at finding themselves on the wrong side. Fielding Hall, Maurice Collis, George Orwell, Leonard Woolf (it is interesting that three of them should have served in Burma) are other examples of intellectual colonial servants who fitted awkwardly into the mould, though Woolf knew he was good at his job and was

---

[1]As Christopher Sykes has somewhat patronizingly conceded: 'Among Arabs of the unpolitical mass an official might sometimes have the agreeable impression that he was doing some good' (*Cross Roads to Israel*, London, 1965, p. 159).

tempted to stay on and rise to the top, and Collis managed to combine criticism with government service for over thirty years. To a greater or lesser extent such people are nagged by doubts whether the benefits an 'advanced' civilization confers on a subjugated one are not outweighed by the injustices and damage inevitably inflicted in the process. And, being intelligent and sensitive people, they are offended by the parochial and insensitive attitudes of many of those set in authority. They will come in the end to find the company of the 'natives' more rewarding than that of their colleagues and to identify with native grievances.

In Thomas's case the grounds for a repudiation of the system had been well prepared by a strong strain of almost Tolstoyan Christianity, perhaps inherited from his Quaker forebears, which he brought out with him. At Oxford this had taken the form of inviting tramps who accosted him in the street back to breakfast in his lodgings. In Palestine he would outdo Saint Martin, giving not half but the whole of his cloak to cover cloakless beggars, and the more such gestures shocked the conventional the better, it seemed, he was pleased. He described himself in April 1935 as 'a bad Anglican pretending to be a good Catholic', but I think this referred more to ceremony than belief, though it is interesting to notice how often he expresses regret at letting a Sunday pass without attending a church service – and this cannot have been recorded wholly to please his parents. He was much influenced by those he was with, and Eric Gill, David Jones and the Richmonds could all stand up intellectually for Catholicism, while the nuns at Tantur and Ain Karim were always there as reminders of the gentleness and humility of Christianity in practice. But as far as I know he never seriously contemplated 'poping'.

Thomas had always, for as long as I can remember, shown an intense dislike of privilege; even, it seemed at times, a preference for squalor. Walking with him through Bosnia in the summer of 1932 I complained about the almost continuous rain and suggested we should make for the sunny Adriatic. Thomas was reluctant to forego more nights in bug-ridden inns, and only agreed to go when he discovered that it was possible to travel fourth class on the train to Sarajevo. That, surely, would be a unique experience! (It was.)

So in Palestine. Though at first he rather enjoyed pomp and circumstance he increasingly came to feel that it was terrible to be paid so much money for doing so little. It was wicked to be driven in a big black car with a Union Jack fluttering on the bonnet instead of going by bus. It was absurd that people despised each other for reasons of race, class, birth, or lack of education. They must be made to see the absurdity of their views. Alas! the world being what it was Thomas was constantly frustrated in his efforts to persuade people to behave sensibly. It was not just that the Arab leaders affected to feel sorrow at the death of King George V (what on earth had they got to thank him for?) but wherever one turned one was constantly coming up against prejudice. Shortly after I arrived to stay with Thomas in November 1935 he invited some of the people of Ain Karim to a party in his house so that I could meet them – the two mukhtars, of course, the priest, the qadi, the schoolmaster,[1] and then, as we entered the village, we passed one of the bus drivers; he was bidden welcome too. And so on to the café proprietor and all the nice people in the café – they must all come. The party had hardly begun when a message came from the mukhtars: they regretted that after all they would be unable to attend. The reason was not explicitly stated but was plain enough: many of the guests were not the sort of people they met socially. To hell with them, was Thomas's reaction – let joy be unconfined!

I hope I have not made Thomas sound priggish, for this was the last charge that could be levelled against him. Life, he believed, was something to be enjoyed, and all he was trying to do was to batter down some of the obstacles which kept others from their natural right to enjoyment. He may have been to some extent a puritan in thought, but never in action. Good food, good wine, good company, particularly of pretty girls – these were things that it was never a waste to spend time and money on. They were a part of the beauty of living, and 'beautiful' was always his favourite epithet of praise – beautiful people, beautiful parties, beautiful letters received, beautiful memories, beautiful prospects for a reunion.

When Thomas returned to Palestine in 1934 it was therefore, as has been shown, to take up a job which above all others he wanted and which he hoped to make a success of. To begin with there were no clouds on the horizon. There were former friends to see again, like George and Katy Antonius and Stewart Perowne, and new friends like Austen Harrison and Robin Furness to be made. He began to put down roots. A house was rented, a horse bought so that he could hunt with the Ramleh Vale Jackal Hounds, and his parents were exhorted to come and pay a visit. He made a good journey on horseback with a

[1]This was Abdel Rahman Sinokrot, a dear friend with whom we both kept up a correspondence for some years until his premature death. There was an occasion, at a time when Thomas was working in the District Commissioner's office in Haifa, when, for some reason I have forgotten, Abdel Rahman, Thomas and I were shown over a destroyer lying in the harbour. As we said goodbye Abdel Rahman turned to our lieutenant guide and, to show his knowledge of English history, asked: 'Was this battleship made in England, or was it captured from the French?'

new Palestinian friend, Anwar Nuseibeh, later to be a minister in several Jordanian governments and Jordan's Ambassador to the Court of St James. He got to know Ben-Gurion and actors and actresses from the Habimah Theatre; in fact I think *The Dybbuk* was almost his favourite play – one he saw probably more often than any other. True, the work was duller than he had expected it to be, mostly shuffling files in the Secretariat, though never as dull as archaeology. Meanwhile there was much to be enjoyed in Jerusalem where people of all races could still meet happily for meals and concerts, and where there was always a good chance of the happy addition of familiar faces from England, like the painter/poet David Jones or Isaiah Berlin.

Then suddenly came a change of jobs, and with it the introduction to an absorbing new personality in the shape of General Wauchope. The High Commissioner's private secretary had been obliged to leave in a hurry under some sort of cloud, and a replacement was required immediately. I don't suppose that Wauchope said to the Chief Secretary 'Send me Hodgkin', but the two had met at Government House dinners, and presumably Wauchope had approved of what he saw, and was therefore prepared to accept the junior member of the Secretariat until a suitable permanency could be found.

So Thomas moved into Government House from the Austrian Hospice in the Old City which had hitherto been his Jerusalem base. He was not to stay there for very long – only three or four months in all – but this short time was long enough for Wauchope and Thomas to develop a marked respect and, indeed, a deep affection for each other.

On the face of it this was odd, because they had little in common. Wauchope was a regular soldier, commissioned into the Black Watch in 1896. He had been seriously wounded at the battle of Magersfonten in December 1899, again during the 1914 war in France and in Mesopotamia. He had commanded a Highland battalion at the Fall of Baghdad in 1917. He was, as the author of his entry in the *Dictionary of National Biography*, Bernard Fergusson, writes, 'a man of high ideals, cultivated tastes, tireless energy and considerable personal fortune. Hospitable and generous and without heirs, he expended the greater part of his fortune in munificence in Palestine; many projects and institutions, Jewish and Arab, owed as much to his purse as to his eager interest in agriculture, education, public health, Arab villages and Jewish colonies . . . There was almost no limit to his interests or to his inquisitive mind.'[1]

---

[1] King Abdullah's description of him is rather nice: 'He was like a burning flame, a man of zeal and energy and an experienced traveller.'

I think the fact must have been that Wauchope was rather bored. He was a bachelor, with no resident company except that provided by the obligations of his office. His ADCs tended to be standard Sandhurst products; most of his house guests were too anxious to please to be capable of stimulating conversation. 'Do you plan to go to the north?' he would ask, as he sat at the head of the dinner table, turning to the lady on his right, and being rather deaf, he would, like his distinguished predecessor, not stay long for an answer. But now he had for company someone who was respectful but not subservient, who was prepared to learn and to ask fundamental questions, who could talk intelligently about philosophy and literature (though not much about music, which was Wauchope's passion), and on whom he could try out some of the ideas about the country for which he was responsible that had been fermenting in his agile mind. Both men were honest, quick to detect humbug, and impatient to pursue what they felt to be the right course of action. Just because the premises on which they built were so different, it gave them a great deal of satisfaction to discover that the conclusions they reached were often not so dissimilar after all.[1]

Soon after Thomas took up his new duties Wauchope was due to go on leave. He would, naturally, be going to Scotland to shoot, and Thomas persuaded him to break his journey at the Northumbrian home of Helen Sutherland ('Aunt Helen'), Thomas's godmother and the patron of the arts and artists. Rather surprisingly Wauchope agreed to do this, and I happened to be staying at Rock Hall when he turned up. I recall him eating his breakfast porridge, like a good Scot, walking around the room, which slightly disconcerted his hostess who, in spite of her own Scottish origins, liked conversation to be static.

Thus a sort of private bond was formed between High Commissioner and private secretary, which was reinforced when Helen paid a return visit to Government House on her way to Kenya. How relations between the two men worked out in practice can be seen in Thomas's letters, and to these I would add an extract from his 1981 Antonius Lecture:

---

[1]Wauchope was prepared to tolerate as an amiable eccentricity his private secretary's habit of falling asleep, not just after dinner when the port and brandy were circulating, but even during dinner itself, or indeed at any time of the day, as more than one letter bears witness. Thomas suffered from narcolepsy, and throughout his life the times when he was asleep and awake often failed to coincide with those of other people, as many of his hosts and guests were to discover.

The morning parade.

The royal barouche (HE's Rolls) arrives, flying its Union Jack, HE, ADC, and I inside. I have the red box with the files HE has read – or hasn't – lots of bits of paper with his thoughts on various subjects. 'Now, Thomas, what's my programme for this morning?' I rummage. HE smiles benevolently. Here it is, thank God: '11 a.m. Dawe [Director of Agriculture]. 11.30 Men of the Trees, Pirie-Gordon. 12.00 Husain Khalidi, Mayor of Jerusalem, acting DC in attendance.' 'Now, Thomas, just find my notes about the Jaffa Gate – what is Johns [Inspector of Antiquities] up to there?' Oh dear! I saw them a little time ago. And what are all these bits of typescript? Top secret reports from Domvile [RAF intelligence], and secret service, go to no one but me. 'You'll be losing them in a moment – don't worry.' HE is in a gay and chaffing mood.

Out we get. The sentries at the Secretariat present arms. HE smiles at them – stops for chats on the way up the stairs and down the passage. First he must have Hall [J. Harthorn Hall, Chief Secretary] with him. I get the lady to bring her boss while I rummage in the red box so as to meet the next three demands for bits of vital paper.

And so the day begins. 'What's the little man like today?' 'Rather chirpy, I'm glad to say.' It ends, with luck, with pleasant talk of love, life, poetry, music, after snoozing through a dinner party for thirty. The ADC is mildly bored, but the loyalties of the Seaforth Highlanders keep him going till bedtime, and HE doesn't like to stay up after 11 p.m. as a rule.

Thomas's affection for Wauchope never wavered, and the rather remarkable letters Wauchope wrote about Thomas's resignation are given here as an Appendix. 'Dear Wauchope,' Thomas used to say in the last years of his life, 'Dear Wauchope, I would like to write something about him. I must get down to it.' But most unfortunately he never did.

Why was it that, in spite of an auspicious start to his career in Palestine, and of this even more auspicious turn of the employment wheel, Thomas should by the end of 1935, only a year after taking on the job, be talking about resigning? The explanation is, I believe, the emotional one to which I have already referred – the feeling, which every day's official business reinforced, that to be one of the rulers was morally wrong. Mussolini's invasion of Abyssinia brought war close to Palestine, and Thomas was one of those who saw the defeated Emperor Haile Selassie step on shore at Haifa to begin his exile. The Arab general strike, which began in April 1936 and led on to the general revolt, came after Thomas's decision to resign had been made, and served to convince him of the rightness of his decision. But it made his last few months in Palestine a pretty miserable time.

There were a few people in Jerusalem who could give Thomas's problems a sympathetic hearing. George Antonius was one; he himself had resigned from government service, and, though his reason for doing so had been pique at being passed over for deserved promotion, he had come to hold as low an opinion of the way in which the mandate was being administered as did Thomas himself. Austen Harrison, the government architect, builder of Government House and the Rockefeller Museum (and later of Nuffield College) was another. He and Wauchope disliked each other, which worried Thomas. Piers Hubbard, Harrison's assistant and later his partner, was a neighbour (he too had a house in Ain Karim) with an understanding ear, as had his wife Frances. I was available off and on for about six months until April 1936, and there were others whose names will come up in the letters.

It may be comprehensible that Thomas should have resigned from the Palestine Government, but it may yet be asked why it was necessary for him to combine this with proclaiming himself a Communist. (He did not actually join the party until after his return to England.) Many people of Thomas's age and with comparable backgrounds have explained what it was about Communism that attracted them in the 1930s. For Thomas, once a political attitude had suddenly become the most important thing in his life, there didn't seem to be any real alternative. You had to be on the left to defeat Fascism and war – that he took to be axiomatic. Social democracy, as represented by the discredited Labour Party, offered no solutions. It was easy by selective reading (e.g. the Webbs and Maurice Hindus) to persuade yourself that Communism was proving itself a successful system in one country and that this made 'Russia the happiest country to live in'. Besides, Russia made the right international noises, and Communists, wherever they were, seemed prepared to do something active instead of just talking. What a source of comfort to think you could rely on finding kindred spirits in every part of the world united by fraternal bonds in pursuit of the classless strife-free world. Above all, his belief in the effectiveness of Communism as a creed was reinforced when, in company with Dr Judah Magnes, President of the Hebrew University and tireless advocate of a binational state, he visited hunger-striking party members in Jerusalem gaol – Jews, Moslem and Christian Arabs, Armenians, thirty of them crowded into one cell. 'This seemed to me,' he wrote, 'the first firm evidence of the kind of anti-imperialist front in which I had come to believe . . . It was, so to speak, my Damascus road.' When he had been expelled from Palestine and was staying in Beirut he met some underground Syrian and Lebanese Communists, to whom he had been given introductions, and them he much admired. These experiences, rather than a careful study of history or weighing of the evidence, dictated Thomas's loyalties.

So here the letters are. It should be unnecessary to state that they were written without thought of publication, and so contain snap judgements and unconsidered asides which easily go down on paper when one is writing late at night, as Thomas usually was. Most of them were written to his parents, with whom he always had an affectionate relationship, though his abandonment of a promising career puzzled and distressed them, and some to me. He had other correspondents, of course, but, except for the few to 'Sligger' Urquhart, I have been unable to trace any surviving letters sent to them. I have also added a few passages from letters sent to me by Prudence Pelham, who accompanied us on a journey in Transjordan and Sinai, written after I had left Palestine and describing the last bizarre weeks Thomas spent there before being expelled. She was, in my opinion, the best letter writer since Byron and the most uninhibited speller since Shakespeare, so I have left her spelling as it is. But I have done a little tidying up in Thomas's own letters, dividing them into paragraphs, which he almost never did, and using rather more varied punctuation than the dash and the colon, which were the only stops he had much use for.

Thomas read through these letters in the last years of his life, and found much in them still of interest. I find them always graphic and often funny. It is my hope that readers for whom Palestine in the mandate period is a hazy or unknown chapter of history will find them of interest too.

E.C. Hodgkin

Editor's Note

Abbreviations used in the letters: RHH (father); DFH (mother); ECH (brother); FFU (Urquhart); PP (Pelham). I have in the notes on occasion, where shown, quoted from the Antonius Memorial Lecture, 'Antonius, Palestine and the 1930s', which Thomas presented at the Middle East Centre, St Antony's College, Oxford, on 17 June 1981. Many thanks are due to Thomas's daughter Elizabeth, and granddaughter Katherine, for their help in preparing these letters for publication. I am grateful to Hamish Hamilton for permission to reprint an extract from *In Search of History* by Vincent Sheean, (author's copyright 1935).

1932–33

Palestine is a country about the size of Wales ('or Vermont' came to be added when the Americans started to take an active interest in its fate). The 1931 census showed a total population of a little over a million, including 759,712 Moslems, 174,610 Jews, and 91,398 Christians. Jerusalem, the capital, had 95,000 inhabitants, Haifa 60,000, Jaffa and Tel Aviv between 50,000 and 60,000 each. Revenue and expenditure for the whole country were between £P3m. and £P3½m. The police force numbered 2,610, including 57 British officers and 650 British other ranks. By 1928 the garrison had been run down to a single squadron of armoured cars under RAF command, but the 1929 riots showed this to be a dangerously inadequate level, and by 1933 there were two infantry battalions in the country, one based on Jerusalem and the other on Haifa.

Palestine was therefore at this time a small country with a relatively small expatriate community. But because of its unique religious connotation there was in it a wide variety of peoples, permanent or transient, not to be found anywhere else. In 1933 the urbanization and industrialization which now disfigure the land had made only small beginnings; the fortress blocks with which Zionism has encircled the Holy City were not there. The walled Old City of Jerusalem was still divided into four quarters, Moslem, Christian, Jewish and Armenian, and in spite of periodic outbreaks of violence the communities could still live peacefully side by side, as they had done for centuries.

The reaction of one visitor who arrived in Palestine at this time, and one whom Thomas came to know, Vincent Sheean, the American journalist, is worth quoting:

> *Jerusalem enchanted me from the beginning by the compactness and precision with which it fulfilled its physical tradition: the Mount of Olives exactly here, the valley of Jehosaphat exactly there, the temple of Solomon (Mosque of Omar) exactly opposite, the Mount of Calvary (Church of the Holy Sepulchre) just up the way, all as marked and visible to the naked eye as are the raised surfaces of a relief map or the bright, sober outlines of a landscape in Italian primitive painting . . .*

3

The Austrian Hospice, where I lived, had a flat roof, and on hot nights it was a particular pleasure to lie there and inspect the floor of heaven, thick inlaid with patines of bright gold – thicker inlaid, and nearer to the view, than in other places . . .

There were mosques everywhere, and Islam's call to prayer haunted the still air of an evening, so that I could scarcely see a photograph of the roofs of Jerusalem afterwards without hearing the long cry of the muezzin as a part of it.

That was, probably, the first impression I received of Walled Jerusalem in the early days: that it was an Arab city. It was as Arab as Cairo or Baghdad, and the Zionist Jews (that is the modern Jews) were as foreign to it as I was.

TO RHH   JERICHO
29 DECEMBER 1932

I mean to leave this hotel as quickly as I can which is I think the horridest that I have ever stayed in counting even the sordid Khans of Albania and Greece: it is pretentious and dirty. The company is cosmopolitan – American, French and a gross old Armenian Monophysite bishop who plays dominoes all day long with the grovelling innkeeper – the atmosphere of squalid tripperiness that is most out of place in this lovely country: for it is lovely though Jericho is by no means the plum. Jericho loses scenically by being a sudden patch of extraordinarily fertile country, and is therefore overgrown with ugly dusty banana trees and has a look half of an unsuccessful jungle, half of an overgrown allotment. It ought to be very beautiful – for there are plenty of orange trees too and now and then an exquisite smell of jasmine: I think it must be its lowness that makes it rather sordid.

Once you get out of the town it's beautiful – the mound where old Jericho stood and the tombs where we work have a splendid view of the valley up and down – the silver Dead Sea – the hills of Transjordan with their rifts shining in alternate light and shade – the hills above Jerusalem when the sun sets and black clouds of rain gather sometimes, but we escape the storm. I mean to go on Sunday to Jerusalem and buy a tent. It will probably be a saving in the long run – over six months will save a lot in hotel bills – the nights are still warm and I think are warm here all the year round. I can work in the

4

evenings in the workroom of Garstang's[1] house – keep my big luggage in Jerusalem – so that it will be easier to keep tidy – the one essential thing in a tent I should think. I hope you think it a wise plan.

The digging so far is most pleasant. On two days' experience I should say that archaeology was a good career: it's reasonably simple and unconstructive work so far which is just as well – on the tombs – Richmond[2] and I each have one. The Professor potters between them – looks at our notes – sits down on our sherds and jumps into our shafts.

[1]Professor John Garstang. Director of the British School of Archaeology in Jerusalem 1919–26. In charge of excavations at Jericho 1930–36. Married Marie Bergès of Toulouse.

[2](Sir) John Richmond. Archaeologist and diplomat. After war service with Special Operations Executive in the Middle East joined the Department of Antiquities of the Palestine Government, transferring to the Foreign Office. Ambassador in the Sudan and Kuwait.

TO DFH   JERICHO
2 JANUARY 1932 [3]

As for news I am chiefly busy with work, for archaeologists seem to work from 7 till 7 and then only to stop because they fall asleep. Also I am learning Arabic I hope – at any rate this charming chap coaches me in the evenings at it – this Christian Arab surveyor called Bulos.[1] Also I am trying to move out of this hotel and hire for the moment a house – only £4 a month – two little rooms and an angelic little green verandah looking immediately over Elisha's fountain. The tent the Garstangs are so unenthusiastic over that I thought it better to move into it by degrees – anyhow it would have to come from Egypt.

Then with a faithful servant to cook me, say, an egg at breakfast and a hot meal for supper – all very simple – but clean and pleasant and of my own choosing (not 3 or 4 bad meaty courses a meal as here) – it will be delightful.

I spent yesterday and last night in Jerusalem. But food and bath were the centre of the day more than anything. Monuments on the whole disappointing, though lovely crusted Norman work in the Holy Sepulchre. Taken round by Richmond, a Papist, so one had to be careful not to say rude Protestant things about relics and suchlike.

Eastwood[2] to dinner – Nicky's[3] friend – a nice sparkling fellow – a pleasant loosening of one's tongue – which tends rather to run in a Middle Bronze Age groove here: though the workmen are charming – one a Druse, who fought with them in the rising and escaped from the French. I am getting very good at Arabic conversation, which is rather stylized, and like this –

HOTEL PORTER: I only get £3 a month for working 18 hours a day. Alas!

I (*sternly*): Allah is merciful.

HOTEL PORTER: Allah is merciful, but £3 is very little for a poor man.

I: Allah the merciful is the protector of the poor.

H.P.: Blessed be Allah the Protector – a poor man *wiv* a wife and family.

I: Blessed be Allah the increaser of families –

H.P.: Wiv an old mother takes half his earning –

I: Blessed is he to whom Allah spares the mother –

H.P.: Happy and blessed. But touching this matter of money –

I: May Allah increase you with riches. (*I go*)

[1]Bulos el-Araj, a Ramallah Christian.

[2]Christopher Eastwood. Eton and Trinity College, Oxford. Private Secretary to the High Commissioner for Palestine 1932–34; later to Lord Lloyd and Lord Moyne when Secretaries of State for the Colonies.

[3]Nicolete Binyon, daughter of Laurence Binyon, poet and Keeper of Prints and Drawings at the British Museum. Oxford friend of T (see p.26).

TO DFH   [JERICHO]
9 JANUARY 1932 [3]   MONDAY

An archaeologist's life is a hard one - he seems to have very little time left for a rational life. When he's not measuring he's cleaning or sketching or scratching or smelling the black air of tombs. People don't seem to think of what an unintelligent and what a dangerous life being an archaeologist is – 'the intrepid archaeologist' sounds comic – but when it isn't a tomb you're afraid is going to collapse it's a wall you expect to give way. Today it was the second, working alternately at the top and bottom of a thirty-foot drop, afraid either of falling over backwards or bringing it all down on top of you. No real danger because the workmen know their business and wouldn't work where they were frightened.

The Bishop of Rochester[1] has come, and is very fine, very much of an Anglican bishop – rowed in his college boat but has put on 3 stone since – lost half of one of them on a sweatwalk with Richmond and me yesterday – dresses like an Arab (the top half of him), the bottom half like a Tommy. His conversation is just him talking – quite interestingly – either of Rochester (his present see) or of Hereford (his last one) or Winwick (the one before). The time between when he stroked the New College Eight to be head of the river and when he became a bishop is a blank. I think they must have made him one at once because he was so clearly bound to be. This [sketch] is him controlling his 10 natives. He was allotted 10 by Garstang – Richmond, 25 – I, 4 – a very reasonable ratio of merit, though I am determined to beat the Bishop before I have done. He kept losing his men – he never seemed to have more than 9, often only 8, and kept counting them like an anxious hen or a teased French master with all his pupils continually pleading nose-bleeds and going out of the room. Indeed it is a little like being a schoolmaster being an archaeologist, but in a school that is a cross between Borstal and a kindergarten.

It was a little frightening beginning my first bit of proper digging – tomb-digging was just getting objects out of tombs and doing it methodically. This was much trickier, and the Professor had gone to bed with a cold, poor thing. To be confronted with a mound like this [sketch] – about 27 feet high with a bit of wall at the top, and a bit of another wall having no relation to it at the bottom, to find something, anything, useful, and if possible not to break anything. The trouble is that there's nothing much to find but brick and brick looks very much like any other sort of earth, not, unfortunately, like Keble; it would have been an enormous help to the archaeologist if it had been, though I suppose Keble for all its purple and green will return to its native mud in the end.

I am now rejoicing in my little house, and all my books at hand on the table, and my cook sometimes at hand in the kitchen, and oranges and figs and olives, and simple plenty in general – the kind of *horrida quies* that the Roman poets used to luxuriate in when they went to the country. Elisha's fountain streams outside – the moon shines on to my balcony.

[1]Martin Linton Smith. Rector of Winwick 1917–20; Bishop of Hereford 1920–30; Bishop of Rochester 1930–39.

TO RHH   JERICHO
16 JANUARY 1933

A good walk yesterday (Sunday) boring into the mountains up the great carved ravine the Wadi Kelt – little hermitages cut out of the rock along the way – great rock basins at the bottom that become beautiful deep pools when the water comes. We walked along the bed and the water-smooth rocks, with the dark crumbling rock closing like jaws overhead, and a goatherd making the hollows of the stream re-echo with his pipe, which he played beautifully, a repeating pattern of about five notes – like Randall's[1] flute. He and his goats against the hillside looking Greek and not Palestinian – and happy to be reminded of that country.

The life is a thoroughly happy one – enough work to take up the body of the day and more, which at its best is most interesting and occupies all one's intelligence, at its worst is pretty dull and occupies none of it, but then one can always look at the mountains and think of possible answers to possible questions in All Souls general papers. And I think I might make an archaeologist, though I don't think a very good one – I haven't enough natural observation; I don't easily see what fitted on to what – a criticism grandfather used to make. I remember his saying at Bamburgh in 1923 (was it?) 'Really for a person of intelligence you are extraordinarily unobservant.' Though I'm sure that can be overcome largely if one learns what it is that one's expected to observe – what sort of things one ought to be looking out for. But I'm not altogether satisfied with Garstang. I think he's being a good deal less use to me (so far) than I to him. He has rather the Pecksniffian quality of *using* one – and he doesn't much bother to teach, though I have had lately about four

8

days with 10 men or so working down to early Bronze Age rooms and clearing them, so that one can't help learning how to cut to find walls and suchlike. Yet he neither much gives advice about the technique of digging, nor much listens to my constructive suggestions (carefully thought out, even if often fatuous) about how the rooms may have gone and what the history may have been. It would be a help to have a person who listened and told you when you were fatuous and when reasonable. I may be wronging old Garstang but he seems so far to think that the only part of archaeology that can be taught is patience. That, though valuable, one doesn't come to a Professor of Archaeology to learn. Don't bother about this for it may be like my stomach-ache quite momentary. He may improve and take more interest. He is kindly and does not I think dislike me, but his nature is wholly opposite: outside archaeology he seems to have few intelligent interests – the difference I think between Liverpool and Oxford. And I rejoice to think how lively and interested and interesting almost all Oxford dons are in comparison.

But I may be being impatient. If I am not I had better tell him after a while that his teaching isn't satisfactory – politely. But I'll wait to hear what you say. As long as I have work that requires some intelligence I am happy. That I think one has a right to demand – after all one comes to offer labour that isn't altogether unskilled. I'll write another letter about the domestic side in a couple of days. How the Bishop came to dinner and was a bore – How a Druse came for a light snack and was delightful – How glorious the sunrises are and how bright the moon – all the pleasant exciting things that are really the substance of my life here, which I seem to have left out of this dull letter.

[1]Randall Swingler. Winchester contemporary and enduring friend of T. A 1930s convert to Communism, novelist and poet. Talented amateur flautist.

TO FFU   C/O PROFESSOR GARSTANG
29 JANUARY 1933   JERICHO

This is a long-delayed letter. I would have liked to write half-a-dozen to you already, but an archaeologist's life is a drudging one, on his feet from sunrise to sunset in the field, and then more fearful planning and recording till seven at night and then he falls asleep. It is a gross illiterate life, but very pleasant as a change from books, to stand with the sun on the back of your neck watching the clouds drift across the Dead Sea, down from the mountains of Transjordan, trying to control forty Arabs who are about as uncontrollable as forty preparatory schoolboys, with the additional difficulty of hardly being able to talk their language, so that one's in a worse position even than a French master.

But they are warm-hearted and forgive you if you become overbearing; a splendid mixture – a core of very ugly deca-dent Jerichans, fine handsome ones from Nablus, about a quarter Druses (these charming), a few nice soft Egyptians, a lonely tall string-shaped man from Italian Somaliland who lies apart from the others pining for Italian Somaliland, and has full lips and a pointed chin like Akhenaten, and, most charming of all, an exiled Albanian, who has been exiled from Turkey too for deserting after the war, and then exiled from Syria for joining the Druse rising. He lives now with the Sultan and other Druse exiles at Kerak. He escorted us there the other day – [with us] a charming old bore the Bishop of Rochester (do you know him, he was at Hereford; his entire conversation is of the antiquities of Rochester and Hereford – but most lovable) – a glorious castle, though I was distressed to be told that all the pieces I admired most were Saracen; one must accustom oneself to thinking that Saracens could build well I suppose. Still there is a great deal of admirable Crusader work left – enormous vaults, a great unbroken pile of a north wall above the fosse – a good fosse – and finest of all the telouse (a word I have only just learnt and don't know how to spell; but you will be able to put it right for me) swinging all along the east face – with a great black tower rising up out of it. We must go again when you come, and you will tell me all about Reginald and Saladin.

Transjordan is a glorious country full of unnoticed pieces of Roman temples and tombs and theatres – you really feel Roman civilization living there as you don't (I think) among the show monuments in Italy – they've had too continuous an existence since. But here you think of the Romans as having only left the country yesterday, suddenly: we drove along the pilgrim road from Amman to Catrani and saw quite often beside the road these Ozymandias-like trunkless stylobates.

You are coming aren't you? – you must. I'd love to travel round with you. I had meant to begin to travel in April or late March myself and shake off the dust (literally too) of the Bronze Age – and think about Romans for a change instead of these measly Canaanites.

I had a pleasant dinner with Christopher Eastwood, at the New Year's Ball when the English were affectionately throwing bread at one another and at the Arabs, and no one was throwing bread at the Jews; he gallantly threw bread only at the Jews, and so soothed their feelings and avoided a national catastrophe. That is the way high diplomacy works. I live happily, not talking much to anyone, spending the day in the sun with the Arabs, and what of the evening I can stay awake for reading Crusader history quietly. I have a small house to myself, white picked out with yellow and green, 2 rooms and a kitchen, and a broad airy passage, and better than all a sunny balcony.

TO DFH   JERICHO
30 JANUARY 1932 [3]

I won't do anything precipitate about Garstang – in fact I shan't sack him: I mean to stay with him till the end of the time which is before the end of March, and, if I decide that I'm still learning too little, tell him so. But he's been better lately; he just is wholly self-centred, and a little infatuated with having a lot of men under his control – depending on him wholly.

Still it's all seeing life, these sly employers. And it is learning archaeology of course – it can't help being that. But I don't think it will be profitable to work in the field after March. My thesis for Magdalen does mean knowing the country thoroughly as well as reading, and anyhow you can read anywhere, and only know the country in the country. I think to spend less than 2 months travelling here and a certain amount in Transjordan and Syria would be a pity. It's not only that I think travelling fun; but you must start with topography – you must know why the provinces were the shape they were, why the shape altered, why some were ruled by procurators some by native princes, and to do that you have to look at them. At the same time I can work in a secondary way at Crusader topography. Again it would be a waste, being here, not to make that as strong a suit as I can – in view of All Souls partly – partly of knowledge in general and the bettering of one's mind.

Therefore only a fortnight's Crowfoot:[1] there's no room in the year for more. And as I say he doesn't want me – has 14 helpers, mostly young women, and has rather finished with Roman stuff and is more at Israelite. You suggest that I should come home in July, but I think I really ought to stay longer if it doesn't get too hot to work properly – partly for the Arabic, if there was ever the chance of a Colonial Service job. I could go on learning it, and read history for All Souls, come home in September, perhaps meet you for that month in Germany and work there. But I do think I ought to stay in this country for as long as is reasonable. It will show 'them' (from Magdalen to the Colonial Office) that I am serious.

I've just been having Bulos – my best friend, the Christian Arab, to dinner – what I thought a lovely meal – bacon, eggs and potatoes fried together, soup, cake, red cheese, oranges. He was a little conventional about eating breakfast foods at dinner though. He talked fierily about Arabic poetry. I was wondering if they could have any love poetry as they didn't seem to have much love. I can't see how in a country where you buy wives women can be the centre of poetry; it's largely their remoteness that makes them so in England. But he seemed to think that they were. But it all seems tremendously formal. You have to have learnt not only grammar and syntax but rhetoric and logic before you can write a sentence, and they are all interdependent. You never mention a woman's name; there are fixed names that must be used – and fixed Devils of inspiration. I must learn a lot more Arabic so as to read their poetry – I imagine at its best sensuously descriptive like the Song of Solomon – a richly metaphorical language – to an exaggerated amount. Meanwhile I am still puzzling at the letters – almost sure of them.

Very sleepy. This letter has to go on to you early this morning – a pleasant crescent moon on the hills with the old one in its arm looking like a walnut made into a boat with thin sides. Hard to settle down to work again for all of us after the

5 days holiday we've just had: the feast of the year – Beiram. Our Kerak expedition was very successful in spite of the rain and the cold. It was a good expedition largely because of the matiness of Richmond and the Bishop and the extreme beauty of the castle; I feel I know double the amount of Crusader history having seen it. We stayed with a Latin Priest who bit his beard, talked beautiful Arabic, but very bad Liverpool English. We argued about Thomas Aquinas and the imagination. He was all wrong but very lively and of Irish blood, admirable for Arabs I should think. Ach I must sleep. It was an 8-hour drive and we only just got through the Transjordan mud – the road becomes soup. But that all made it more of a holiday. Then the other two days in Jerusalem, writing the novel mostly – even dancing, after dinner with the Richmonds – *Blue Danube* with daughters of Commandants of Police and Chief Commodores. Not my line a bit, but interesting to see for a change.

Expenditure for month:

House	£4–5
Cook	£3½
Groceries	£4
Fruit, meat, etc.	£3
all local things & cook's food	

[1]John Crowfoot. Director of Education in the Sudan 1914–26. Director of the British School of Archaeology in Jerusalem 1927–35. T's future father-in-law.

TO DFH   JERICHO
4 FEBRUARY 1933   SATURDAY EVENING

Tomorrow blast it the High Commissioner is coming – which spoils Sunday as a walking day. But I will not be organized into a picnic to the Dead Sea which threatens. We all see quite enough of one another in the week (as archaeologists); I shall stay on the balcony of my little house and read and write and watch the life beneath.

The Professor is as conscientious about not talking shop on Sundays as he is about talking it at every meal in the rest of the week – so chat is strainedly gay. Tomorrow I mean to beard him. I'll suggest going on working full-time to the end of the month, and then half-time through March, so that I could get at least three hours reading a day done. If he doesn't like that he ought to take more seriously *his* obligation to teach me. There is really so little time for all this glorious country. But I shall certainly not let him down if he wants me; it is only the belief that he doesn't particularly want me (inferred from the fact that I have to make work for myself or bully him to give it me) that makes me feel it a waste of time to go on giving him all my time to the end of March. But I shall be gentle. I think he has the kind of beard that is beardable – gentle if you really force a serious human issue. We'll see. I shall not be precipitate though.

The Emir Abdullah came over for the afternoon with a lot of his wives – himself dressed in bright orange, they in coal black. He is unhappy because he hasn't got enough money to go to England with, which he longs to do. If he was Charles of course he would just put on Ship Money or Tonnage and Poundage. In the Turkish times he would have confiscated the estates of the 20 principal citizens and exiled or beheaded them, like Ahab. Now with the British Hampden at his gates he has to govern constitutionally and simply pines.

TO RHH   JERICHO
8 ? FEBRUARY 1933

I find to my shame that I don't know how to work my own primus – a stupid position to be in – so I can't wash my feet tonight as I had meant to. I have simply blackened my hands to no purpose. Even my silly cook can work primuses, but he's gone home.

It's 10 in the evening – a lovely full moon – I've just been out in it; we are all opening like buds but with the sun and moon not with the rain. The rain we are sick of and it looks as if it has stopped – off and on for a week – no warmth no gay shirts no pleasure in out-of-door work and not much work anyway. Even the land and the fellahin seem almost satisfied. All the ground is mud and pools – an unknown waterfall has broken out down a cleft in the Mount of Temptation opposite. We shall soon be like Port Meadow and up to our necks in it: it's splendid for the wells and crops but apparently

too late for the cattle; most of them have died already they say
– no fodder.

Now even the deserts have clothed themselves with grass.
The wilderness on the way to Jerusalem has covered itself
with a thin green plumage, still showing rather naked,
though, like a newly born bird, but a glorious emerald. Now
the sun has come, shone through this afternoon – drove the
clouds in piles up into Transjordan, and looks promising.

Little news. This life moves with an even pace like school,
small and restful. I regret that I do so little reading. But
Arabic goes better; I am beginning to understand the
structure a little – and to learn the grammar properly. I shall
beat it in the end. I sit with four grammars and a note-book
learning, or have my Arab in to talk to me. But as a rule we
get interested in the matter of our conversation and break
into English.

A beautiful procession the other day. A feast – real pomp –
flags – darwishes grimly stuck with knives to cut themselves
and one another with – everyone joining in – hollow kettle
drums – the damsels with the timbrels going after. A whole
body of them going to spend the day in revel up at a spring
nearby, in glorious gay clothes.

Reconciled to Garstang. Talked to him seriously on
Monday. Great thing to be firm with one's employers. He's
been very gentle since, much more explanatory and helpful,
giving me more instructive work. It's fearful how far a little
gentleness goes though. I am now prepared to take back
almost all the ill I ever said of him – he certainly has a warm
kind nature, but a bit lazy about using it.

The Governor or whatever he is came and looked at the
dig on Sunday – told Garstang apparently that I wanted to go
into the Administration. It's nice of Furse[1] to have taken the
trouble to tell them here. He asked Garstang what sort of a
fellow I was. I trust he didn't too much believe him. It was
rather like Herod noticing a likely looking Jew in a
chain-gang at the stone quarries. If the Colonial Service are
really taking this seriously all the more reason for staying here
as long as possible and learning Arabic as well as possible. I
couldn't get a better job for the time being at any rate. I feel I
ought to be pulling strings or something; but I obviously
can't. It will turn out as it will.

[1]Sir Ralph Furse. Director of Recruitment at the Colonial Office 1931–48.

TO DFH   [JERICHO]
14 FEBRUARY 1933

In five weeks I ought to be able to get away I think – only three or four more actual digging. Not that it's not a pleasant life, but a stupefying one – saps thought – and the standing and worrying round all day is tiring without being exercise. I noticed as I bathed yesterday that I was obviously fatter – a Titian stomach and no longer a Mantegna one. Nor did a gallant walk from here to Jerusalem through Saturday–Sunday night help much.

I went with young Richmond, pleasant in his silence and his Popery, friendly and intelligent. He takes too long a stride though, being 6½ foot high about – 'tallest but one in Jerusalem' they say (sounds like a Philistian boast). He meant it to be full moon, but all the way to the end the moon was cloud-wrapped; it was clear enough to see though. I took my whip against wild animals – alas we saw none wilder than quite tame barking dogs – he his cudgel.

But noises of jackals, owls and curlews all the night; and a good dawn just below Bethany, the first red striking the young grass tufts, and a golden line over Transjordan. I was very tired by then as we had hardly rested – had had only two hours' sleep – and a tiring day behind. But it was good to arrive like a pilgrim and not a tourist for once, all the more realistic for the accursed Jericho nails which began to come through my feet. We started at one and arrived at half-past seven – for a glorious breakfast – beginning with porridge and *cream* – my first I think since England, or Trieste anyhow. I'm glad to have done it – but not again. It must look quite far even on the map – at least 21 miles by our road.

Jericho smelt scented and splendid as we left it – a hot perfume; good to get into the cooler inspiring air of the hills, and eventually find a fierce wind against us, as we came across the Mount of Olives. The whole way deserted, not a village till Bethany, only a ruined Crusader fortress and the half-way inn where the Good Samaritan put the man who fell among thieves. Thieves go to bed at nine o'clock now in this country; the man who fell among them ought to have known that. Dusk is the time that they hold up cars, but in quite a quiet way, and then ride off and hide in the wilderness.

Slept most of the day in Jerusalem. Walked around the town a little at sunset to see the red clouds pile on the hills. I tried to go to church at the Holy Sepulchre but kept losing my way to it, and by then it was dark. Ended by dining with the Richmonds – a charming family, especially the father – Director of Antiquities here – thin, like a knife, always ill, an architect, aesthetically cadaverous cheeks and nervous fingers – incisive talk – far the cleverest of the family and an artist. He very kindly suggested my living in a tent in their garden and taking meals with their family while I lived in Jerusalem, which would be cheap, and not dirty with baths. But I think one ought to be independent, get more work done, and other reading. It might be a danger to be too sociable. But helpful to have friends.

Garstang like a lamb after my talking-to. I really often like him – he is human and pathetically fond of hens, but Hogarthianly awful when he jokes. Domestic comfort is his aim. It shows how nice and polite I must be to them that Mrs Garstang suggested (if I wanted to sack my cook) my taking meals with them – another hit – but not a temptation like the Richmonds. Anyhow independence I think is worth keeping.

TO DFH   JERICHO
27 FEBRUARY 1933

After a week more the digging stops – tho' I fear at least three weeks more of office work, and awful packing of pots. I trust that Mrs G thinks both Richmond and me unfit to pack them – we have broken one apiece (she wept at mine – very embarrassing – showing lack of proportion. But she softened quickly afterwards – these hysterical Latin races.) Thin new moon today; so I trust that I shan't do much more than see this moon out here. Though I shall be sad to leave my little house – happy to leave my little cook. I have sacked him twice in the last week, but neither of his successors turned up so he still stays. The second, at least, called romantically Ishak (the part Devlin[1] played in *Hassan*) came and looked very much the man about town with a small military moustache and a long white trembling face; but he would only come for five months. So gross Saleh will stay I suppose. He cooks me nice soup every evening, and does liver a treat. (I have two proper courses for dinner always – soup, meat, then cakes, figs, oranges, cheese, ginger biscuits – whatever there is. So I live pretty richly, and add a course or two when visitors come.)

Rather a week of visitors. Beginning the week with the disturbance of our circle with the Jewish minx, Judithe. Then I had this Arab youth, minor inspector-of-antiquities, Baramki,[2] to stay for a couple of nights – brought his own bed – delightful – *allegro vivace* – a bit wild in thought having picked up (as intelligent well-bred natives do) a little Darwinism and a little humanism and a smack of out of date higher criticism, and then mixed them haphazard, and let the confusion resulting do for a philosophy and a religion. But his odd principles didn't harm him much. Anyhow, he had a car and drove me and Richmond both nights he was here to the Dead Sea. They sat and talked on the beach – I looked at the stars and went to sleep.

Then for the weekend I had the Keeper of the Museum, called Iliffe,[3] for a night, full of interesting ideas, Roman and Socialist. We had a good walk in the sun up a lot of mountains; he a good fierce walker – the kind that always wants to go up rather than round – and up over this wilderness under this sun means sweat and stumbling over a thousand ill-placed stones. We could eat little but oranges. Not much new country but relating old bits; a few green cracks in the hills where scarlet anemones grew like single drops of blood – like the meadows near Marathon; the only wild flowers so far except meadow ones here, like vetches and poppies. I'll look near Bethlehem next Sunday. Ended by coming down the gullies of the Wadi Kelt again, greener and more pleasantly overgrown now, more like Arizona, with all its canyons, and suddenly a great Byzantine waterway on six fine stone arches high across the dry bed.

[1]William Devlin in the 1931 OUDS production of *Hassan*. T had been Second Gentleman in the 1929 production of *Othello* in which Valentine Dyall played Othello. Devlin subsequently became a professional actor of note.

[2]Dr Mitri Baramki. Later excavated the Umayyad Palace near Jericho.

[3]J.H. Iliffe. Keeper of the Archaeological (Rockefeller) Museum in Jerusalem.

TO DFH   JERICHO
22 FEBRUARY 1932 [3]

This horrid mistiness goes on – sunshine but you can't see
Transjordan, and thickness of atmosphere that makes
everyone cross. The thickening and thunderstorm atmosphere began spiritually too on Sunday with the dropping into
our mill-pond of a little French milliner, really a little French
Assyriologist, half Jew, chic, Parisian to the pinks of her
finger nails, rustling black silk, at least half her arm exposed.
No one but a Frenchwoman I think could combine being
such a bluestocking with being such a minx. The scandal of
her is that she was turned out of Jericho last season after
working here for a month or two by that harpy Mrs Garstang
because she went for a sunset walk unchaperoned with the
poor Professor. There's a Fielding sort of story for you: very
much the same sort of thing happened to Mr & Mrs
Towwouse in *Joseph Andrews*, except that the Professor was of
course as innocent as a lamb, which no Fielding character
ever was. His wife a real serpent though often (and always so
far, for the last month, to me) with the manners of a dove.

Anyhow the poor young woman arrived here on Sunday
with a *thèse* and the backing of Baron Rothschild to work for a
fortnight, but thanks to steady rudeness has gone in three
days. Comic, though rather sordidly so, to hear the Professor
repeating to her the arguments that he had just learnt up
from Mrs Garstang against her staying in Jericho; while she
hovered like a female vulture just outside the door, pretending to mend the pottery, and shouting insults to the Professor
in English (which the young woman is supposed not to
understand) if she thought he was flagging, or becoming too
polite. Bulos, my Arab friend, was ordered to keep a watch on
her while she took notes 'for fear that she would steal the
pottery'. Pathetic to hear him warning us against her and
begging us to discourage her the place. I frankly encouraged
her it as fresh blood and fresh conversation is just what I most
want. But they won as I knew they would.

Three copies of that awful essay book[1] have arrived. I shall
burn two – give the third to Richmond to burn. I'm
comforted by Sigle[2] liking mine (read the proofs): certainly
it's better than what I've read of the others, but they are

mostly simply childish, formless in construction, peevish in matter. Lionel[3] is the only redeeming companion. Heaven help Oxford – no wonder the press think us a decadent university.

[1]*Red Rags: Essays of Hate from Oxford.* Edited by Richard Comyns Carr and published by Chapman and Hall in 1933, it contained eighteen essays by former undergraduates and undergraduettes who had been invited 'to write upon an object of his (or her) peculiar detestation'. The result was said (by the blurb writer) to be 'a series of attacks upon rotten conventions and modern fads, narrow prejudices and false enthusiasms'. Some of the contributors, such as Derek Walker-Smith, Robert Speaight, Quintin Hogg, John Boyd-Carpenter and Giles Playfair survived the experience without irreparable damage to their careers, as did T. His essay was called 'Hating Italy' (a country which he loved) and he feared that such a title by an author so named might give offence to some of his aunts – as indeed it did.

[2]Sigle (Sheila), elder daughter of Robert and Sylvia Lynd. A Zuleika Dobson-like figure at Oxford. She worked for Victor Gollancz and became an elegant pillar of the Communist Party, as did her younger sister Maire.

[3]Lionel Hale. Balliol friend of T, sharing lodgings with him. Journalist, playwright and broadcaster.

TO ECH   HOTEL FAST
4 MARCH 1933   JERUSALEM

I am having a small holiday. I really couldn't go on working at the intense pitch which old Garstang whips out of us without 2½ days holiday. I have almost finished the first of them and have retired like a pleasure-loving Emperor from the provinces to the comfort of the capital. Talking about intoxication – I come in for the feasts of all three religions. The Arabs shouted like the Bullingdon under my window last night (Friday); today, Saturday, the Jews will be drunk; and tomorrow, Sunday, the Christians. It makes a lot of extra noise and I wish they could come to some agreement on which is the properest day to drink.

What Jerusalem needs is an Acropolis; there's nowhere peaceful and architecturally fine that you can look at the country round from. Yet it's good country – hills in every direction, and a line of mist lying over the deep Jordan valley – more mountains reddish behind. I met a Jericho Arab friend here. We embraced in the middle of the street and greeted one another for about five minutes. I am getting good at greetings – they're what the Arab language chiefly consists of. You can get along on a visit without anything else. It must be the most formal language in the world – there's an absolutely set shape which your meaning must fit into, almost no scope for inventing remarks, and yet the forms, though they exist apart from you and have gone on for so long, don't seem ready-made. You make them yours though you don't construct them – a good language I think; and interesting to leave out the vowels, for they are the noise I think on which poetry chiefly depends; you can't imprison them in symbols as you can consonants. So there you have room for personal variation to make up for the language's great impersonality.

TO DFH   [JERICHO]
8 MARCH 1933

An admirable time for writing to you. I've just washed my feet after dinner – a good moon outside – charming Egyptian inside, sitting peacefully in the comfortable chair, not interrupting, and catching moths for me in a sprightly way whenever they become troublesome: he is more bloodthirsty with them than I dare to be.

But, like Henry (?I or II) with Becket, I connive at the murder till it's safely done and then blame him for it. He is said to be a Hashash (the knowing word for a man who takes hashish), but he's not taken any here yet nor offered me any so I expect he only does it in quite a mild way. We've been having a chat about the hard times and the wicked price of oranges. Now he has gone to his cold bed on my wall (I tried it the night before last, but it was a great deal too uncomfortable, though dawn and moon were nice, and I kept slipping off the wall into a dry ditch).

On the whole everything is gayer. Lovely shining weather – hard not to fall asleep after lunch. But otherwise only pleasantly hot - except for the workmen, who all have headaches, and eat aspirin like hot cakes; they have long ago finished all mine. The Professor has a cheap brand – a bottle of 500 – but they are almost through that. I almost think they like the taste of it.

I dined on Saturday with this chap Iliffe. Music afterwards, a local quartet, half Jews to listen to the music, half English to give tone. Some Brahms that sounded quite pleasant – most of the rest I went to sleep in, though keeping an expression of alertness. On Sunday evening a cinema with Bulos Effendi (the Arab clerk of the works here – the nice one that teaches me Arabic), though I disapprove as a rule on Sundays, but because it was *Ben Hur*, having seen it in Corfu and Klagenfurt, I thought I ought to cap it by seeing it in the city of its origin. It was great fun – film apart. Feeling ran madly high. For 'Roman' everyone read 'English' of course: besides it says some stiff things about Jews. When the Roman officer Messala remarked to Ben Hur: 'You are a snivelling sneaking Jew and your race will always be trodden, as it has always been trodden, in the dirt', all the Arabs shouted and stamped like a Bump Supper. But when Ben Hur with flashing eyes replies: 'My afflicted nation has shaken off its other persecutors before now, and the day will come, be sure, when it will rise up and shake off the yoke of Rome', then all the Jews in the audience joined in a splendid seditious cheer. Finally in the awful sentimental bit at the end when Ben Hur's mother and sister, who seem to have been lost in the city drains for the rest of the film and have caught leprosy, are healed by the hand of Christ (who repeats some text from the Sermon on the Mount as he heals them), the whole Christian audience (plenty of Christian Arabs) hallooed and stamped and shouted so as to beat all the others. It was really rather awful, though comic. It's a good picture of the way the town population at least seems to distort everything into conflict.

Most of Sunday I spent with Baramki. First lunching for an almost Oxford length of time, then going into the country – Bethlehem direction – looking for a village with a Crusader church in it which he couldn't find – or rather found was an hour and a quarter's walk off – which he thought an expedition rather to be planned than actually attempted. So we went to Solomon's pools, in the hills nearby, and wandered. There were flowers, red anemones above all and masses of cyclamen hiding under rocks and in crannies, where goats couldn't eat it I suppose – all colours from white to red and full purple, with every exquisite shade of pink and pale purple in between.

We took a charming female cousin of Baramki's too – with almost all the virtues except that she would pick all the

22

cyclamen, even where it was rarest. Beautiful, great round eyes – with heavy under-lids, not browner than an Italian otherwise, in face not as brown and rosier, reserved, humorous, English just broken enough, enjoying nature (like Jane Fairfax). Her chief virtue is that she is called Nastasya. I have always intended to know a Natasha. I think she'll be worth knowing more of – at first sight the pleasantest female Arab, if not the pleasantest person, I've met in this country. Like Byron and Teddy I'll try to learn my languages from a young female – said to be the most satisfactory way.

Baramki (and Nastasya) are directly descended (they hope) from the Barmacids, viziers to Haroun-al-Raschid, and all through the 8th century, flew to Byzantium in the reign of the Empress Irene, were forced to become Christians, have remained Orthodox ever since – till this (Dimitri) Baramki turned pseudo-Darwinist, poor chap. They received the envoys of Charlemange. A charming Dominican in Jericho, Père Vincent,[1] the man who always disagrees with Garstang's conclusions – he has come to disagree with this year's. He was lovely to us, about our notes and things, and said to Garstang, 'Vous devez être très satisfié avec vos assistantes' – to which the old brute replied, 'Ah oui – pas mal'. Bah. But we are still fond of one another.

[1]Père Vincent OP. Member for many years of the Ecole Biblique et Archéologique Française in Jerusalem.

TO DFH   JERICHO
13 MARCH 1933

I came back from a very happy Dead Sea jaunt yesterday, the best two days of all my Palestine time so far: Eastwood's plan – the exquisitely mannered crisp brown-haired smiling but rather serious-minded friend of the Binyons.[1] We went on a great flat-bottomed barge three-quarters full of Germans. We were the final quarter, the cream, and the most influential quarter, and the bravest in any adventure. As a result whenever the fat pink big-bodied organizing little German summoned a meeting to decide some question of plan, we could always pack the assembly, and sway it by our influence into voting our way.

It was extraordinary with those Germans, with their hairy knees and efficiency and guide books – it seemed like a piece of Germany stuck down in the middle of this wild Eastern country. The lake one could imagine a German lake, the mountains on each side Bavarian mountains, and above all the little pink man who kept blowing his whistle to make announcements, archaeological or human. He loved discovering mistakes – was at his best when pointing out with derisive roars of laughter to an American Latin priest that his thermos was broken and soaking through his shirt: a typical German joke.

We were an admirable party: a little well-born and bred but not offensively. Poor Eastwood couldn't help having and keeping a lovely crease down the front of his grey flannel trousers, put there by the Government House butler. He brought a splendid man called Jarvis,[2] cousin of Watson's – the High Commissioner's – Etonian too – in a bank rumly enough having three months leave being Honorary Secretary here – really simply gadding, but charming and a wit. Though a real Cambridge undergraduate he could imitate one magnificently – could turn somersaults beautifully. His sparkle put life into all of us.

The weather was foul (as it has always been on our expeditions) grey and close; no views. At first very choppy (I didn't think the Dead Sea had it in it to be choppy) but the boat was too flat a shape to be able to toss much. At any rate we never didn't want our meals. Stopped first at hot springs – really hot, the kind of water you could shave in: I always thought hot really meant tepid, like the taps in your room in foreign hotels. I took a bathe in the Dead Sea – horrid – water in my nose and mouth and eyes, – which Baedeker particularly says Avoid, but doesn't say how to. Foul taste, and it smarts, and one can't swim on one's front because one's legs are chucked up in the air – a silly sea. I washed the salt which caked my face off in the hot springs.

Then we stopped again on the Transjordan side to look at the gorge of the Amun; again intrepidly we went ahead up it. It is the most exciting bit of scenery I've ever seen; a narrow crack four or five hundred feet deep with this swift river at the bottom; walking along in almost darkness, dark as a cathedral, with the same towering Gothic walls hewn out of

dark red rock like Liverpool or Chester – most like Liverpool
– a little winding band of white light at the top.

We waded up it as far as the waterfalls, ridiculous in
bathing shorts below and shirts above, I in my brilliant green
one for the fiesta: wading up to our waists in water and
feeling like old Neptune. It looked like Rider Haggard or
Jules Verne – *King Solomon's Mines* perhaps. This great
underground river – and Eastwood and Richmond like a pair
of intrepid Alan Quatermains standing small but dignified at
some bend in the river looking up at its towering walls, as if
they had just observed a plesiosaur or a lost goddess,
Richmond with a very Livingstone-like sort of broad-
brimmed hat.

We had a brave and exciting time climbing the waterfall at
the end too, as each time you tried to get up and failed you
were swirled along in the water back beyond where you had
started from, bumped against rocks as you went. However
with one behind balanced in mid-stream upon a slippery
stone to shove – and one above to pull we all managed to get
up. The women being simply put up, like plates on a shelf, in
a splendidly primitive way. Getting down we were swirled
away again but worse. Large stones bumped our feet, small
stones got into our shoes and cut our feet: the river fought us,
going at a tremendous rate. That gave us a good appetite for
tea – which had to be at half-past one, owing to our
disarranged day. It had started at half-past four and we got in
about four major meals and three minor meals. All the good
food contributed of course by Government House. I brought
oranges and a simple leg of mutton which we hung at an end
of the boat and in spite of looking like an albatross it tasted
delicious when we fried it over the Primus stove.

Then in the dark of that evening we came to the south end
of the Dead Sea, explored great caves of salt – again the first
and boldest – ugly great stalactites, foul-smelling hot air. We
shoved the American Latin priest up a shaft of loose stones.
We found no end though there is said to be one, where you
look up and suddenly see the stars. No stars that night
though. The Germans of course got lost with all their
efficiency. We had to rescue them with fresh lanthorns like
pickmen, but got no gratitude from the brutes. We slept on
deck which was no worse than bearably cold, except for half

an hour's tornado in the middle of the night, when I thought our anchor cable would break.

Then yesterday was really best of all, climbing to the top of Masada, where Eleazar's last Jews held out in the war of 70, killing one another on this great plateau about 3000 feet up. No way up that the Romans could find – Heaven knows how the Jews had got there. The Romans had built a tremendous causeway, earth and stones, against the sheer face of the rock. With the help of that we climbed it – a difficult walk really, not a climb, only needing scrambles now and them. There was always a bright young bare-legged German whom we named Andreas Hofer to give us – me rather – a tug. We left our women behind with Eastwood by one of the Roman camps – from above they stand out clear and beautiful. We took 6 hours walking. Our mouths when we got back were like the grit we walked over. Thank Heaven Richmond's sister had brought ginger beer.

[1]Laurence and Cecily Binyon. Frequent guests of Helen Sutherland at Rock Hall. Parents of Nicolete (see p.6).

[2]R.G.E. Jarvis, of Doddington Hall, Lincoln. Later with M. Samuels, the merchant bank.

TO RHH   JERUSALEM
21 MARCH 1933

I gave a dinner to about a dozen of the most charming workmen when digging ended on Wednesday night. We had a sheep roasted whole, truly Arab. Not a very large sheep though, but a beautiful meal, cooked in boiled rice and flavoured with pine – very rich. They played pipes and sang sad love-songs and danced (at least the Egyptians did) odd dances which used the bottom in a wonderful way – waggling it grotesquely – and half falling down and pulling themselves together again. A happy evening – and they cheered me like a House Supper at the end. Sad to see the last of them.

TO DFH
27 MARCH 1933

C/O THE MOTHER SUPERIOR
TANTUR HOSPICE
NEAR BETHLEHEM
PALESTINE

For the last fortnight there has been nothing heroic, just this dull winding-up record writing, editing messy old notes, sketching plans sections and elevations, explaining for the fiftieth time to Old G exactly where room 63 is and why he had called it 63, and where in it this particularly interesting sherd had lain. But I mustn't say a word of even mild ill of old G. Bless his heart he has just given me my first archaeological earnings – ten pounds. I doubt if Schliemann himself had made as much by the time he was my age; in fact I know he hadn't. It almost makes me feel archaeologically self-supporting. Of course three digs a year at £10 a dig wouldn't go far to support a wife and family, but a bachelor of simple tastes might manage it. It's exactly what I would have made if I'd been working all the time as a pickman at 13 piastres a day (high wages for a pickman). I don't feel I deserve it as much as a pickman. Still it's very pleasant, and warm-hearted of him – shows that we haven't quarrelled, and that he's content with me. It's nice to part amicably. In fact at parting with this cheque in my pocket and his kindly words in my ears I felt a devil for all the offensive things I've thought and said about him. However they were most of them true. And we hadn't much in common. But these partings make one wish that one had followed a saintly, not a rational human, course. And when he thanks me for 'loyal service', I fear I've not been as loyal as all that. But it's nice that he should think so.

Never mind. A new circuit is beginning, and it looks as if it's going to be a more happy and profitable one (not that Jericho was *un*happy – only a bit moth-eaten in places). I've seen my nunnery, returned for some shopping and a dentist. It's most lovely, among a garden, sweet-smelling, rich red olive-grown hills all round, more flowers among them, Bethlehem and Beit Jala and two hills beside it. My window looks out over the garden and its bright green fir trees, and tall black steep pines, like blots of Indian ink, standing on black narrow stems. A charming sweet-faced nun who spoke English took me in and showed me to a glorious breezy beery (no not beery really but red-scrubbed and nurselike, warm and busy) Mother Superior – who (Hurray) can speak no English so that my Italian will go like wildfire. I will read my Croce and rub it up. Already she says it's jolly good, though under the influence of Arabic it was at its most puerile. My plan at present is – most days to walk into Jerusalem (3 or 4 miles – keep healthy with the exercise, as Uncle Lionel[1] used to at Baghdad) read in the admirable library there Josephus etc; I can't take the books out. My chief modern authority is a German, but he looks tolerably easy.

Anyway I'll attack that language again too. My long-curbed energy ought to be able to tackle three languages as well as Jewish history and take them in its stride. The thought of being at Greek texts (Josephus and the rest) again excites me almost as much as it excited the dead-from-the-waist-down grammarian. I shall work in Jerusalem from half-past 8 to half-past 1 say – then walk back to my Nunnery – eat – read variously till dinner – All Soulsish sort of subjects. At the novel[2] after dinner if there's time or strength left. A joyful programme. This will do for a couple of months or so – varied with expeditions to places. Then a general travel in June – up to Syria particularly. Boase[3] may be coming I hear. Nice if he did.

I stayed with Baramki last weekend. I liked his Byzantine home. They were at various levels of social development – him at the top, his mother at the bottom. Arab mothers seem always to be kept rather in the background – the distinction between a cook and a mother doesn't seem to have been properly drawn. Even in Christian homes she seems to be locked up in the kitchen while her children go out and scour the world for culture. Only two of the family besides Baramki were allowed to come in to dinner; the rest were shut up in little rooms off the main hall and kept scuttling out like rabbits, and having to be captured and repenned by the flustered Baramki. Some of them though were too timid even to scuttle and would only put their noses out, see me, and quickly draw them back again.

The trouble with the English church is that it imposes no religion though it suggests one to the children it teaches. But no Arab is clever enough to understand a merely *suggested* religion. The result is that he gets hold woollily of a lot of secular ideas (scientific or political – Bertrand Russellian Huxleyish pseudo-philosophical biology Recreate-the-human-race-and-break-down-old-stupid-standards sort of stuff) which without any principle to interpret them by turn him to the silliest materialism. That happened to Baramki and is the trouble with all his family except his mother who remains Greek Orthodox, comfortably and wisely. It's very tricky all this teaching of Arabs.

But there ought to be either a compulsory religion or a compulsory philosophy at the root of any teaching I think.

[1]Lionel Smith. Adviser to the Iraqi Ministry of Education, 1921–31. He always walked to work from his house in Alwiyah to his office in the Baghdad Serai, a distance of four miles, and as often as not walked back again when he had finished work.

[2]The novel T was writing, like his thesis, never saw completion.

[3]T.S.R. Boase. Fellow of Hertford College, Oxford 1922–37. Later became Director of the Courtauld Institute and President of Magdalen. 'He, John Richmond and I did a wonderful Syrian expedition together.'

TO DFH
18 APRIL [1933]

C/O THE MOTHER SUPERIOR
TANTUR HOSPICE
BETHLEHEM

This Holy Week has been an interrupted time for work. I was all the time torn in my conscience between work (which I have none too much time for anyway) and watching services (thinking that it might be the only chance, and one would call oneself a fool afterwards). In the end I saw about half-a-dozen. This religious maniac Ferguson[1] ('fanatico' the Mother Superior called him) went to everything – saturated himself with worship, up at seven and back at one, and taking beastly little notes all the rest of the time. He was fearfully tolerant and fearfully Protestant; a seeker after sincerity. He didn't want to condemn the Roman Church but he had to. He suspected that they didn't really mean half they said, and all this dressing up was all very fine but surely it was a mockery. I don't mean that I'm a Papist, but he had such silly narrow reasons for being a Protestant, and the typical broadminded way of always hoping that he was going to find Papists right, but always knowing that he would have to find them wrong.

Certainly all the services I saw in the Holy Sepulchre were

rather shocking, but I wanted not to find them so, as I could hear all the time the rustle of my countrymen being shocked. I went to Tenebrae once as I remembered Lothair (the Disraeli one, not the Holy Roman Emperor) had gone to it and been impressed. But it must be different in the private chapels of luxurious English country houses and in the Holy Sepulchre. There it was hideous: the rotunda is full of boxes round the walls, about three tiers of them, and in them people camp and take their families, their noisy babies and larrikin youths. They sit all day – and all night often – with picnic baskets, sucking oranges and eating peanuts, throwing the peel and husks at their girl friends below, or shouting at fat uncles who are arguing with one another on the ladders that lead to the upper tiers of boxes. Small boys waggle the ladders at the bottom to make their fathers fall off. Armenian priests lounge and shout. The parties of Americans come in waves with hideous-voiced guides showing them round with a roar. The place is full of guides sneaking up and trying to show you the sepulchre – that is in the middle of this rotunda – tall and domed like the Albert Hall.

What they all sit longest for is the Holy Fire – the Greek rite. It is as people say 'supposed to be a miracle' meaning that the poor Christians (very little better than poor heathens) think it is one. The patriarch goes into the sepulchre on Saturday at noon and the light that comes through from the sepulchre into the church represents Christ risen from the dead. All the Eastern churches come and process – Syrians, Armenians, Copts and lovely Abyssinians. Very early in the day people begin to get tremendously excited – the whole court as well as the church is packed full. Our brave troops occupy the place. There is a slow procession three times round the rotunda. It is beautiful to see the troubled faces of English policemen as smoking incense is swung at them in a censer. Boy scouts are somehow part of the processions, they manage to get in where there is any faction or swashbuckling to get fun out of. They march round singing a hymn which means:

O Jews O Jews
We are the blood of Christ:
You are the blood of monkeys.

The people in the boxes clap and cheer and shout to people they know in the audience.

[1] An unidentified 'nice rum archaeological hanger-on from the Indian Army'.

TO DFH
2 MAY 1933

C/O THE MOTHER SUPERIOR
TANTUR HOSPICE
BETHLEHEM

The Catholic atmosphere in which I live makes one feel that every Sunday is a Festa. I had my proper, much postponed, birthday dinner then – a lambkin roasted whole (as for the workmen, but smaller). And my better class of acquaintances – the Dead Sea ones, except for Eastwood who was in Transjordan. It combined my birthday with a farewell to Jarvis, the most pleasant of Cambridge men – the High Commissioner's nephew, handsome and witty, so he gave tone. We had salt, and I, John Richmond and a highly cultured Syrian called Mrs Antonius[1] (the kind who has read more of the sort of books you pride yourself on reading than you have – and all French, Italian and German literature – or at least has the air of having done so) sat below it. And Anne Richmond, Jarvis, the nice Gräfin that Richmond rather moodily and abstractedly woos, and a charming sister of the ADC who had just come to Palestine and was rapturously excited with everything.

I found that in the course of too many Arabic telephone calls I had accidentally invited twelve natives too; and Farraj, the blanket-thief, was there kissing my hand devotedly, as only men who have your blankets know how to be devoted. He has taken on the bit of stony desert where old Garstang used to brood over his potsherds and stolen some seedlings from Mrs Garstang, and now runs the patch beside their house as a market garden; he came late having just caught, he said, a thief in the cucumber beds.

The children of Galilee are rude.[2] We spent most of our time quarrelling. The leader of the Dominicans, a beautiful man called Barrois,[3] very athletic, ran after and caught and cuffed a small boy who was making rude gestures at him – a magnificent righteous Old Testament sight in his flowing white habit.

[1]Katy Antonius, wife of George Antonius (see p.33). Daughter of Faris Nimr Pasha, editor of *Al Mokkatam* and a member of the Egyptian Senate. She dispensed superb hospitality at her house in Jerusalem or anywhere else she might be. Witty, generous and courageous, she was a steadfast friend to those who, like T, were fortunate enough to be taken under her wing. 'There was something of Mrs Dalloway about Katy – seeing her parties as an offering – though a much more lovable person' (Antonius Lecture).

[2]T had been on a ten-day excursion to the north.

[3]Père A-G. Barrois OP. Archaeologist working at the Ecole Biblique.

TO DFH   C/O THE MOTHER SUPERIOR

9 MAY 1933   TANTUR HOSPICE

                                             BETHLEHEM

Your letter only came this morning instead of yesterday. This lazy rurality of only sending for the post every other day becomes annoying – I must speak to the Mother Superior. But she is so gentle and beautiful for all her slight hairiness that I hate even to make a quiet suggestion. Their extreme saintliness makes business very difficult for them. Sister Matilda waited a week before asking me if I minded being given my bill for April, and then apologized for a minute or two before I realized what it was that she was asking. She said she didn't want to give me pain, in case I couldn't pay – beautiful of her. I'm sure they'd rather never be paid at all than paid money which it cost one a moment's anxiety to lose.

It remains a perfect place to live in. Every now and then I *do* walk to or from Jerusalem, but it takes time, and I feel there isn't much time to spare. I ought to begin to try to know Jerusalem properly.

I ought to begin to get to know some important Jews. How else can I face Sir John Simon[1] over All Souls' dinner table (if I do have to face him) unless I can gossip with him about what the Zionist leaders have most recently been thinking? So far I don't know in the least what they've been thinking. Tomorrow I mean to call on the Head of the Hebrew University – perhaps one Jew chum may lead to another.

[1]Sir John Simon, perhaps the most disastrous Foreign Secretary of this century (1931–35). Fellow of All Souls. Candidates for a fellowship are invited to dine to be looked over by existing members of the College.

TO DFH   TANTUR HOSPICE
16 MAY 1933

This last week was mildly social – a moonlight picnic by the
Dead Sea – then the evening after a 'small dance' which, as
there was a great deal more talk than dancing, I enjoyed,
given by rich Syrians called Antonius,[1] a man with rather the
manner of a young Fellow of All Souls and a mysterious
profession, controlling governments – travelling expensively
round, interviewing Amirs, Sultans, Grand Rabbis and
Secretaries of State, and opening all their eyes. His wife has a
social sense, and the exquisiteness of her small late food
almost rivals Aunt Helen's[2] – platefuls of truffles and
asparagus-tip sandwiches.

[1]George Antonius. From a Greek Orthodox family in Alexandria. Educated at
Victoria College and King's College, Cambridge. Worked in the Palestine Government Education Department until he resigned in 1930 after being passed over for
deserved promotion. Middle East representative of the Crane Foundation and author
of The Arab Awakening. Secretary to the Arab Delegation to the 1939 St James's
Conference on Palestine. T spoke in his 1981 Antonius Lecture of George's 'genius
for mediation . . . a role for which he was admirably equipped by his essentially rational
way of looking at the world and belief in the rational solution of problems, the lucidity
of his reasoning, his Henry-Jamesish sensitivity to the undertones and overtones of a
complex situation, his imaginative power of grasping, and indentifying himself with,
conflicting points of view'. He also spoke of George's wit: 'It was a very pleasant, gay,
but at the same time critical, mocking kind of wit.' There was nobody in Palestine
whose judgement T more trusted. Married Katy Nimr (see p.32). Died in 1942.
[2]Helen Sutherland. T's godmother. Daughter of Sir Thomas Sutherland,
Chairman of the P & O Company 1880–1914. Patron of the arts and artists,
particularly of David Jones and Ben Nicholson, whose paintings she bought long
before they were generally known or admired. After living in London (4 Lowndes
Square) she took over, in 1928 at the age of forty-seven, the lease of Rock Hall in
Northumberland, belonging to T's uncle by marriage, Carr Bosanquet. Here
privileged guests could expect to find interesting company, intelligent conversation,
good food and wine, and long walks on moors and hills. This sensitive, tough-minded,
generous, strict, humble, exacting, affectionate hostess exerted a strong influence on
the life of T and many others.

TO ECH   TANTUR
17 MAY 1933

I have this interval between sleeping at a lecture and sleeping
at a play. Père Barrois, the delightful Dominican who took us
to the Jebel Druse, had been lecturing on the Jebel Druse:

the mixture of slides, French and a wet steamy atmosphere kept me asleep throughout. From time to time a little black Jesuit beside me propped me up in my place and I saw half a slide – but always out of focus. This getting up at half-past five – though healthy – makes me very sleepy at almost any hour of the day. You will find me when we meet I'm afraid almost more slothful than when we parted.

In a few minutes I go on to sup on a simple Wiener Schnitzel with an intelligent but lonely friend from the Museum called Lambert, and then to see the Habima act a play called *Rahab*: rather my subject I feel, to see if I can pick any archaeological holes in the production. They are Bolshevik players I think, modelling themselves on the Russian Ballet – intense stylization. But I'll tell you about it afterwards. They've done *12th Night* which I wish I'd seen, partly just to know that it wasn't as good as us.

I must tell you of my Sunday's ride – a rather shameful thing. Really a judgement for riding on Sunday during Church time, which I'd forgotten when I ordered my horse that it would be. And had to slink past the English cathedral looking like a Jew who had kept a pious Sabbath yesterday, or a Moslem who'd kept a holy Friday the day before. I rode up through Hinnom (I think it's Hinnom, but any divinity note will tell you) up towards the Hebrew University, having promised to see a professor, don, there called Billig[1] ('alles noch billiger' – do you remember, in Klagenfurt?) who has made up his mind from a chance enthusiastic remark that I am going to Persia, and loads me with German books about it which I am very grateful for but have no time to read.

I tethered my horse (a large well-built chestnut) to a post in a shed, carefully choosing for him a nice bit of shade, and went to find Billig. But as soon as my back was turned I heard a crash and saw that my horse had detached the bit from his mouth and was cantering away. I tried to go after him gently and entice him to come back to me, but when he wouldn't be enticed I ran. But of course he being a horse could run faster. When I was tired of running I luckily found a little Jew student bicycling quickly in a hurry to get to his lecture, and borrowed, or rather commandeered, his bicycle. What's the use of belonging to a ruling nation if you can't be a little high-handed in an emergency?

34

Meanwhile my horse had broken out of a canter into a gallop. A procession of mixed Jew students was parading, as they often do, in gay clothes, with over-healthy bare legs and arms – about 200 of them, rather truculent, some arm in arm, a great many playing mouth-organs, all marching jauntily down the road to Jerusalem. My horse careered through the middle of them (being an Arab it was obviously fiercely nationalist and anti-Jew) while I bicycled at a tremendous pace a couple of hundred yards behind shouting to the young women to get out of the way, and the young men to catch my horse – curse them all for cowards.

Then I, like Pharaoh but more successfully, tried to dash through the gap made in the children of Israel by my horse before it closed up again. I got through but my horse easily gained on me. So I saw a passing taxi, hailed it, and told it to drive like the devil – throwing my bicycle, that is to say the little Jew student's bicycle, to a little Arab boy to mind. We drove on after the horse, having lost sight of it through all this, asking each policeman which way it had gone, and cursing him for not stopping it. It was a bit foolish of them. Surely the first thing a policeman learns is how to stop a runaway horse.

Anyhow in the end we found it frothing and sweating caught by a bold young Arab townee outside Barclay's Bank. But even then I had to go back returning everyone their property and compensating most of them. I had to give 5 piastres (I felt it would let English horsemanship down if I gave less, and I had already let it down far enough) apiece to:

The man who caught the horse

The man who happened to have a bit of old rope about him and led it back to the stables (where I was too ashamed to appear)

The boy who had looked after the bicycle

The boy who rode the bicycle back to the owner of the bicycle

The owner of the bicycle (hot cross and late poor fellow. He'd had the worst time. But, honour to Jewry, he was the only one of them who refused my five piastres).

---

[1]Levi Billig. Jews' College, London University, and Trinity College, Cambridge. Lecturer in Arabic literature at the Hebrew University (see p.132).

TO DFH   C/O THE MOTHER SUPERIOR

6 JUNE 1933   TANTUR HOSPICE

                                        BETHLEHEM

Today I have spent mostly in the shelter of a closed car, a luxus Chrysler, belonging to a Russian Jew with the typically Russian name of Joshua Gordon.[1] Have I mentioned him already? Very fat and square, a huge bulgy face with small blue eyes shining like a pair of expressive sultanas in a rather nondescript helping of suet pudding. He is the showman and liaison officer with the Government of the Jewish Agency, so that one can feel that his motor car was ground off the faces of poor dispossessed Arabs.

He's a friend of Eastwood's; that was how I first got to know him – took us both the other day to look at Jewish life and culture in Tel-Aviv. It's all very efficient but gruesomely go-ahead – what I imagine England must have been like in the Lancashire parts in the last century, and America till quite lately. Rather like the five towns – everything bubbling over with expansion – great maps of Tel-Aviv showing in coloured inks how huge was the increase in the increase of population every year; ghoulish German architecture. Sprightly people, but all fearfully dignity of labour conscious. Of course it is very dignified – and these trodden people from the ghettos have a right to be proud, but it's rather nauseous in a way, this bristling prosperity – and absolutely unscrupulous. They even say that there are times in any nation's history when it must simply go straight forward and realize itself as a nation and let everything else – the rights of other races – go to the devil. All this civic pride is very healthy I'm sure. We had tea with the Mayor[2] who gave me a signed picture of his bust, as ugly as sin, and the town-clerk, and the conversation was all the time of this sort:

Pause

ONE OF THEM: Yes – there is a greater average consumption of water per head per day than in any of the great capitals of Europe.

I: Really?

ANOTHER OF THEM: Yes, Sir. Let me tell you that every Tel-Aviv citizen consumes 500 pints of water a day. Berlin comes second with 400 pints. London, third with 250 pints.

Paris, last with 40 pints.

ANOTHER OF THEM: When one of the children runs home dusty from school or from Kindergarten the first thing he does is to demand from his father or mother a thorough shower bath. 'Mother,' he says, 'I want a good wash all over.' – and so on.

But it grates on one when one belongs to a country becoming poorer, and it makes one feel thankful for poverty, and almost for dirt. One can understand how all this bumptious prosperity must grate on the Arabs who see it. For the ones who profit from the Jews being here (which Jews say everyone must do) are only the town ones, most of them Christians, who drive buses to Jaffa, that sort of thing. The labourers have their lands sold over their heads and become really unemployed, but so long as they have a patch of ground they're not registered. So Norman Bentwich[3] in the *New Statesman* can still point proudly to figures. Yesterday (it's now Wednesday morning) this Joshua took me to Tel Mond – 900 acres of oranges and a statue of the late Lord Melchett, in the position of a policeman on point-duty, as Progress. The idea is that you begin working for the company with a back garden and your back garden increases and by degrees you become a private owner – hence no proletariat. That they seem sensibly to aim at everywhere, giving everyone an acre or two for their spare time so as to have a part in the land. To see them in the streets it is almost what one expects Moscow is like – all of them being so consciously not proletariat, swinging along with open shoulders, open necks and girls on their arms. But yesterday at Tel Mond they were discussing an eviction of a Bedu from ground he thought he had rights on – and probably had – and being told they had better keep Jews out of the way on eviction day. All this they excuse by saying that the less civilized must always give way to the more civilized. Probably true but wicked.

I'm sorry – but you don't often have politics. I expect I ought to mention these topics more often. But as you know they're not my strong point, though my increasing admiration for Gladstone makes me feel they ought to be. Anyhow I feel I can face the politically minded in England now without utter ignorance.

I've had a busy week and done too little ordinary work,

alas. Friday and Saturday at Sebastiya, Samaria that is, Crowfoot delightful – friendly in a rather gnarled way – gave me very kindly almost a day of his time showing me buildings and explaining them, which is more than that old curmudgeon Garstang would have done for anyone short of a Duke. And the people seemed pleasant there, mostly young women. The daughter[4] seemed a delightful and well-featured young woman. Mrs Crowfoot[5] very ill-mannered and never passed the cake. Some sprightly little Jews like sparrows. Mr (? Dr) Lake[6] with his trembling lower lip talking about the Shakespearian *variae lectiones* and thinking how lucky he was not to have got a fellowship at Oxford because it had left him so much more time for writing. Enormous Mrs Lake, the housekeeper, providing excellent food, so that one really looked forward to meals.

A fairly profitable expedition from the thesis point of view – and some jolly 12th-century Byzantine paintings of John the Baptist. It was there, you remember, that poor John the Baptist lost his head, and the fact has been commemorated with two tasteful shrines. I am becoming (like Teddy) excited by early Christian architecture and mean to read Stzrygowski – at present I have only got as far as reading about him. There are very good 5th and 6th-century churches near Aleppo which I mean to visit, either with Boase or alone – a glorious one for Saint Simon Stylites to judge from the pictures. I feel that he will be a good object for a pilgrimage.

I am thankful to hear that my devoted native servant, Isma'in the Turk, is willing to leave the Sultan's employment for mine for that month, which will be useful if we cross the frontier over into Turkey, though I'm certain that he'll be arrested there poor fellow:

> This face of his I do remember well . . .
> Here in the streets, desperate of shame and state
> In private brabble did we apprehend him . . .
> Notable pirate, thou salt-water thief,
> What foolish boldness brought thee to their mercies
> Whom thou in terms so bloody and so bold
> Hast made thine enemies?

(I hope Isma'in won't get into any private brabble. I told you about him didn't I – deserter from the Turkish army after the war – killed 70 Frenchmen with a machine gun in the Druse revolt, when he was part of a small sniper force and they were a battalion marching in column. A price on his head in both countries. A charming absolutely faithful and lovable person in spite of this bloodthirsty record.)

Other events have been a happy dinner and a miserable garden party at Government House. I have enough snobbery to revel in going there. Beautiful singing we went to afterwards, a Yemmanite (Jew from SW Arabia), a lovely actress, a little like Ruth Draper but less varied, singing love songs like Theocritus and battle songs and songs about flowers – beautiful sudden subtle changes of mood and character. She sang with bare feet and a great shapeless dress high at the neck so that only head and feet showed. We agreed that we'd never seen anyone with a more beautiful inside to her mouth, like a Cathedral with nave and choir – a dark choir and a brighter nave – she opened it wide as she sang. We sat gloriously in the front row so could see into it well. We were almost clapped too when we entered but just not. These Yemmanites were expelled from Spain in the 15th century and one can see that part of their history from their singing, and shawls that she danced with and things. Tonight to a Jewish satirical drama – Gordon taking me again – he promises that it is like Aristophanes.

[1]Joshua Gordon. Born in Lithuania, attended universities in Germany and America. Sergeant in the Jewish regiment in the 1914–18 war. From 1931 in the political department of the Jewish Agency.

[2]Meir Dizengoff. Founder and first mayor of Tel-Aviv.

[3]Norman Bentwich. Attorney-General in Palestine 1920–31, and then Professor of International Relations at the Hebrew University. A moderate and ecumenically minded Zionist.

[4]Probably Joan, second of the four Crowfoot daughters, not Dorothy, the eldest, who was to marry T.

[5]The failure of T's future mother-in-law to pass the cake can be attributed to her mind being on other matters than acting as hostess to greedy visitors. Grace Mary Crowfoot was the world's greatest expert on ancient weaving. Later she and T became very fond of each other, and much cake was passed between them.

[6]Dr Lake was from Harvard. The Samaria excavation was conducted jointly by the British School in Jerusalem, the Hebrew University, and Harvard.

TO DFH   TANTUR
19 JUNE 1933

A fairly hot very windy dusty ill-tempered sort of day – the
kind that makes you unpleasant to servants, and, alas, in
Palestine there are always plenty of servants to be unpleasant
to. It was on the whole a satisfactory visit [to Beirut].
Baldwin[1] was a beautiful host – a lovely man, simple and
most hospitable, if anything too ready to love worms – the
usual Junior Consular sort of worm. He had one living with
him with a small moustache, small stature and what he
believed was a dashing manner.

I hardly know how to travel or when or with whom. No I'm
not really as hopeless as I sound, but it is hard to combine
places that I must see with any particular route. At last
though I have decided that I shall go from Hama to Aleppo
and leave Transjordan and SE Syria – they're both very ugly
(or SE Syria is, all volcanic rock). I've seen part of them (the
Jebel Druse) already, and finally I must be content to be an
amateur in travelling. It's no good trying to travel to find out
things that other people don't know. I must simply try to find
out some of the things which they do. And I might as well
look at the best, and they (as far as early Christian churches
are concerned) are almost all in this district N of Hama.
Neither journey would really help my thesis; so I might as
well go for my own pleasure, through lovely country and
buildings. It's perfectly safe. I asked a high French official at
Beirut about that – a diplomat with a bent nose. He
guaranteed me Hama to Aleppo, and he knows.

Another trouble is that I have half hired two faithful and
devoted bearers – more than one I can't afford. Besides if
there were two they would probably intrigue with one another
and stop being faithful. And one is at Kerak– he's the one I
like most but that's so hard to get at and the other is at
Samaria and that's not much easier. God will send some
beautiful and easy solution – or I shall find some bad one.

My present idea is to go to Jerash (good 2nd- and
3rd-century Roman town and nice churches) the day after
tomorrow early (Saturday), return Sunday evening, set off
with one of the Devoteds on Tuesday, have all my luggage
sent on to Alexandretta, be met in N Syria about the 17th of

July by Boase and Richmond after a month's dirty travelling, have a week's clean travelling with them, and then about the 25th set off for Europe.

Yesterday was a long exhausting bargaining irritable day here. I'm afraid I became rather the intolerable sort of Englishman who curses quite ineffective quiet people to prevent his being taken advantage of. Of course I always was taken advantage of.

Then I travelled the last part of the way with a fanatical Moslem from Hebron who had strong views about the immorality of the Jews. I think he was really shocked by them. He categorized me about who sent us food and money and who sent the birds food and the Jews punishment and I after a few hesitations realized that I was expected each time to answer 'Allah'. But I was scored off when he asked if Allah didn't see the differences between his life and a Jew's, and I answered 'Surely God will reward you for your holy life and will punish the wicked Jew', and he pounced on me at once and said, 'How do you know that? Only God knows who will be rewarded and who punished. Who are you to say that I shall be rewarded?' Which was very crushing. He also gave me a list of the Four Things which man would never know but God knew. They were:

(1)   Whether you will get money tomorrow
(2)   Whether you will die tomorrow
(3)   Whether the child of a pregnant woman will be a boy or a girl
(4)   Whether it will rain tomorrow.

The last seemed rather bathos. We discussed a little the immorality of Americans. I offered sententious remarks about riches not making you happy or good, which he thank Heavens approved of, but most of the time we discussed his own morality – very like a Cromwellian. I quoted some of the first verses of Saint John's Gospel (the only Arabic I know by heart) which seemed to bear on the subject, but he didn't seem much affected. Perhaps I pronounced them wrong.

[1] R. de C. Baldwin, British Consul-General in Beirut. Had been at Queen's, and so knew T's father. An easy and accommodating friend to T in good times and bad.

I can't think why I didn't write from Jerash, except that I was
bothered with trying to find my Abd-el-Fatah, who I fear now
is irretrievably lost anywhere between Jerash and Amman. It's
really his own stupid fault, except that I suppose I shouldn't
have relied on his intelligence to come and meet me, but
should have attached him firmly to me before I started. But
that's all a long and not very exciting story.

I had quite a useful couple of days at Jerash – lovely green
slit between yellow sandy mountains – all Circassians – said
to be unpleasant and treacherous race – they seemed quite
gentle. Probably the Arabs dislike them because they have
most of the best bits of land in Transjordan. The trees in the
river valley are beautiful white poplars which flutter in the
wind all day and show alternately the green and the grey side
of their leaves.

I stayed two nights with the American expedition there, on
the ground of the camaraderie that binds all brother-
archaeologists. They were an inhospitable lot, never offered
to show me round, insisted on not understanding or taking in
some silly literal way everything I said. A brute of a child who
talked continuously and was brutally treated for it by his brute
of a father.

Lovely to be among the exquisitely mannered French
again. I found to my delight Schlumberger[1] – the Inspector
of Antiquities that I met in Beirut – here, taking notes on the
coffering of the temple of Bacchus on a plank supported by
ropes about 60 feet above the ground. I was made to go and
look at them too which I did in terror, supported from both
sides. It was a great help having him to explain things: and
apart from archaeology he's a beautiful person, with manners
as well as charm of manner – gaily dressed in bright
sleeveless shirt and beret. But even the less godlike here – the
architect and the director of the dig – are beautifully friendly
and waste all their precious time showing me things.

I feel this a friendly town though the Syrian inhabitants are
pretty decadent – sleep all day and then in the evening parade
up and down the main street with their wives and children –
all in the same row if they are Christians, men, women and

children in separate rows if they are Moslems. But even the Moslem women veil pretty transparently if they are good looking and even let it hang negligently down till you are right up to them when they pull it quickly up like a railway carriage window as you go into a tunnel.

It was warming as I walked home last night at dusk to be greeted by and chat with first the Chef des Charpentiers (of the excavations), then a charming Hindu dressed just like Gandhi in a sack with three buttons. I had met him earlier among the temples. He looked like a tramp (so if it comes to that do I) but was a Professor of Geography from Allahabad – a Hindu. I was sorry that geography isn't my strong point, but perhaps by geography he just means visiting foreign countries. I asked him to dinner but he seemed to fast at mealtimes. Then I met the architect and his wife and we had about 10 minutes of taking off our hats to one another and shaking hands. Then I was introduced to a photographer from Aleppo who had studied photography at the Polytechnic in London, affianced himself to a girl in his boarding house, set her down to have a 2 years' photography course and will then return and claim her. He was a Moslem, so remembering *A Marriage in Burma* I talked to him seriously about the sort of life Western women were used to.[2]

[1] Daniel Schlumberger, French archaeologist. Excavated the Umayyad desert palace of Qasr el-Hayr el-Gharbi.

[2] *A Marriage in Burma* by Mrs M. Chan-Toon, author of *Under Eastern Skies*, *Told on a Pagoda* and other works. She introduces this novel, published in 1926, with a note: 'In the following pages I have endeavoured to sketch the life of any English girl who married a native of Burma, to show, if only in outline, how vast is the gulf that divides the Eastern from the Western.'

TO RHH   IDLIB
2 JULY 1933

I'm afraid you're being rottenly supplied with letters and even postcards. But not only are there no post offices that I've seen between here and Hama, nor roads, nor any conceivable way of a letter ever catching up with civilization, but my manner of life makes letter-writing impossible too – a whirl of constant entertainment; having no tent I have no privacy. At midday we call on a chap to rest and have (with luck) lunch; at night we call on a chap to sleep and dine. What of the day isn't spent in riding (as a rule about 6 hours – 9 yesterday when we lost our way all morning) or making notes on churches (mostly so far mediocre aesthetically – a lovely one at Ruwaha yesterday – but anyhow profitable to have seen I think) and trying to photograph them, with the inescapable native propped against a lintel, is spent in sleeping, and trying more and more fatuously to chat in the houses of mukhtars, sheikhs, mayors, fat men who own cattle in a large way, thin men who raise cucumbers in a small way, and wild bony men who own nothing at all and take it very badly.

I was talked at for 1½ hours yesterday by a man from Ruwaha sitting backwards on his donkey while I rode forwards on my horse, telling me what a shame it was that you had to go an hour for water from Ruwaha. So it is. But a one-subject man in a language which you only understand slightly is horrible. On the whole though everyone is beautiful; I am magnificently healthy and I think (having just looked at myself in the first glass for 5 days) bronzed, thinned and handsome. Certainly I have never ate less or more wholesomely. Breakfast – what of last night's coffee one can pinch; lunch – Arab bread and some slop, like what of the apricots were too rotten to sell made into a mush. We sit round and I as guest of honour dip first, hold my breath, lick my lips and make one of the few compliments I have to the host.

Hunger forces one to swallow the most nauseous things. Last night my exquisitely mannered host, Abu Ahmed, piled up the part of the dish opposite me with sheep's eyes and the whole nervous system which I had to eat patting my stomach for pleasure. Today here I lunched off French red wine and buttered beans with the beautiful hospitable Commandant – a glorious change. He had even rather absurdly insisted on my taking two soldiers tomorrow; really no need he admits. On principle I share Gertrude Bell's dislike of having them. However as they like it, and it relieves him, and I hope pleases you (though you could really be perfectly comfortable without), and doesn't do me any harm (in fact pleases me too in that I like clattering into a village being mistaken in my khaki breeches, for a 2nd lieutenant), it seems to be altogether a satisfactory arrangement.

Tomorrow we start for the Jebel Barisha – I, the two soldiers and my faithful man (a little like Corporal Trim – about as much as I am like Uncle Toby). Better churches there, working up to the glory of Simon Stylites, and then back to Aleppo. That ought to be at most another week. All these happenings I must one day write down: forgive me for not doing so now. Only I must tell you of the fat delightful sinister old man who entertained us royally because it happened to be harvest festival, who looks like Clemenceau. I promised him the hand of Diana Bosanquet[1] – he wanted an English wife whom I could personally recommend as his 4th has just died and he is very Anglophil. He offered to take most of his cattle and horses across to England as a present to his future father-in-law. He would ride around in front of him to show how young and strong he was. I suggested Diana because he particularly wanted my family and I know her sporting nature. It would be a lovely interview wouldn't it between Uncle Carr B and his herds and this fat old Syrian and his herds bargaining with beautiful but firm politeness in the fields of Rock. Like Jacob meeting Esau.

[1] Diana Bosanquet, second daughter of Robert Carr Bosanquet, owner of the Rock estates in Northumberland and a successful breeder of pedigree rams.

TO RHH   TRAIN FROM JERUSALEM
24 JULY 1933

I had a hurried last breakfast with the Bowmans.[1] (We have grown very fond of one another. He even calls me 'dear Thomas', in spite of a slight brush about braces which I borrowed and then mislaid. Curiously however they turned up at Tantur and I bought him another very smart pair. So he is a brace to the good as a result of my visit.)

[1] Humphrey Bowman. Director of Education in Palestine, 1920–36, who had started his career in the Egyptian Ministry of Education in the days of Cromer. 'A kindly, snobbish, bumbling, Polonius-like Old Etonian. He had good stories about the past. I was fond of him in my earlier period, when we went on some good walks together, down the wadis to the Dead Sea' (Antonius Lecture).

1933–34

Thomas came back to England at the beginning of August 1933 and started looking around for a job. One he was offered, and accepted, though it did not offer great prospects, was at Cleator Moor in Cumberland, one of the 'distressed areas' where the Quakers had set up various sensible projects for the unemployed, including adult education classes. These were people, and a part of the world, Thomas was to remain all his life especially fond of. Then for a term he joined the philosophy department of Manchester University under Professor Stocks, whom he liked and admired, as an assistant lecturer. His parents were naturally delighted to see his foot at last on the academic ladder, but no permanent post offered itself in Manchester or any other university, and all the time his heart was set on a return to the Middle East. I give extracts from a few relevant letters of this period.

TO FFU
12 DECEMBER 1933

C/O J. GIDLEY
HIGH STREET
CLEATOR MOOR
CUMBERLAND

I still partly curse myself for wasting time in Palestine, and for going there at all. But I don't believe it will make an enormous difference really: it's quite a good stimulus to fail: the stimulus of success always goes to my head. You also wrote very interestingly about Christopher [Eastwood], Palestine and nationalism. It is too late at night to embark on them now, and this is after all a long enough letter already. But don't you think that intense political consciousness is a stage that any person or community must go through? Even if you had given Arabs and Indians a much wiser more cultured less factual education, and encouraged them much more to enjoy what was theirs – encouraged them in their own life rather than twisted them into ours – wouldn't the dislocation in their lives which our mere presence caused and our commercial relations and whatever book education we had to give them forced them to think in terms of ideas like self-determination, Arab countries for the Arabs, Parliament for the people? These ideas being so thick in the European air weren't they bound to infect any backward race that Europe came into any sort of contact with: e.g. Japan which seems to have learnt all our xxth-century ideas, without our having actually settled there to teach her them? But I don't know anything about imperialism, I'm afraid.

TO RHH   MANCHESTER
[MARCH 1934]   WEDNESDAY EVENING

Sleep is almost overcoming me – I'm invigilating over my first examination. They seem to be behaving very well – no cheating I think. But as I am most of the time half-dozing over the Archbishop's proofs I probably shouldn't notice even if they did. Thank you tremendously for your wise and helpful letter about Palestine. I agree with all the disadvantages that you suggested (except that Jerusalem at any rate is just as healthy a place to keep a wife and family at through the year as Manchester – healthier I should think). But I do think that they are easily outweighed. What chiefly moves me to apply for this job is simply its objective importance. I don't know that I shall really be any more fitted to do this than to lecture about philosophy – not specially fitted to do either. But I do think that an ordinary tolerant sociable sort of person can be of use in Palestine – unofficially as well as officially. Nationalism being most of the trouble, and that being due a good deal to sentiments as well as to interest, and sentiments being alterable by social intercourse. And it is an advantage to have on the whole a liking for Jews – which not all, I think, of the officials there have.

Palestine is bound to reflect what happens in Europe immediately and violently, so that one couldn't feel oneself cut off from the real movement of events. I agree it would be foolish to intend to go only for 10 years. As you say, after that sort of length of time one would be or ought to be beginning to have a good deal of responsibility. And that would be one of the great advantages – the amount of scope that one should get in a small service like that, compared with Africa for instance, to alter things.

This may be over-optimistic. But I do like the thought of the possibility of practical activity, partly because I'm so bad at it – a good discipline, and a good foundation for theory of any sort.

Thursday. Another letter from you arrived this morning – I'm very grateful – it bears out what I was saying when I had to interrupt this letter last night. The practical life of a government official ought to be the best possible discipline for removing my unbusinesslikeness. Even if painful it must be possible. In a lecturer's life it seems easier to scrape through without real efficiency. I realize too – what you suggested too – that one has to discipline one's opinions a certain amount. One can't be actively a socialist or even I suppose actively a pacifist as a government servant. I don't suppose that that will do any harm for some time to come.

What political views I have are quite undeveloped. As long as one doesn't let the official atmosphere develop them in a wrong direction – let oneself become reactionary – it ought really to be only useful, giving one data for a sounder judgement about politics than one could ever get by simply reading and thinking. In fact it is not the glamour of the East particularly that makes me want this job, but the glamour of trying to put beliefs into practice, and of modifying beliefs by experience of what happens in practice. Which may turn out to be not much more solid than the East. But I don't see how one can take other people's word for thinking, either that Arabs are hopeless people, or that administration in Palestine is bound to be simply a hand-to-mouth giving of sops to alternate sides without principle in order to avert disaster that is bound to come eventually. Even people there who have had experience don't all think that, e.g. Humphrey Bowman.

TO ECH   TREWORGAN
3 APRIL 1934   FALMOUTH

I ought to hear tomorrow I should think about Palestine, or soon after. I am fairly equal about it with a certain amount of preference at the moment for Palestine; but that may be glamour and immediacy. I am prepared, more or less, to regard it as equally suitable in its own way if the Colonial Office makes the mistake of not selecting me and I return to Cleator Moor. But it's silly to begin philosophizing provisionally about both futures when one will quite soon know which will happen and can then begin to philosophize about that one and save half the labour.

TO FFU   20 BRADMORE ROAD
4 MAY 1934   OXFORD

Today week I am going to set sail for Palestine again, if all goes well. Thanks probably to the friendly influence of Christopher, the Colonial Office has given me the job that I always wanted – cadet in the Palestine Civil Service. I am relieved to have given up my not altogether satisfactory wandering Prodigal-son sort of existence – for a time at any rate – and thankful that it is this work that I am giving it up for. The prospect of having admirable language, history, and architecture all there to be known, and with luck a good length of time to try to know them better, or at least to be less ignorant about them in, is a happy one. The only grief is the leaving of family and friends – you among them. I don't think a two-year gap is a bad one, and Palestine is a fairly accessible place – and I don't think not seeing one's friends for a while is a bad thing – keeping the early, school, sort of structure of life – 'routine punctuated with orgies'.

TO DFH   TANGIER
15 MAY 1934

I have just learnt what if I hadn't been an idiot I should have learnt long ago – that we get to Gibraltar today and not tomorrow – so that I'll have to put off the long spacious letter which I meant to write to you. I waited till today in the hope of finding some event to put in it – but I have scarcely any – neither friends nor storms. The Feilings[1] and Donald[2] I eat with – that is pleasant. He makes good jokes; she is friendly, and (like all the friendly women that I pick up) a cousin – you probably knew – through those princely ancestors the Lloyds of Dolobran. So that is a connection which does credit to both of us.

Donald is pleasant and quiet and serious and when we talk it is usually about the importance of keeping off whisky in hot climates. I must say any regrets that one has at the thought of Palestine for two years vanish when one compares it to Singapore for five.

This is Jim's[3] place and it does look gay and jolly – great dark rainy hills in the distance, bright green slopes by the sea covered with black blobs of trees, and the town of Tangier shining with white houses. It might be a South Italian town and countryside, I think, but some lovely Arabs have just come alongside in little white boats. It was glorious to hear their voices again, selling leather pouffe-covers, lovely gay colours. The whole sea on one side of the boat was bright with all the colours, and great open hulks coming alongside too to take cargo on shore – and the harbour full of jolly little boats. The hulks fouled one another and the little boats with pouffes in them at once, and they cursed one another magnificently, so that in a way I felt I was among my own people again.

It is exciting to have this outpost of Araby, outside the Mediterranean, making one think of the time when they were all over Spain. It warms me to hear their language. I wanted to shout remarks down to them as they shouted up. The beautiful genial way they came round with all these monstrously priced things shouting, 'Half-price – everything half-price', knowing that you can catch an Englishman if you offer him a bargain, even if he really knows that you can get the same things for a quarter the price at Harrods. I was tempted to buy you a scarlet handbag, but didn't.

Now we're getting near to Gibraltar – in fact have reached it. Feiling's imperialist heart beats quicker, so I'm afraid does my bourgeois-intellectual one. I have weakly consented to go on shore with Donald – a waste of a few precious hours. I know exactly what it will be like – Cyprus without the beauty. But the rock is fine, a lion couchant, like the Lion Rock[4] only twenty times as big and with a great left paw extended. A lovely warm day as all of them have been – with a gentle tepid breeze – this launch rolling on the water, and glib evil-looking men disguised as hall-porters trying to make one do something one doesn't want to – have a cab for an hour round the town, buy oranges, or stay at the Hotel Cecil.

[1](Sir) Keith Feiling. Historian, Student and Tutor of Christ Church.
[2]Donald Erskine-Crum, former Captain of Boats at Eton, then on his way to start a business career in the Far East.
[3]H.S. (Jim) Ede. Art historian and frequent visitor at Rock Hall.
[4]Familiar landmark on the Belford Moors in Northumberland.

TO ECH   MARSEILLES
18 MAY 1934

How horrible Englishmen are in countries not their own. I know we have decided that often before, but I realized it more clearly than I ever have before this afternoon. Shouting in the tram – a great broad-bottomed lout – quarrelling with the conductor in shocking French, reading out all the notices and names of roads aloud in mock French, swinging along without a hat and with greasy hair in this nice respectable town, jarring on the place. Luckily I shook all of them off by attending a lovely confirmation service at a church on the top of a hill – not a good church but a good hill, with a view over all the hills and the islands and the water. I understand your love of the French and preference of them to Germans. These were beautiful – bulging mothers with their *confirmandi* and *confirmandae* children herding them up this steep hill to the service, sweating and late, with these charming children, the girls in white muslin with white veils, white wreaths of artificial flowers and white silk shawls, the boys in sailor suits, the most holy in pure white, as sub-lieutenants, the rather less holy in white blouses but blue trousers, as petty officers, and the hardly holy at all wholly in blue except for their white collars, as able seamen.

The boys had white armlets on too, and strayed most of

them over the hill-side after flowers, while their sisters, forgetting that they were just going to promise to be full members of the Church militant, scolded them back – 'Antoine, Antoine, renverse-toi!' It is lovely the way all the time half the Frenchmen in the world seem to be trying to make the other half do something, while the other is refusing to pay any attention.

It was the same when some little girls came in a quarter of an hour late for the service and sat at the back, and a whole row of little girls sitting further in front scolded them into the front pews. It was a lovely off-hand business altogether; everyone talked and came in late, so no one could hear what the priest was exhorting them to do or be. The relatives chatted at the back, while just outside the church a man as unconcerned as the uncle in *The Cherry Orchard* who goes in off the white kept looking at things through a telescope, absolutely absorbed.

TO ECH   PORT-SAID
24 MAY 1934

In the course of my so far nine hours' stay I have come to hate this place, charmingly oriental though it is – engaging pedlars selling foreign stamps and photographs of naked women, appealing to two opposite poles of human taste; but it is silly of them to try to sell one both. They ought just to make up their mind which kind of thing one looked as if one collected and then offer one whichever it was.

Other signs of this being the Levant are the flies (on my nose as I write) and this huge pretentious dirty hotel – like all large Arab hotels, the architecture of Euston combined with the furniture of a fourth-form room and the garden of a Cleator Moor allotment in which a lot of geraniums and a palm or two have happened to come up. There are always about six men in shirt-sleeves leaning against things in the hall too – yawning and scratching their scalps – and someone in the downstairs lavatory in pyjamas using all the face towels to wipe the sweat off after his siesta, and a miserable little boy dressed up in a red uniform, who is sent everywhere, on all the errands, and then thumped for getting his uniform dirty.

A man is talking German and English to me at once to explain that he only talks French. I've been walking down the pier – fishermen bored with fishing asleep on their nets – soldiers on guard lending their rifles to small boys to point at one another – women leaving their children to scramble over the colossal statue of Lesseps – Benefactor Humani Generis – who invented the Suez Canal. I'll post this and look for my train.

From 1920 onwards, when a civil administration replaced the military government set up at the end of the war, the policy towards Palestine pursued by successive home governments was what was called 'equality of obligation' – that is, the Balfour Declaration must be implemented and a 'national home for the Jews' built up, but 'the existing non-Jewish communities' (Arabs) must have their civil and religious rights protected. In spite of the manifest impossibility of giving both Arabs and Jews what they thought they were entitled to under the mandate – let alone in terms of absolute justice – it was not until the 1936 Peel Commission recommended partition that the irreconcilable nature of the dual obligation was admitted.

The years 1931 and 1932 were relatively quiet in Palestine, but 1933, with Hitler now in power, saw a large increase in the number of legal and illegal Jewish immigrants (30,000 legal immigrants compared with 9,500 in 1932 and 4,000 in 1931). The Twelfth Zionist Congress, meeting in Prague, demanded that the National Home should be built up as rapidly as possible 'and on the largest scale'. It also voted large sums for further land purchases. The Arab Executive Committee demanded a complete stoppage of Jewish immigration and declared that the Palestine Government 'will be looked on as the true enemy which the Arab people must get rid of through every legal means'.

In 1934 there was still no major clash between Arabs and Jews, though there were skirmishes between rival Zionist groups (Revisionists and Labour). A superficial prosperity generated by the capital brought in by Jews escaping from Hitler (42,000 legal immigrants and probably half as many again illegal ones) encouraged official optimism, but it was largely the towns which benefited and expanded while the villages suffered. As the Annual Register *commented: 'With two largely self-contained populations it is possible, and it happened, that while one mainly prospered the other largely suffered destitution.'*

On his return from leave in November the High Commissioner reiterated his intention of initiating a Legislative Council as soon as the newly elected municipal councils had started work. But, owing this time to Zionist objections (it had been the Arabs who objected to the scheme in 1923), this never got off the ground.

TO DFH
27 MAY 1934

AUSTRIAN HOSPICE
JERUSALEM

A nice sunny Sunday: it still seems odd to write Jerusalem at the top of the note-paper and look at Jerusalem out of the window, and walk through Jerusalem. I think I value the city a good deal more this time than last – absence and thinking about it and having missed much of it before, all teaching one to value it more. I feel it a privilege to be walking through its streets – which I usen't to. That is partly because of the tremendous advantage of living in the old city, so that the first part of all one's walking is through the city, along a lane that leads to the Damascus Gate, where there are bearded grandfathers kissing enthusiastically a favourite grandchild, donkeys with four or five carcasses of fat sheep just flayed swinging about in their panniers – the flesh rolling over the ribs and rolling back again as they jolt – small boys teasing bigger boys – bigger boys making smaller boys cry – men with trays cooking disgusting sweets that look like syrupy bran – men sitting down on chairs in front of somebody's house to spend the day there ordering at eight in the morning their first coffee and first hubble bubble, who will keep having fresh ones till they can decently go to bed – men with camels and a wife coming in from the country unloading the wife and cucumbers from the camel in the middle of the Damascus Gate and being told to get out of everyone's way – men being shaved with a razor in the street in everyone's way too and squealing when the barber cuts too close – an old rabbi in velvet hurrying and muttering.

It's very good to have all this to go through whenever I go out, and there are hundreds of complicated little streets, so that one is never likely to completely unravel them and find one's way about easily and dully. The Secretariat where I work, though, is only a quarter of a mile or less from here – opposite the Damascus Gate – useful, though it may make one lazy. It's rather horrible to go past these beautiful slovenly people every day so tidily dressed – it makes it not easy to stop and chat with them. I don't mean that their beauty is their slovenliness – they must have a disgusting life, all the time in muck and idleness. This island of German cleanliness and Catholic godliness seems strange and out of place and over-privileged in the middle of it all, with a garden of rosemary and a stone terrace to walk along, high up above the streets, the Via Dolorosa, and the firs to give shade – trees to look at out of one of my windows and houses thick as flies with domes and towers sprouting and the Dome of the Rock half hidden by a cypress out of the other, a lovely great green horseshoe-shaped dome.

As for actual happenings, they're still almost too vague to begin to talk about – the work is at any rate. I think I'll leave it till it is rather less of a mystery to me and talk about it then. So far my work is *drafting*, which means writing these difficult letters of the kind that I have grown used to getting – the ones that begin by referring to your letter of some time ago. I suppose like all beginnings it is a matter of learning a new language, and that is a long business. I had a kindly chat with the acting Chief-Secretary, Moody,[1] who said that he didn't expect me to become a good secretary within three months, which gives me some rope at any rate. The acting Assistant Chief-Secretary is a man called Thompson[2] – very genial, talks a lot, an old Balliol man, a fact that we both dwell upon. It is he that delegates most of my work to me. I like him, particularly because he has married a Cypriot. He tends to praise everything in a way that is reassuring at first.

I have been told by a kind female English clerk how I must call in on about a dozen different officials' wives, or they will talk; a hideous prospect. I began it by dropping in to the Anglican Bishop and leaving my name – I won't be bullied into leaving a card – at worst I'll get pieces of pasteboard and write my name on. But it does seem silly and a waste to have the things printed just for a dozen officials' wives don't you think?

Socially Jerusalem has been very genial so far. I dined with the High Commissioner on Friday night which I regard as an honour, but it was an unsatisfactory meal – he, the ADC, two very Cairoish Cairoans (army) and one very sporty English-woman (army too – just back from India). She dated events in England by partridges; I tried to date them by bluebells, unsuccessfully. HE couldn't hear what I said – and as I could only talk to him on my right by avoiding the young Englishwoman on my left it embarrassed all my conversation with him. But my opinions were quite respectable – in fact sheepishly and treacherously Tory, so that I was ashamed of myself. Probably in fact it was the obvious deceptiveness of views which you express when they're not really yours which spoilt our conversation. And though of course I should never have the courage or folly to label myself Communist here (knowing what a red rag that is to people – not even Socialist, which means the same but is a degree less frightening), probably in the long run it would be better to express one's views to a High Commissioner – or, if not that, at least not express others for the sake of conversation.

Anyhow I went at 10 punctually which is said always to please him, and walked home the last couple of miles with two friendly Arabs. Last night I dined with Iliffe, Keeper of the Museum, and liked him, having for a while ceased to last year: hospitable of him to ask me so quickly.

Today I lunched with Mrs Antonius – nice except that at about half-past three she became passionate about Arabs and dragged me into an argument which I tried very hard to avoid. Not a good thing to talk politics with people who are interested very definitely in one direction, I know, but one can't simply let a stream of passionate attack on Jews flow past one and not attempt any defence when one knows that a lot of what's being said is just 'not true', and when only a fortnight ago one was dining with Frankfurter.[3] I expect one has to have one such talk and get it over. But with the best will to be discreet in the world I don't see how one can avoid defensive argument sometimes even if one manages always to avoid offensive.

[1]S. Moody, Assistant Secretary. 'A poor fish. I had an embarrassing interview with him when he sent for me having found an anti-imperialist poem I had written lying around' (Antonius Lecture).

[2]D.C. Thompson. Had married three years earlier Marie Tacos. 'A sweet character. Regretted somewhat by the ruling class since he had married a native – not a Palestinian native, true, but a Cypriot native . . . Not terribly hard working and didn't mean to be . . . A rather unhappy character, who met his noble end when the King David Hotel was blown up' (Antonius Lecture).

[3]Felix Frankfurter. Justice of US Supreme Court. Eastman Visiting Professor, Oxford 1933–34.

TO DFH

30 MAY 1934

THE AUSTRIAN HOSPICE

JERUSALEM

CORPUS CHRISTI EVE

A few bells have begun to ring though it's only eleven o'clock, which reminds me what tomorrow is, so does David Jones,[1] who has just gone up to bed and asked for Mass specially at 7 and got it (it's usually at 6), and then cursed himself for not having asked for 8, which he thinks now that he could have got if he'd asked the priest when he was friendly and full of dinner.

It's a great thing to have David here. The history of his coming is that for the first day or two I saw about the hospice a strange great bearded man like Tolstoy dressed in yellow and black striped silk, an Arab skirt, with Arab headdress, who could only talk English, and discovered by degrees that this was Eric Gill.[2] Then when he spoke about a friend from Cairo coming by aeroplane I eavesdropped and guessed it was David, as it was. Now he has come I have beautiful company – for Gill is a friendly man – and though we don't see much, any of us, of any of us during the day we meet at dinner and then sit and talk and drink in my room afterwards.

David is less ill mentally he thinks but just as ill if not iller physically. Egypt has given him mosquito bites as big as billiard balls and perpetual stomach ache – he can eat little – loathes the hospice food, which is all right but untempting, about Tantur level. He is a stone lighter and naturally troubled about his lightness. He does look ill, but then he always did, and he talks as much and as gaily as he ever did, I think. He thinks Jerusalem a bad place for him as it probably is, but he was swirled away on the tide of Eric Gill's enthusiasm – knowing that he knew what was best and the only thing was to make David do it, as one often does with ill people.

I pottered about the town in the evening yesterday with David, he obviously hating it, so that one felt that Jerusalem was all dust in your eyes and stones that you trip over and small boys that you trip over. Till then I had been loving it. Gill agrees that David has that effect on the place. That's unfair to him – he loves looking at the town from his window, but when we begin to walk in it it becomes a burden, though he doesn't complain.

I'm not sure he hadn't better go to the Fast Hotel where he'd at least be well fed, though the people are nicer and odder here – the beautiful shy Bishop (now acting Patriarch) with red buttons down the front of his suit who runs the place – Gill calls him a bad hotelier, which is true. Dinner is full of silences. Seven of us meal together. The Bishop, we three Englishmen, another Englishman, Gill's prentice, who helps with the lettering of the Museum inscriptions that Gill is here for, a hilarious Italian, and a strange soft priest – the kind of beard which looks as if it was the result not of design but of a very long illness.

We are waited on by a kind old woman, beautiful and thin and her hair drawn back from her forehead and held with a black velvet band – a Tyrolese – from what is now Italian and was Austrian Tyrol. I said that I had stayed a night in Bözen, as my blue suit-case witnesses. She was very excited – 'Ach, so, Sie kennen *Bözen*'. I couldn't be as enthusiastic about it as she since all that I remember of it was walking round and round with Teddy and Berlin[3] looking for Derek in the registers of hotels, and almost missing our train next morning. But she was delighted by it and told me how unhappy the Tyrol was, and both her brothers out of work, and we both shook our heads over Hitler, and she obviously would have liked to do the same over Dollfuss with his pro-Italian policy, but was too patriotic actually to.

This is office hours. But I still have on the whole so little to do during mine that I see nothing wicked in finishing off a letter in them. They are very friendly and tolerably encouraging, but though all overworked they find it hard to give me things to do – the natural dislike of surrendering things you know how to do to someone who doesn't I suppose. Even if you don't want to do the thing yourself you don't want anyone else to. What I do is still simply drafting – some of it interesting – rum men and rum companies wanting rum privileges and rum concessions. By degrees probably I shall be able to tease them into giving me more to do. As it is I don't much mind but sit and read things like reports which may come in useful eventually.

[1]David Jones, poet and painter, had worked with Eric Gill at Ditchling and Capel-y-ffin, and for a time been engaged to marry his daughter Petra. He had

become a close friend of T's – another of those friendships nourished at Rock Hall. One of the comparatively few portraits he painted was of T, done at Rock in 1930. David's journey to Cairo and Jerusalem was supposed to be part of a cure for a nervous breakdown, but, as will be seen in the letters, was not in this respect particularly successful.

[2] Eric Gill had been invited by Austen Harrison, the Government architect, to carve ten panels for the courtyard walls of the Rockefeller Museum, each to represent one of the ten peoples, starting with the Canaanites and ending with the Crusaders, who had had a cultural impact on Palestine. Gill often wore the habit of a Dominican Tertiary in England and Arab dress while he was in Palestine. 'On the night before he left Jerusalem Eric was entertained to dinner by Sir Arthur Wauchope, the British High Commissioner. He was prepared to dislike any proconsul, and this one in particular, but he thought him "really ready to be decent and not unintelligent". Wauchope's secretary, Thomas Hodgkin, became a close friend of Eric; and the breakfast table at Government House was enlivened for some weeks to come by arguments about whether Beauty could really be left to Look after Herself [the title of one of EG's books]' *The Life of Eric Gill* by Robert Speaight (Methuen, 1966), p.252.

[3] (Sir) Isaiah Berlin, OM. Oxford friend of T's.

TO DFH
3 JUNE [1934]

THE AUSTRIAN HOSPICE
JERUSALEM
SUNDAY

David is sitting on the divan reading the *Anatomy of Melancholy* which I lent him as suitable, but what he wants is the *Last Chronicles of Barsetshire*, which I might have brought if I hadn't been an ass, and thought only of what I would want to read and not what other people might. Could you possibly send it do you think, that old two-volume copy? Burton's arrived too, the other Burton,[1] and I mean to read him before the summer is out: it's beautiful of you, but I'm afraid frightfully expensive, as it boasts on the wrapper that it is very cheap indeed and only costs seventeen dollars: I'm afraid that's a lot, even with the dollar what it is.

This is a warm good day and full of chirping birds. At lunch today I pay my first state visit to the Bowmans, to be formally forgiven I suppose, though from the one short meeting that I've had with him so far I gathered that I was unofficially forgiven already. Then I thought that I might try to bully David into coming to tea at Tantur, by motor-car, the kind of gentle exertion that he might be able to manage: I'm afraid he hates Palestine though. How can one do anything else when one's stomach is out of order, let alone one's soul?

There seems no solution, and it is no use trying to arrange treats.

The man I work under is an old Balliol man called Thompson, enormously genial, married to a Cypriot (?Cypriotte), a die-hard, talks a lot, hates work, smokes a cigar every day after lunch, a thorough bureaucrat. Otherwise I know no one there yet at all personally, though I like at a distance and admire Duncan Macgregor's[2] fine brother-in-law Champion, just back from Äden and was in the Beersheba district, the right sort of picturesque desert-hankering Near-Eastern Colonial servant.

I was at the eye-hospital this morning. It is horrible to see all these people, herded in-patients and straggling out-patients, all with the same miserable thing wrong with them. A comfort, of course, that they do get treatment now at all from good doctors, but obviously far too few, and one just presses past because one is English and wears a tidy suit. I went because of the insulting things that Doctor Glen Liston said about my left eye: this man didn't seem to think much of it, treated it as David says the country priests treat him when he says he has nothing to confess.

I put on my lovely tails to watch this damned king's birthday parade, I mean this excellent king's fortunate birthday damned parade. I must run and lunch with the Bowmans or be late and have to be forgiven again.

[1]Sir Richard Burton the explorer. More likely to be his *Personal Narrative of a Journey to Al-Madinah and Mecca* than his translation of the *Kama Sutra*, though not clear why he had to be paid for in dollars.

[2]Duncan Macgregor. Fellow of Balliol and T's tutor for Greek and Roman history. His brother-in-law was Sir Reginald Champion, a Divisional Officer in Palestine 1924–28 and Political Secretary in Aden 1928–34.

TO RHH   THE AUSTRIAN HOSPICE

14 JUNE 1934   JERUSALEM

I want to write twice a week yet seldom do, it is this mixture of longish hours, Arabic, David, and the heat I think that takes time away from writing letters. Governing seems to usually till about six, Arabic then till seven, and David the rest of the evening, or rather for the rest of the evening the heat and he contest for my soul, the interestingness of his conversation against the overpoweringness of the heat. Up till about ten the heat seems usually to win and I am three-quarters asleep and make imbecile replies to all his remarks. But then when he has despaired of me and begins to go to bed I become ashamed of myself and wake up and begin to talk, and though I grudge time not spent in writing to you and the few other people that I very much want to write to and don't, yet I have no chance of seeing David during the day and he is very good indeed to talk to. And since he came to Jerusalem against his will under the pressure of friends who thought that they knew what was good for him, and is wretched and grows wretcheder as the heat grows intense, I feel conversation is the least one can do for him. Besides he is learned and wise and interested in the things that I am interested in, Jews and Crusades and the British empire, and makes admirable judgements about all of them, having Catholic wisdom without those particular Catholic prejudices that one doesn't like.

Alas, idiot that I am, the air mail goes in half an hour and I must dress and run with it. What a wretched scrap to send off to you. I am ashamed. But last night when I meant to write it I had hurriedly to dine with the High Commissioner – more glory – and arriving back here at eleven having walked the three miles back from his palace, full of moselle and old brandy, roast pigeon, crème brulée and green figs, I could do nothing but fall immediately asleep, swearing that I would write this early in the morning. And now it is seven already or more and the post goes at half-past.

It seemed a very successful dinner with HE, good conversation leading off from Andy MacCulloch[1] who I boasted of, and he thought a lot the better of me for that connection and I loved him for being even remotely a Jameson, and the hot wind had gone and we sat on the terrace for dinner with a cool wind like cold wine blowing in our faces.

---

[1]General Sir Andrew MacCulloch. Elder brother of Johnny Jameson (see p.67). Changed his name to MacCulloch to inherit the Ardwall estates in Kirkudbrightshire.

It's after dinner and there's the faint noise of Arabs singing or praying through the city, a nice cool windy evening, after a quiet and pleasant day. Again to the Benedictines with David and the Gills in the morning (at this rate I shall be at Rome before Teddy even). A most beautiful service they have, simple and admirably drilled. Germans they are so that's natural, and high Mass is an admirable rite though without a missal very difficult to follow even with David's whispered helpful comments. He is very bold with them, as people tend to be at their own forms of worship, where oneself being ignorant is shy of doing anything but inconspicuously praying. Rather like Uncle Johnny[1] he was, and when they sang a *Te Deum* at the end said, 'It's probably because the Germans have taken Paris.'

We went on from there to look at the splendid Armenian church, full of bright tiles all the way up the walls, almost like a mosque, and lovely childish but good and Giottolike wall-paintings of Hell and Heaven, a little like Fairford too, glorious black demons and scarlet flames. Last Sunday, when David and I went alone there, there was a glorious christening of a naked child looking like a piece of red uncooked beef by a crimson-robed gold-crowned priest looking like the Red King, everyone very off-hand about it all, especially the godfathers dressed up too in very smart vestments and giggling about wearing them to one another.

After that visit to the Armenians (today I mean) we went on wandering through the town stopping to buy nuts and beer and a fresh red Arab handkerchief for Eric Gill like the one I wore on my journey last summer, a very slow progress since we kept stopping not only for real shopping and because Mrs Gill had just seen something that caught her fancy, but for Eric Gill to stop and offer nuts to any of the many small boys that he knew or liked the look of.

By after lunch I became strange to say extremely sleepy and lay down for a moment on my bed meaning to sleep for half an hour and then wake, write to you and after go out on a picnic and walk beyond Tantur with the Bowmans, a kind invitation of theirs. But a kind of devil seems to dog me in my relations with the Bowmans, bad as I sometimes am with other people like Tom Boase about appointments, there is no one that I am invariably so hopeless with as the Bowmans. This time I was half an hour late for I slept Heaven knows how for two hours and had to telephone at once for forgiveness, which I received immediately from Mrs Bowman and eventually from Mr. It is a damned malign fate, or my own damned stupidity merely perhaps, that makes me always do something wrong with the Bowmans though always meaning to behave so very rightly.

However this meeting was a great deal pleasanter than the one a fortnight ago, a really lovely walk, a very gentle one along the paths near Tantur that lead nowhere or back to where you were before or exactly in the opposite direction from the one which you were aiming at. And it was beautifully clear, the Transjordan hills as pink and as detailed as they used to be from Jericho in the winter before last. We picnicked on a rock which was out of the wind and out of the sun and out of the view, after a lot of dispute about which of the three should be sacrificed to which, and wall after wall to jump over and down as though it had been Rose Castle[2] or the moors anywhere.

A quarter of an hour before this ought to go to the post. I've managed it a little better than last time, anyhow, but this isn't the sort of long letter that I'd meant to write. While the visitors are here that is bound not to be easy. But you mustn't think that it is at all more wretched than delightful having David here. Though he hates the idea of any kind of activity he is magnificent company and not neurasthenic in that kind of way. Talking seems to be about the only thing that he enjoys doing, and he is so learned and witty that I always enjoy these conversations that go on intermittently from six till eleven at night. It's been a very good opportunity for getting to know him which I'm thankful for. I only regret that it means I scamp my Arabic and my letters to people. But you mustn't feel that he's a burden at all except that I feel that I ought to be trying to do something about trying to cure him and that I don't know what to do about it, but really I think one hardly ever can do that for other people. But I'll consult you about that in my next letter.

Work goes slowly, but at least I have so far secured the friendship of Thompson, the rum Old Balliol man that I work with and under who is therefore I suppose responsible for my progress or regress. I disagree with him about so many things that I don't know whether we shall be able to keep our embryo friendship up, perhaps vaulting ambition on my side will do it. Anyhow I have asked him and his Cypriot wife to dinner on Tuesday.

[1]John Gordon Jameson. Married to Margaret, fifth daughter of A.L. Smith. Tory MP for West Edinburgh and Sheriff Substitute for the Lothians. A preacher of the Gospels at every opportunity, particularly at the Edinburgh Mound, a Scottish Speakers' Corner. Mary, his elder daughter, inherited her parents' beauty, wit and originality, but not her father's politics, after the war embracing Communism with a zeal of which T thoroughly approved.

[2]A high point on the Chatton moors in Northumberland overlooking Chillingham Park and the only herd of wild cattle in England. A favourite picnic rendezvous.

TO DFH   AUSTRIAN HOSPICE
25 JUNE 1934   JERUSALEM
                                                  MONDAY

In a week David and the Gills are going, they think, and though that will make this place a lot less pleasant for me it will have the great advantage of there being more time for writing letters in. As it is every evening after dinner when I am in I spend talking with them till eleven or so – admirable but means there's not much time for other things. But I shall miss them. So it seemed sensible to escort them to the North when they wanted to go. And they are such magnificently enthusiastic people that they made the places and people alive and beautiful for me – the olives over the reddish earth, the bright skirts of Bedu women, the lovely first blue then green colour of the Sea of Galilee, like a bit of Italian sea, as bright as Porto Fino.

The sad part of it was though that Eric Gill started the journey with bad tooth-ache which grew gradually worse. Being a Tolstoyan sort of man in regard to his principles he bore his tooth-ache about as embarrassingly courageously as David bears his illness cowardlily (only cowardly in the good sense – in that he's always ready to talk about it – and likes to show how miserable he is). We stopped at Nablus to drink

Araq and eat cucumbers and goaty pastry – then stayed for the night at the north end of the Sea of Galilee – the Mount of the Beatitudes it's called – a pleasant Italian Hospice, but extremely hot as you can imagine. A lovely place to be with the more-than-half moon making the whole west half of the lake silver – looking at it from a balcony.

There it was almost cool, but in the bedrooms sweating hot – an alternative between mosquito nets which made you even hotter, got tied up with the bed-clothes and were too small to stay on the bed, and actual mosquitoes. I began by choosing the latter but was eventually forced into accepting the former. Still I slept better than the rest of them, at least four hours, while Eric and Mrs Gill slept only half an hour between them, and their daughter Joan two hours. Besides they had to get up for half-past six Mass while I was sleeping.

By then his tooth had grown very bad – an abscess it was – and he went to a little bearded Jew dentist in Tiberias who belched every time just before coming into the room. He had an injection, but it meant a lot of wrenching and must have been very painful. I watched for the good of my soul, and also being vaguely interpreter and master of ceremonies. It was a tough old one and broke. But the man used a stronger instrument and got it out at the second whack. A filthy shop he lived in in a repulsive bye-street, the shop full of noisy sewing machines and spare parts of bicycles, the consulting room reasonably clean though, and he seemed to disinfect his tools.

Late last night we got back, having left Eric Gill to sleep at Nazareth, and ourselves climbed Tabor – lovely, square and oblong shapes of fields below, a mixed gold and green pattern all over the land.

When the Gills go I shall I hope begin to walk in the country and know it better – an increasingly good country I think as one stays in it longer and begins to possess it more and know pieces of it more intimately. Spread out in front of me (as it might be Moses) on Tabor this afternoon it did look splendid, and the exciting pink and misty hills of Transjordan disappearing into desert beyond.

Now this must be posted. I'll try for another one in the middle of the week. I dined on Thursday with the Bowmans very pleasantly. I think we are wholly friends again. Some not

very good charades but a good dinner and good stories from
Bowman – three young women so young and so innocent that
I felt like an uncle and I'm afraid talked like one.

TO ECH   GOVERNMENT HOUSE
1 JULY 1934   JERUSALEM

Here, Heaven help me, I am in my sixth occupation since I
left the university – though last in time not least in station – in
fact easily the most exalted, and certainly the most uncomfortable. I am acting Private Secretary to His Excellency: the
other one went mysteriously back to England yesterday. I am
here till the Colonial Office gets another one (and you know
as I do the sort of pace at which the Colonial Office works) or
till I lose a treaty of peace or a declaration of war. I find
myself leaving everywhere in the most exposed positions
letters in bold handwriting saying 'It ought to be easy enough
to do this without the French hearing of it', and 'Of course it
is vital this should be kept secret *vis-à-vis* the Italian
Government', and 'I agree on condition it is realized that
neither the Grand Mufti nor any of the Saudi pan-Arab party
get to know of it, yours very sincerely P. Cunliffe-Lister'.
This is perhaps too serious a subject to jest on, but it is the
only way I think to prevent myself from losing all the
important documents, not to mind too much if I lose any of
them.

I am very frightened indeed of the ADCs. I have never
known any experience since that has been so like my first
term at Winchester; except that my hair is shorter, that I am
better dressed, and that I have the *savoir-faire* which going
through the OTC, to the extent of being honorary lance-
corporal seconded for duty to the Boy Scouts, gives one. At
least one ADC is kind to me in a J.D. Marstock[1] sort of a way
– the other is simply cold and handsome, a Seaforth
Highlander of alabaster. Ah Teddy, uneasy lies the head that
is even the third degree removed from the crown.

I am ravenously hungry because, in spite of sumptuous
viands, I am almost always too frightened to remember to eat
any of them. This little room full of maps, paper-clips, red
and blue pencils and telephones I share with the ADCs.

They haven't yet taken advantage of this proximity to tweak my ears, put glue on my chair, or throw ink bombs over my most confidential files, but undoubtedly they will. They were here this morning sorting out gramophone records under names of composers – very troubled by there being a Schumann and a Schubert. In the end they decided to sort them both under head SCHU, sub-heads MANN and BERT.

[1] A horrible public school character in Harold Nicolson's *Some People*.

TO DFH
1 JULY 1934

GOVERNMENT HOUSE
JERUSALEM
SUNDAY

I have explained my slap-up address in my letter to Teddy and I think of you as in Brittany when you get this letter. That may be quite wrong and I several days behindhand, but if you are together then I won't repeat to you the story of why I am here. It is an odd business, exciting and terrifying, useful and a bore, allatonce (that accidental word looks rather a good one and might be used again).[1]

It is a great bore having to leave the beautiful day-to-day life of living with the Gills and David for what would have been the last ten days of it. That is particularly a pity as I had promised to escort them again on a journey this weekend probably to Carmel and Athlit, which we missed last time because of Eric Gill's tooth. That has now ceased to be the swelling it was, and though it would have been certainly impossible to persuade David to move out of the hospice it would have been a good plan for the rest of us.

Now I can only creep back like a rather reformed Prince Henry very rarely to my old associates: usually in the afternoon which is a bad time for David and he hardly ever feels like talking then. On the other hand he doesn't like it if you take half-an-hour's silence between you as a reason for going away. That happened yesterday afternoon: he was too wretched to talk, but he wanted me to stay. Joan Gill says he is beginning to realize how in this state he gets on her father's nerves, who for all his gentleness has such robustness himself that he looks on all spiritual malady as sin and shows it. So there does seem point in not making David any more miserable by taking the same pull-yourself-together-man-and-do-a-decent-job-of-work sort of attitude, however gently, oneself.

Anyhow in the end yesterday afternoon he fancied a motor drive to Bethlehem, so I pampered him and we went, and looked at the exciting new mosaics which they are finding under the floor of the Church of the Nativity, thought to be Constantinian though I admit that my only authority for that view is Sister Matilda, who said they must be because they had Greek on them and the English gentleman's son who was digging there knew Greek and Saint Helen (Queen Helena) had spoken Greek. On the way back I visited Tantur, a beautiful interval.

I haven't told you much about this new work because I haven't really done it long enough to be able to say anything, it and the whole existence surrounding it are still very rum and unreal. I went last night to Bowman to ask his advice about the thing and he was friendly and gave helpful advice interspersed with grim stories of awful things done by previous private secretaries.

There was an MP[2] here for dinner last night, for Blackpool. That was a link though I didn't get a chance of asking him about Lucy. He talked about himself in strict confidence all the time. He was a most horrible capitalist, and had come out to Baghdad to spy into the possibilities of a trans-desert railway (the route to India you know) but had been previously in the Black Watch, HE's own regiment. He got moved with brandy, stayed much too long getting more and more confidential, and finally when he had been showed out he came back into the room to whisper to HE: 'The Black Watch is my religion, you know, my religion.' HE patted him kindly but non-committally on the back.

[1] This letter was, unusually, typewritten.
[2] Captain A.L. Erskine-Bolst. He defeated Edgar Wallace, standing as an Independent Liberal, at the 1931 general election. Lucy Bosanquet, a cousin of his own age to whom T was particularly devoted, was married to another cousin, Michael Gresford-Jones, then Vicar of South Shore, Blackpool, and later Bishop of St Albans.

TO DFH   GOVERNMENT HOUSE
15 JULY 1934   JERUSALEM

No chance of getting much of a letter written tonight I'm
afraid, though I shall use every available moment. But the
trouble is that there don't seem to be many moments going to
be available. Tonight is another slap-up dinner party – or
pretty slap-up, though I am told they can be slapper, for we
are not wearing our decorations tonight. The reason is that
there is only one admiral when there were meant to be two. I
must say I don't at any time feel that admirals are very big
game. One can't help feeling that an admiral may only be a
sort of maritime Uncle Harold[1] – a general which lives in the
water but still feeds its young and comes to the surface to
breathe.

The Italian admiral was called Novaro and was delightfully
Italian. One advantage of this on the whole rather terrible job
is that people like the Italian Consul-General ask you to
things ex-officio without knowing or caring who you are.
Hence I in my Barker's tails (valued the butler told me with a
pained look at 45 piastres – but very useful all the same – and
they arrived just when I needed them most), and the ADC in
his green kilt red stockings red jacket and buckled shoes,
went to the Italian dance on Saturday to meet old Novaro.
Hence we had a lovely Italian conversation mostly about the
excellent condition of the roads between Genova and
Livorno (the favourite road, Teddy will remember, of Binda,
il Rei delle montagne).[2]

I fear I talked indiscreetly about the French too to an
Italian Jew who teaches Hebrew at the Hebrew University. I
cannot help first beginning to talk politics with every foreign
stranger I meet, second, always running down the country
which I imagine he wants me to run down. But European
politics are safer to talk of than Palestinian ones anyhow.
Those I have almost learnt to avoid I hope. The great evil of
this life is that I have almost absolutely no time to myself, and
therefore no time to read, or, which is worse, to write to you
or to anybody, or, perhaps worst of all, to be at peace to
reflect on my sins and try to amend.

I took lunch peacefully out by myself and began to read
Tancred – as suitable for this present temporary greatness and

for Jerusalem. I feel I almost am Casilis or Ormsby myself – one of the fainter respectable people who lives quietly in the background of society on his £20,000 a year. Then I meant to settle down to writing in the afternoon, but this damned ADC made me escort HE and the visitors (a kind major with stomach-ache and his frightened wife and a proud Etonian district administrator) to Bethlehem to see the new mosaics, and that all took up the rest of the day till dinner time. To have the fun of jumping out of a car with a flag on it, springing to attention, being saluted by policemen and gaped at by burghers crowding round to get a glimpse of their Governor is fun, but the devil of a nuisance since it prevents me from writing to you. Then this damned dinner party last night.

[1]Sir Harold Hartley. Married Gertrude, eldest daughter of A.L. Smith. Brigadier-General, adviser to 3rd Army (Allenby) on chemical warfare. Science don at Balliol until spreading out into the wider world of affairs as Chairman of BOAC, President of the World Power Conference, President of the British Association, etc., etc.

[2]A leading Italian racing bicyclist of those days, whose name was painted in large letters on many walls.

TO DFH   GOVERNMENT HOUSE
[21? JULY 1934]   JERUSALEM

I write from among princes. Abdullah[1] has just arrived and has been excitedly describing to HE his adventures, how he saw over the Humber factory, how he went to the House of Commons and sat in the Distinguished Strangers gallery and got a wave from Sir Herbert Samuel, how he went to the aeroplane display at Hendon and watched men coming down from aeroplanes in parachutes and had to hide his eyes till the parachutes opened, how he went to Edinburgh and was met by the Lord Provost, and to Peebles and stayed in the best hotel. He told all this like a boy of 14 just back from Wembley,[2] trying all the time to think what was the most exciting thing that he had seen. He had a beautiful childish power of description, especially when he began to imitate the aeroplanes and the fizz of the bombs they dropped hitting the ground.

He had brought presents for HE in the proper oriental way

– photographs of himself in a striking attitude, cigars, tuffets, and (his best present) an iced cake in the shape of a mosque from McVities – to remind HE of the Dome of the Rock whenever he ate it I suppose. But unfortunately the dome had been smashed completely on the way, and the walls of the rotunda were badly caved in on the east side.

Abdullah travelled with Fuad Pasha,[3] his (I suppose) adviser, an agitated man who meant to do the interpreting but always just forgot the English word which he wanted at the critical moment. His two great virtues were that he was friendly and that he knew Haji,[4] had been (he said) a great friend of his when Haji was at Jedda and he himself Foreign Minister at Mecca. That was a pleasant link to carry us through what might have been otherwise a rather strained lunch. His doctor too was there, a plump man who ran round with Fuad and was said to have eaten so much in England that he had come back weighing 150 kilos. Then he had a lovely English captain with a scarlet uniform and a twinkling blue eye as ADC. Finally a Chamberlain (he had left Palestine as a personal servant but came back a Chamberlain – I suppose because Abdullah decided when he was in England that his suite would look better with the addition of a Chamberlain) with the typically Mahommedan name 'Mahommed'. He wore a splendid dagger in his belt, had four long pigtails, a nice smile, and was thickly perfumed with the kind of scent that cabaret girls use.

The little Amirs[5] had come to meet him here the night before and were rather bores – great bores in fact. They wore swords and spurs and one heard them rattling at the far end of the passage, like *Punch* ghosts, before they came into the room. The larger one had been to Sandhurst so had at least the merit of talking English and was moderately friendly: the smaller could only snigger (in Arabic) behind his hand. They played hide and seek with their father along the passages till midnight – or that was the sound they made at any rate – and were up at half-past four in the morning to have the Koran read aloud to them by Dad.

All this is fun but it uses up time and wears HE's temper. The Abdullah day was a bad one, but the anger of generals is an easy thing to meet on the whole. Besides, [he has] these continual large dinner parties where he has to be tactful to a dozen ticklish nationalists at once. For me they are a relaxation. It is easier to talk to a rascal who has just bribed himself into being Mayor of Bethlehem and another rascal who is meaning to edit a paper with him and learnt enough English in four months to be able to talk about any political subject but not about anything else, than it is to talk to HE really. Now everyone has gone. I hope I have been able to 'walk with kings, and keep the common touch'. From my limited experience (rather short meetings with few rather trivial kings) it seems a fairly easy thing to do.

After lunch we are going, by aeroplane, to Athlit – the Crusader castle, south of Haifa. I stayed there with Boase and John Richmond. So you will be the only one of the family who hasn't done it – I'm a bad third. It will be lovely to watch water and land. I hope I shan't be both sick and frightened.

Later: My first flight over. I was more frightened than sick, but not enough of either to spoil the beauty and excitement of it. Over the hills first (the kind pilot passed me a note saying he hoped I wasn't finding it bumpy; I said No so long as it didn't get any bumpier). The ADC and I in a tiny cockpit – the whole aeroplane tiny and most unsafe, I thought. HE by himself in another aeroplane; a police escort in the third, they and we one each side of him.

It was lovely flying along the coast: patterns of deep olive groves staring up from the yellow soil – a thin band of golden beach, and then the brilliant green sea. We entered Haifa in fine style – circling round above the town first all so close that I thought our wings would buckle. They knew best though; we didn't.

It is very happy and almost peaceful to be here: very like Bamburgh. We had a bathe as soon as we arrived. The castle wall a glorious black silhouette against the pale sky. Almost night now: in a moment I must change. (We are very simple and only change into dark suits in the evening here, and dine very early, at eight: altogether rather vulgar.) The ADC thinks this a romantic spot, and would be suitable for a honeymoon. I agree. My tent is as big as my bedroom in Beaumont St and about five times as comfortable. It is an Oriental model with an anteroom for the harem at the back.

[1]Emir Abdullah of Transjordan. Son of King Hussein of the Hejaz, brother of King Feisal I of Iraq. Murdered in 1951.

[2]The Wembley of the Empire Exhibition of 1924, rather than of cup-finals.

[3]Fuad Pasha Khatib. Abdullah liked his company because they were both poets. When Fuad Pasha deserted to Saudi Arabia, Abdullah used to send him reproachful verse telegrams.

[4](Sir) Reader Bullard of the Levant Consular Service. Known to his friends as Haji. Married Miriam (Biddy), fourth daughter of A.L. Smith. Later became Minister to Saudi Arabia and wartime Ambassador in Teheran.

[5]The two sons of Emir Abdullah, Talal and Naif.

TO ECH   EL A'AL

[22? JULY 1934]   SUNDAY

A most exciting visit – the non-committal address which I have given you is the name of a great stretch of high flat fairly fertile country called the Belqa. It comes into books on the Near East a good deal – Gertrude Bell was quite often in it. Now I am gate-crashing (with HE's leave) on a party of the Amir Abdullah's, so easily does British gold buy the invitation of princes.

But the Amir is very genial about it and beautifully welcoming, and even didn't mind my going to sleep at dinner yesterday during a very long fairy story which he was telling – the kind about a virgin, and a future husband who suspected her virtue, and a riddle, and an old man with second sight who lived in a cave three years' camel journey off, and spasms and bleeding at the nose whenever his second sight worked, and a happy ending with the virgin proved innocent, the husband repentant and an answer found to the riddle. A lovely story in Arabic, so far as I could understand it, but a bit of a bore in English. So I began to nod asleep, which the Amir noticed, laughed at, and forgave. By that I won the affection of Naif, his younger and duller son, who felt that was the right sort of attitude to have to his father's conversation, having been groaning yawning and stretching at his father's stories all evening. He then took courage from me and frankly went to sleep in his chair. I thought that rather shocking – he was sitting on his father's left too, young cub.

Now Sheikh Fuad Pasha who is Haji's friend – I asked him to come for a walk but he can't poor chap because of his kidneys, and anyhow can't see why anyone should want to walk if they have the good luck to know an Amir who owns three bright yellow cars – Fuad Pasha means, very courteous-

ly, to take me in a car to look at a Circassian village. I might
buy one if I had enough money with me.

Returned: We rolled over the country in one of these yellow
cars enjoying the obeisances of the village, drank coffee with
a principal merchant (obviously well off because he wore
European trousers as well as a European jacket) and refused
(after about 20 minutes' politeness) melon.

It has been a lovely occasion – more like May Field I
should think than anything. About six tribes are gathered
here to honour the Amir and HE and to get free food. The
honouring consists mostly of firing live rounds nominally up
in the air whenever the Amir or HE or anyone else of
consequence goes past – to the great danger of the
aeroplanes when they do go off into the air and of the rest of
us when they don't. Half of the tribes, mostly Beni Sakhr,
had arrived last night, and we stood on the top of the hill
where this camp is and chatted to them and watched the
sunset and let the cool wind blow on us: very pleasant.

The rest arrived this morning. One could see them early
streaming over the hills miles off like a swarm of insects,
singing their monotonous perpetual chant, and galloping as
soon as they came to within about a mile of the camp. Then at
about eight this morning they held their great celebration –
that was to form up in line along the plain. We, the monarchs
and their trains, stood under a canopy with chairs enough for
four of us, and watched them stream past – galloping their
horses, trying to fire, gallop and shout loyal and self-
congratulatory remarks (a sort of mixture of 'God save
Abdullah' and 'look at me riding') at once. Most of the ones
that did manage all three fell off.

A major diplomatic *faux pas* was committed by HE looking
the other way just as the Amir Naif rode past hallaoing at
him. As a result Naif has cut all meals since. The
performance was a mixture of the gathering of the tribes
before passing over Jordan, the Field of the Cloth of Gold
and the Fourth of June. Had it been a charade it might have
been guessed as any one of them. It was a lovely sort of show
– no expense or fuss but admirably spectacular.

I was introduced to a nice old man who looked like a
Bombay nationalist, called Sultan Adwan,[1] very small, dried
up, black beard and spectacles. His tribe used to rule the

Belqa I was told. I was also told that his age is 100, that his beard is dyed, and that he has a new wife every year. He wore a tremendous long gold-sheathed scimitar like all of them, hundreds of cartridges hung round on a ferocious bandolier.

They do carry arms extraordinarily young here. You go into cartridges long before you go into long trousers. I've seen boys of ten or less looking like young armament firms – but so far thank Heavens all the firing has been up in the air. It is odd to be in a tribal society, though. I feel it very ungermanic – no need for socialism in a community where everyone knows his king, from time to time has a slap-up meal at his expense, and where many can chat to him. I think I begin to see a point in favour of Social-Democrats as opposed to Communists, for the latter seem to say compel people into Communism whatever point of development they have reached, whereas Social-Democrats I think say that you only want Communism when a state has developed so far that it must be communistically organized or burst.

Lovely yesterday, flying from Jerusalem, looking down all the length of the Dead Sea, and the tongue that sticks into it, and far away towards the desert.

Home again – well, humble and simple though it is it's nice to be back in the old place – dear old Guv. Cottage. It has at least the advantage of water-closets as opposed to fields of thickly growing maize – and no bed-bugs such as infested the silken counterpanes of the Amir.

[1]He had rebelled against Abdullah but been reconciled. Perhaps not a hundred, but certainly very old and uxorious.

TO DFH	GOVERNMENT HOUSE
29 JULY 1934	JERUSALEM
	SUNDAY

I am afraid we do not stock any paper cheaper or lighter than this and as I must display the coronet I think I'll go on using it and damn the expense. After all it will only be for another month: my boss leaves for England on the 26th. Then I shall be simply an abandoned favourite – return to turning the spit in the Austrian Hospice, lucky if my arrogant manner while in office has not stirred up a plot to stab me as soon as I fall from power among the old Heads of Departments whom I used to lash with ill-bred gibes while the High Commissioner applauded.

Today has been quiet. I have written letters a good deal, walked for a couple of hours over the wilderness towards the Dead Sea, chatted with friendly natives, one with a voice like all the bass stops of an organ and a pretty daughter, read more than a chapter of *Curzon*[1] – for which I am tremendously grateful to you both, and for *Civitas Dei*,[2] which the papers have praised and which looks as you say a good book to lend to one's Arab and Jewish friends alternately. I'll have a shot at it when I return to obscurity and the Austrian Hospice.

As for this last week it has been quiet too and pretty full of affairs of State. HE is very much occupied with the question of a Legislative Council, which the Government has been trying unsuccessfully to establish for twelve years. Now it is pledged, and has been pledged since 1930, to establish it even if it is boycotted by one section of the community. It is the Jews who are particularly against it now: they want to wait until they are in a majority in this country – though not everyone supposes that they ever will be in a majority. But their experience of being a minority under representative government in Europe since the war has been so unhappy that they are naturally frightened of having the same thing happen to them here. It is unlikely that it ever would of course since no Legislative Council in which Arabs, as the most numerous section, dominated, would have power over questions which concerned the carrying out of the mandate – e.g. over immigration. But that doesn't prevent them fearing, and the Arabs hoping, that it would. HE has spent this week having interviews with prominent Palestinian Jews, trying to find if they would co-operate, and if they think Palestinian Jewry would co-operate in a Legislative Council. One Jew, a lovely white-haired Labour man, a Russian idealist who mumbles and came over with the second group of pioneers in, I think, 1907 or so, is here tonight. He talked interestingly about what non-orthodox Jews nowadays mean by the idea of a Messiah – a sort of ethical message to the world: a bit indefinite and Russian and symbolical and idealist and beautiful and hopeless like the ideas of most Russians, his was.

(I finish this letter in bed, Monday morning.) I'm afraid it sounds as if the Jews are very likely not to co-operate, which would mean a Council with only Arabs and British officials in it, therefore not properly representative, and probably consequently a wider division between Arabs and Jews.

It is rather glorious to feel oneself one of the only three or four people in Palestine (I think) who know the numbers which HE means to allot to Arabs and Jews and British officials, even if I don't do more to the numbers than blot them. Yet it is fine talking (as I did yesterday at tea with Bowman) discreetly on the subject, making now and then a minor revelation and implying all the time a vast reserve of information which it would be indiscreet to reveal.

The only other politically interesting thing which happened was two Syrian nationalists – one a Druse and very wretched, the other very bright, a little like the mock-turtle and the griffin – both under sentence of death in Syria. They came to tea here, and the Druse talked French rather dreamily, recollecting his childhood and the advance of mechanism among Arabs. He'd just been on the peace mission to Ibn Saoud who apparently had over 200 machine-guns. Unfortunately the French ('The French' you know) got upset, and all the exiled Syrian nationalists began to come to Jerusalem to chat with these two, and there was a wild morning of interviewing the French Consul-General and this poor Druse, the Amir Shakib Arslan[3], alternately. And in the end he had to go, but with great diplomacy it was discovered that the first boat which he could get a berth on was the one which he meant to travel on anyway. So the French were satisfied and the principle of courtesy to Arab exiles even if they are plotting to shake off the French yoke was maintained.

[1] *Curzon: The Last Phase*, by Harold Nicolson.

[2] *Civitas Dei* by Lionel Curtis.

[3] Druse leader. 'Emir el-seif wa el-qalam' ('prince of the sword and of the pen'). Prolific author. His daughter married Kamal Jumblatt, the Lebanese Druse leader and politician, founder of the Progressive Socialist Party, assassinated in March 1977.

TO DFH
11 AUGUST 1934

GOVERNMENT HOUSE
JERUSALEM
SATURDAY

This is a beautiful peaceful evening. My boss is away, gone to celebrate the 12th with shooting sand-grouse at Beersheba, and much though I love him it is jolly to be on one's own in this vast house full of exquisitely smelling flowers, carnations and lilies above all, pink lilies with a subtle smell that I don't know, and the flower-beds in front of the house bright with rock-roses of every colour, as thick and varied as tiddlywinks.

I have been working a little, walking in the garden rather less, sleeping not a great deal, and writing odd letters this evening: a couple of rather humbugging ones, one to Mrs Richmond thanking her for Papist tracts, and another to the Austrian Consul-General thanking him for a horrible propaganda account of the death of Dollfuss, with some admiration of the Heimwehr and the operas which I didn't see last summer at Salzburg thrown in. I have now dined alone in immense state – dressed – reading the life of Curzon, with a soft–footed Berberin slave ministering to my wants, padding behind me with hands full of tureens of rare green vegetables sacked from every horticultural station in Palestine, and decanters of sherry and white burgundy sacked, thank Heavens, from the vineyards of Xeres and Burgundy, not of Palestine. I ate and drank so much that I am afraid I fell asleep from immediately afterwards until now, and now I really ought to go to bed, for I have arranged to be called at 4 tomorrow morning – foolishly – intending to motor to Hebron and walk back via Jebel Fardis (towards the Dead Sea, also called the Frank Mountain, a flat-topped hill that sticks up from here and which I have therefore always wanted to go to – the ancient Herodium, I am told). The slave that wakes me (the same I am afraid that tonight fed me) gaped when he heard that I should be walking when three stately well-bred Humbers were eating their bonnets off in the stables – like Fuad Pasha last week. As it is now midnight that means I have at most only 4 hours more sleep tonight, and I need them all. So I'll say goodnight and bless you now.

TO ECH   GOVERNMENT HOUSE
19 AUGUST 1934   JERUSALEM

I think I am just going to catch your birthday, by the skin of
my teeth; this should reach you on Friday at latest, perhaps
Thursday, so it will have a day to recover its breath. I try to
think of appropriate quotations for a 21st birthday. But
though I try to remember how 'long expected one and twenty'
goes on, the tune in my head is *Dies irae, dies illa*, and has
been ever since we mourned Dollfuss[1] with it in the chapel of
the Austrian Hospice, a tune appropriate for the world
situation but not for your birthday.

Jerusalem had been enriched for me by the return of
Perowne[2] and Antonius. The latter you remember talking
passionate politics at the Maison Basque.[3] He is even more
charming here than in England, because in England there are
more people rather like him, whereas here there are very few
– no one that I have ever met that so admirably combines the
passion of the Syrian patriot with the lucidity of the
Cambridge don in stating his patriotic beliefs. It would be a
jolly good thing for the Arabs if they had some more people
equally clear-minded to put their case. As he says, the Arabs
do lose from having no Englishman practically competent to
understand their point of view, and no Arab competent to
express it.

It looks almost as though there might be going to be the
usual summer riots. I hope not. But an Arab boy has been
stabbed by a lot of Jew boys (not to death – though it is said
that the Arab youth leaders are anxious that he should die, so
as to give them a good excuse for a row). The trouble now is
all this illegal Jewish immigration: anything up to about 2,000
come in every month by avoiding frontier controls – there are
no coastguards to stop them coming in by sea, and too few
police by land – with the result that Arab boy-scouts have
formed themselves into an illegal body to prevent illegal
immigrants coming, with the result that the Jews have formed
themselves into another illegal body to prevent Arabs from
preventing illegal immigrants coming in. And then both lots
meet on the beach, which is how trouble begins.

This is very dull and heavy and imperialist. I am sorry. My
letters are bound, I am afraid, to become increasingly so, as I

become increasingly bureaucratized. You must stop me from writing them when they are.

A lot of French about lately, including an admiral. They dined here and we all talked English very loud and very slowly. It is an odd feeling, talking to Frenchmen, for they always seem to make you feel that England is committed to France – that we are both in the same boat, that we govern Palestine as repressively as they govern Syria, and that we shall both be fighting shoulder to shoulder before long – a horrid idea.

The kind-hearted butler has given me an enormous lunch up in my room – smuggling me out of the lunch for the Director of Agriculture. Pray for his soul.

[1]Engelbert Dollfuss. Austrian Chancellor, murdered by the Nazis in 1934.

[2]Stewart Perowne. Joined the Palestine Government service in 1930. Later Oriental Counsellor in Baghdad and author of books about the Herods and others. Witty and scholarly product of Anglican bishops, Cambridge and Harvard. 'After George [Antonius] and John Richmond my dearest friend in Jerusalem' (Antonius Lecture).

[3]A very good but expensive restaurant in Dover Street, long defunct. Used for entertaining by Helen Sutherland when in London, and by T and others when they could afford it.

TO DFH   THE AUSTRIAN HOSPICE
27 AUGUST 1934   MONDAY

I moved in here last night. The horrible prospect confronts me of having to unpack before I can dress. It is cloudy cool damp early morning – very unusual. This will be very little of a letter I'm afraid, but never again as far ahead as I can see will High Commissarial bustle curtail my letters to you. HE went off yesterday afternoon. His ex-ADC and I went to the aerodrome to wave him off. I've never waved anyone off by aeroplane before and didn't realize the cloud of dust and earth and small pebbles that is spat up into one's face. So there wasn't much waving – more like the ascension of Elijah.

I was really sad to see him go. It has been a happy period on the whole – the tension of his rather exacting ways probably helped to make it so – and I grew very much to enjoy evenings alone with him, when we talked as freely as Mary or Aunt Helen about Shakespeare and Eternity. I will send you the letter which he gave me at parting – a beautifully friendly one, and a comfort to know I hadn't written it myself.[1]

As for meeting him in England, I should very much like you to. He will be near Hawick staying with Walter Elliot[2] (Agriculture), and near Yetholm staying with I don't know who, some time in September – about the middle of the month I think. Perhaps Aunt Helen would invite him over. But I know that he hasn't much time now. It isn't that it's not the thing for headmasters to meet the parents of their boys, but I think it will probably be easier to leave it till this time two years hence, when his time in Palestine will probably be up, and we shall all be in England together.

Now the sun is up and shining into my room. I found that it was not cloudy, only an hour earlier than I had thought, a pleasant and rare thing to find. Now I must settle down to trying to really do all the things which I said I would do, if being a Private Secretary and living at Government House didn't occupy all my time – above all learn Arabic. And I must learn my trade too. But there is now a better man than before to help me, just come back from leave, called Nurock,[3] an Irish Jew, an unusual combination, well spoken of, and Perowne is in the Secretariat too for a month which is fun for me. But he, like a hot-blooded young pro-consul detained in Rome on suspicion by the Emperor Tiberius, keeps looking towards the mountains and pines for his province.

You ask when and how I get your letters – at lunchtime usually, when I come back from the office. At Government House there was never time to read your letters before lunch. HE used to race into lunch leaving us hardly time even to wash. But when we'd finished lunch, usually at about three, then we were dismissed for the afternoon, and I could relax and read peacefully while the ADC went to sleep in a corner of the room. A very happy time.

[1]The letter reads:

> Government House
> Jerusalem
> August 25

My dear Hodgkin,

I feel very sorry to say goodbye to you today.

You took over the job, which is no easy one, at very short notice; you have been of the greatest help to me in every way possible – always so ready to work, to carry out my wishes as to what should be done, and constantly to put forward some jolly good ideas of your own. Apart from your work as Private Secretary it has been the greatest pleasure to have you as a companion in this house.

I only hope you have found people and things to interest you. In spite of the dullness inherent in an ancient and much occupied gentleman of 60 summers, I hope I may think that we have made good friends this summer and will continue to be so.

I wanted very much to give you a present, not so much for all the work you have done so willingly for me, as for the good relationship and interesting talks we have had together – but I have no idea what you would like, so I hope you will accept the cheque I enclose and get some books or anything else you want.

You have been too busy lately: so try and take plenty of afternoons off this next month, and I hope some weekends.

With many thanks for all you have done for me,

Yours,

Arthur Wauchope

[2]Walter Elliot. Minister for Agriculture. An ardent gentile Zionist, he leaked cabinet secrets to Dr Weizmann.

[3]Max Nurock. Assistant Secretary in the Secretariat. 'A brilliant historian from Trinity College, Dublin, with whom I had a very happy relationship – a kind of Zionist opposite number to George. He taught me much about administration – how to keep a tidy desk, make the files move around. He had a contempt for most of his colleagues' (Antonius Lecture).

TO DFH AND RHH
2 SEPTEMBER 1934

THE AUSTRIAN HOSPICE
JERUSALEM
SUNDAY

(Monday) The effect of a long walk and a hot bath and, curiously enough, sleep following on the bath interrupted this letter yesterday evening. It was a quiet and unadventurous but fairly active walk, and I am all pink again. But alas my cochineal, like other people's bronze, will never last. We went over the hills deviously to a place called Ain Karim, a pretty cypress-grown village looking down into a valley full of olive trees growing in lines as if they were marking the contours. From there up a great hill which made me repent all my good and evil living at Government House, and only prevent myself from vomiting by eating grapes on the top. Then down into a valley called Walagy (which may be called Bettir in your historical atlases as the Jews held out there in their second revolt, the Hadrian one, the last place), across the railway line, up to Beit Jala, and then on in extreme exhaustion to Tantur, where we were met with all the love and wine from

Matilda and the Mother Superior which I had longed for for the last four hours of the walk.

Iliffe, the man I was with, and I between us drank two bottles of not normally very delicious wine, but mixed with water and accompanied by potted meat and cheese sandwiches it was delicious, and I spent the second half of the day in a state of intense physical comfort. It was lovely in the garden there without future close enough to trouble one, with the satisfaction of six hours' walk behind and all one's appetites appeased. How good about drink nuns are: they would have brought us a third bottle if we had let them, and didn't mind in the least our sitting boozily there on their front lawn while the troop of tiny orphans in brown smocks was led in front of us to Mass and back, while a tall grim priest lounged after them with bell, book and candle.

Now it is six in the morning. I am happy to find that I can get up quite easily at this hour or even earlier, though of course it makes me go to sleep all the quicker during or after dinner. It is as you said very good to have friends back here. Antonius I have had one or two happy meals with, and the same with Perowne who to his disgust having got himself seen off and dined off from England as the young pro-consul finds himself now for a month temporarily in the Secretariat because there are so many people still on leave and such a great deal of work.

This is rather the riot season of course, especially with HE gone on leave. People who respect him personally, and behave nicely to please him, are not restrained by a Chief Secretary acting for him. The trouble at present which might lead to riots if anything did is all this illegal immigration of Jews. About 800 used to come in a month illegally, either by getting smuggled in by sea or by evading police posts on the northern or eastern frontier, both quite easy things to do. This has been infuriating the Arabs for very few of the illegal immigrants ever get deported, it's so difficult to trace them. When over 30,000 immigrants are coming into a country in a year legally (as have been for the last two years) it's understandable that you shouldn't want a lot more coming in illegally. The result has been that the Arabs have been organizing what are practically private armies, patrols, to watch the coast and catch Jews as they are smuggled in. The

Jews have of course replied to that by starting their own patrols to prevent this and to help the Jews who are trying to enter the country; which is a bad situation. 'The situation has deteriorated' is what they say of it. So far there has only been I think one actual clash when an Arab was stabbed by a Jew rather badly. Fortunately he has recovered, to the disgust it is thought of the Arab leaders. And the Government is being a lot more active about catching the immigrants themselves, with coastguards newly enlisted and even aeroplanes to look for ships bringing immigrants in, which has great moral effect one is told. But obviously so long as the immigrants aren't being caught the Arab argument that they are there to co-operate with otherwise rather ineffective justice is a strongish one; so of course morally is the Jews' case, considering how miserable a time they are having in Europe. But as in Germany and in any other country to have conflicting bands of illegally organized youth is a danger.

TO DFH   AUSTRIAN HOSPICE
8 OCTOBER 1934

It was beautiful to have your letter arriving just at lunchtime yesterday. I was giving lunch to a pleasant young Jewish Labour leader, extremely sensible and astonishingly hairy, called Zaslani.[1] As I was punctual and he was almost exactly an hour late I had plenty of time to read and re-read your letter while waiting for him, satisfying my hunger with potato chips. I was delighted and excited to hear that after all HE is going to, was about to be going to, stay with Aunt Helen. They will like one another I am certain, being both by nature Liberals, lovers of the North and probably many other good things in common, and he'll love Aunt Helen's drink as well as herself. I am proud that this plan should really have worked out, and it will be a beautiful bond in the future that he should also have stayed at Rock and looked out on the stream and the little wood and the cows in the field and almost the Cheviots if he craned his neck (I am supposing him the best bedroom of course), and walked down the avenue and down to the lake to feed the ducks. It is admirable of Aunt Helen. In a way I feel it is rather cheating since it will make it a lot more difficult for him to dismiss me from the service if he ever wants to, knowing my pitch-up[2] and having eaten their salt.

It has been a very quiet week; the only thing that stands out for me in it is that I have bought pictures – some or one of them was intended to be the remains of my 21st birthday present to Teddy, but I get such extreme satisfaction out of all of them that I shall find that difficult, unless by the time that Aunt Helen arrives I have managed to get bored with one. Two are Persian, not old, 18th century I should imagine; one (which I meant for Teddy), a lovely Watteau-like man with a face like a French diplomat standing on one leg in a red jacket and blue breeches, nothing else in the picture; the other Persian one is a wooer in a yellow suit reciting a poem to a coy and exquisite mistress about the size of a sparrow and dressed in violet and gold and at the back are trees full of pomegranates on which bolbols sing (or I suppose that they are bolbols). I have also bought two icons, one of which gives me the greatest pleasure of all – that is simply a Madonna and Child, not earlier than the 17th century I should think, but a glorious amplitude about her. I think Aunt Helen would admire her and I think you too. The last is a triptych of the kind that Aunt Gertrude[3] brought back from Athens but again newer, a most beautiful French Madonna and four saints, very lively, flowing cloaks and prancing horses. I should like the opinion of someone not necessarily who knows but who enjoys, e.g. you or Aunt Helen or Teddy. All this is not too expensive except that it drives me even more definitely to try and look for a house so as to have walls fit to put these on instead of these present ones, corrupted with one tremendous hideous holy picture.

---

[1]Reuven Zaslani. Born in Jerusalem. In 1933 joined the political department of Histadrut (trade union federation) dealing particularly with Arab workers in Jaffa. In 1936 joined the political department of the Jewish Agency and became one of those most responsible for liaison with the mandate authorities.

[2]Wykehamist notion for boys' families.

[3]Wife of Harold Hartley (see p.73).

TO DFH   AUSTRIAN HOSPICE
15 OCTOBER 1934

The sun just rising, a quarter past six. Fairly soon I shall have
to begin putting on my top-hat and tail-coat for Alexander.[1] I
hadn't much admiration for him, a tyrant I think; on the other
hand it means all the more tension in Europe, suspicion of
Italy I suppose, and one naturally compares Sarajevo. And to
have had two Sarajevos in a single summer (Dollfuss the
other one I mean) is unhealthy. But I suppose there may be
truth in the idea that anything, like this event, which tends to
distract attention from the increasing antagonism of Germany and the anti-German bloc is wholesome in a way.

So many sceptres and crowns have tumbled down this
summer that there has been a glut of memorial services. This
one is to be in the Holy Sepulchre, of which I am glad, but it
will be the Orthodox rite for which I am sorry, as these
Orthodox are from the little I have seen of them shoddy
about their services. Ruhi Bey Abdul Hadi,[2] a Moslem in the
Secretariat, my superior, an ex-Turkish diplomat and highly
polished who has spent most of his life attending memorial
services for royalty and that sort of function, refused to go to
this on the ground that His Beatitude the Locum Tenens
who will be officiating has an illegitimate child. I tried to
convince him of the greater reasonableness of the Catholic
Christian belief that the priest can be a vessel of Grace
however naughty. One advantage of that belief ought to be
that it prevents gossip; anyhow I believe it to be right don't
you? Do Quakers? I should think probably not.

[Refers to the visit of Wauchope to Rock Hall, where
RHH, ECH and David Jones had also been staying.] It does
sound to have been good but I am thankful that Daddy was
there to manage the conversation and do the honours; I agree
with him that David, though beautiful, would have been
hopeless. I wish, fool that I am, that I had remembered to tell
Aunt Helen that she ought to speak very clearly and quite
loud to HE: her voice is so gentle and Cordelia-low. That is a
frequent snag with visitors, for as a rule when he can't hear a
person he curses him. It has been the undoing of honoured
heads of departments before now. I had a letter from him
yesterday saying that he had very much enjoyed his visit to my

'Fairy Godmother', and seeing Teddy and Daddy, as I am certain he did, and asking Aunt Helen[3] and myself to stay with him here for a few days when she comes; beautiful of him and without doubt the best place to stay at in Jerusalem, in fact the only place really where Aunt Helen could be kept in the station of life to which she is accustomed. But as she said in her letter to you awkward in a way, since it gives the false appearance of an ulterior motive to her invitation. But that of course HE is too sensible to suppose.

Alas no more time, only to say that the first rain fell last night, a great hissing sheet for a few minutes, and that of my own will I took a day off and went with a man to where Bedouin rendered landless by Jews were being settled (there are not in fact many of these but a great fuss is being made of them and they know it) – after to an excellent lunch of stuffed partridges with an Arab farming family near Jenin that had spent much of last year in prison for murder. But they are rich and genteel enough to do it like Macbeth through other people.

[1] King Alexander of Yugoslavia. Assassinated in Marseilles, 9 October 1934.

[2] Senior Arab official in the Secretariat. Served in the Mandate Government until its end. Was later Jordanian Minister for Foreign Affairs.

[3] Helen Sutherland was on her way to Kenya, where she was going to set up a German refugee she had befriended as a coffee farmer.

TO RHH   AUSTRIAN HOSPICE
21 OCTOBER 1934

Anyhow it [Katherine Mansfield's *Journals*] is an extremely comforting book to read, a good change from *Tancred*, which after three months I have read 3/4 of, and the speeches of Stalin which after 11 months I have read hardly an eighth of, and the Koran (in Arabic) of which I have read two chapters at the rate of about ten verses every Sunday, about the rate at which I used to read Judges in the lower forms of the Dragon School, I should think.

My most striking and adventurous news is that I have bought a pony. I think you will approve on grounds of health especially; it is really the only possible way of getting horse exercise in this country where there are none except the most miserable to hire. This means that I shall get exercise twice a week I hope – huntin' it on Sundays and hackin' it on Wednesdays. And that will be good for me and I hope all right for it. The rest of the time it will be exercised and groomed by what they call a syce, which I thought at first was either a misprint or a piece of mechanism, a part of the bit perhaps, but now know is only the Colonel[1] for groom.

It cost £30, which I am told is a fair price. It is the more likely to be as the actual deciding on the price was done not by me who would probably in my greenness have paid a hundred, but by an, I hope disinterested, third party, the Chief of Police, a ridiculous man called Spicer,[2] whom Berlin will like to be reminded of, another of his old schoolfellows which grow as thick as cinnabars here.

The real expense will be the upkeep of course; but for £4 a month I have everything done, grooming, exercising, feeding, medicines and so forth at the polo stables, without of course having to involve myself in that expensive and class-conscious activity. There is also a £5 subscription to the Hunt; and that if I neither buy a red coat with buttons saying Ramle Vale Jackal Hounds nor have inscribed and mounted the rather gruesome jackal's pad, which Spicer (our Master, God bless him) with real kindness of heart gave me when we killed yesterday (only just around the corner from where we started from, so not much credit to have been there for it, but a kind gesture, welcoming an outsider), and which now waits on my dressing table to have something done with it, ought to be really all the expenditure which this pony will involve, and that I think, from looking at it, my balance in this country will stand.

I wish I knew what to do with this poor creature's foot. To bury it I feel would be unsporting, but apart from the expense I don't think I would have the face to hang it in my house and come home every day to its reproaches, like a stag's head on a small scale: I don't think I'm a fit person for stags' heads.

---

[1] One of the impersonations which T enjoyed giving, though in this case based on little first-hand experience, was that of an Indian Army colonel.

[2] R.G.B. Spicer. Inspector-General of Police and Prisons, Palestine, 1931–38. Isaiah Berlin had been at St Paul's School.

TO DFH   AUSTRIAN HOSPICE
29 OCTOBER 1934

I went out cubbing again yesterday. I wonder if I shall ever be
able to write that without embarrassment and some shame: I
don't say it but cover it behind 'riding', since most of my
friends are either aesthetes or Jews enough to resent such a
Philistine and British activity. But yesterday it was remarkably
beautiful. I went with a nice quiet Jew who can be a bore (but
has no chance at a concert) to a concert at which I regret to
say that I slept through what I would have enjoyed (Chopin)
and stayed awake for, or was kept awake by, what I disliked
(Debussy). This and a supper of eggs and bacon after with
the Jew and a talk about Persia kept me up till eleven, no
twelve, when I put on my breeches and went to sleep on the
sofa till half-past three – then an hour's ride in the dark in the
car of a pleasant clever almost over-cultured man called
Wolfson to the meet.

That was still before dawn; lovely as we stood round the
covert, I praying to Heaven that the jackal would be directed
not in my direction since I knew that if it slunk out opposite
me I shouldn't know how to deal with it or what to say to it,
whether to charge it and holla or to hide and stay silent, as
uncomfortable as fielding at mid-off in cricket; one feels
horribly exposed. Fortunately no jackal came my way; one
came the way of an Arab police officer who was out and he
charged up the hill after it; that though a most natural action
was treated as a great joke by our lot. We told each other and
retold the story about half-a-dozen times each to each, 'That
native policeman, did you see what he did, makes me laugh.
Jack went up the hill, hounds not in sight, and that native
went galloping away after him'; 'Well did you ever, what a
joke.'

It was a perfect morning, the copse bright green, the sky
extremely blue, and red huntsmen's coats against white Arab
ponies; the air sparkling and smelling here and there sweetly
of orange blossom; the earth tomato red like going through
Devonshire; low grey hills on one side and the sand of the sea
on the other, pale yellow and distant.

We finished or whatever the word is at ten, and I stayed
talking with the English policemen of Ramle who are the

nerve of the hunt till twelve or so, drinking their hospitable beer, learning to call drinking deep dyeing scarlet and when you belch in the pottle to call hem and cry it off, like Prince Henry you remember. The sergeant who had chiefly befriended me on the hunt turned up; he had led me on exciting canters over tricky country and prevented me falling off. He gossiped and his plump charming bread-coloured wife and his stiffish sister who refused beer and drank a very genteel quantity of fizzy lemonade came in. The sister wore a muslin gown and an artificial flower in her button-hole. She didn't like Palestine, was thankful she didn't live in it, pitied her sister-in-law who did, but if it was ever to be God's will that she should live here she hoped that she would have the fortitude to make the best of it.

The sort of bridle which I am told I should like most is called a Half-moon Pelham (no port) bit, with a martingale – sounds nonsense and I may have spelt it wrong but I am assured that that is the sort of bridle which a gentleman ought to have.

TO DFH   AUSTRIAN HOSPICE
5 NOVEMBER 1934   JERUSALEM

How much of this letter I have wasted already with no news given yet. The saddest piece is that Stewart Perowne, using the warm spot which he has secured for himself in the heart of every Chief Secretary there has been in this country in the knowledge that he was likely sooner or later to become a Colonial Governor to help him up another rung of Young Ambition's ladder, is going as Assistant Secretary to Malta, curse him. I curse him only because I shall miss him, and because I think he was a valuable person to have in this country since his love of it and his social graces both tend to reconcile the people that he comes in contact with, and they are hundreds, to English rule. But I mind more for myself, I'm afraid, probably.

I went down with the hunt again yesterday in the very early morning with the far waned moon just rising, and the shapes of riders and hounds when the dawn was just beginning, the dark outline of one's pony standing waiting for one under trees, and cantering across ploughed land to meet as the dawn became pink, trying not very successfully to make it distinguish between the quiet controlled canter that I wanted and the bolt that it wanted. That is still as Mr Fairchild would say its besetting sin. Indeed when the hounds actually ran out of the wood (BROKE COVERT, I believe is right , with the T not sounded) and streamed down a rocky valley after a real jackal my enthusiastic pony charged ahead quite out of my control, cutting across the horses of respectable colonels, passing both whips, although whenever I saw an open place I tried to make its awful speed less obvious by taking it round in a semicircular sweep, but even so it always came back again to the front of the hunt, and I only avoided riding like Mr Briggs[1] with the Master on one side and the principal hound on the other (not the thing to do) by riding against the face of an almost precipitous hill which couldn't be galloped up.

Such speed is not thought highly of by real hunting people as one would have thought, but they are very tolerant: 'He's young of course' they say; 'Needs a bit of licking into shape; but no vice in him, O no vice whatever.' I am never quite sure whether they mean all this to apply to me or to my pony: I think to both.

The Colonel whom I rode down told Perowne that he was sorry to hear he was leaving for Malta: 'You won't get any hunting there of course, but plenty of polo, though they say the ground's very hard, like a brick. The 60th Rifles are there you know; you'll find them very keen, but no hunting, none nearer than Gibraltar.' Stewart suggested that they might always hunt an Italian. The idea was taken seriously, considered, and rejected as inhumane.

That was all yesterday. I finished the day with two large meals. (Lunch I gave to the Pasha-like son-in-law[2] of the Prime Minister of TJ, in case that might be useful when travelling in the country; dinner I was given by Domvile,[3] a romantic Kiplingesque intelligence officer, who loves to moralize about life, the passions and God, and that we do very pleasantly together. Isaiah will describe him further to you.) For the rest of the day I fear that I chiefly slept. Alas I must dress and breakfast (that meal I have given more meaning to by buying a pot of Zionist honey) and go to work. I hear an unpleasant rumour that I may have to go back and be PS when HE returns. I pray not though I love him. I am bad at the job and I want to be independent; those are two very good reasons, but of course neither will have any weight if they once make up their minds. It would have advantages, but I think more great disadvantages.

[1]The stout *nouveau riche* cockney pictured in sporting and other embarrassments in *Punch* by Leech.

[2]Ihsan Hashim, Arab private secretary to the High Commissioner. Later Jordanian ambassador in London. His father-in-law was Ibrahim Hashim, many times Prime Minister of Jordan.

[3]Pat Domvile. Formerly with the Military Mission in Iraq, and later with RAF and other intelligence bodies in Arab countries. A charming, gregarious and boozy Irishman.

TO RHH   AUSTRIAN HOSPICE
12 NOVEMBER 1934

I'm afraid that this will be only a short letter, for the rain has come; and though that sounds inconsequential the fact is that I have been relying all through the past months on the sun waking me; as it has got later I have got gradually lazier. But now that the air is heavy with rain there is no sun at all, and I have stayed on happily in bed thinking of my letter to you and waiting for it to rise – a stupid thing to do.

It was lovely to get both your letters yesterday afternoon, as I stayed in hoping that they would come, reading William Temple and my Arabic Grammar alternately and watching the noisy rain and smelling the hot rich smell which came up from the garden after it. All the children in the streets came crowding round our garden wall where the rain poured out in a waterfall from a gutter at the top of the wall into the street below and bathed in it like the people of Rome in Caesar's blood in Calpurnia's dream, and flung it at one another and carried it away in tins in order to fling it in the future. It was a very uniting event, and every Arab that I talked to for the rest of the day we began by asking one another, 'How are you? How is your work? How is the rain?', and one always answered, 'Beautiful thank you'.

It is lovely to find that the saddle is all bought and coming so soon. It is beautiful of you to have taken so much trouble, even to buying a ridiculous thing like a No-port Pelham. (It sounds like a titbit of eighteenth-century history that doesn't it? The younger and less distinguished of the two sons of Lord Pelham who chose to enter a political career, Aubrey by name, was always known among his associates as 'no-port', an affectionate soubriquet (but how far founded upon fact we are not informed) which served to distinguish him from his greater brother, 'Three-bottle' Pelham, the trusted adviser of Fox and of Sheridan.) Thank you extremely too for taking the trouble to ride and even to sweat in it, and so to help it escape Customs Duty: I hope that it will. But the Director of Customs is my friend and has a great admiration for Winchester as a school, so that and the sweating and Aunt Helen's innocence ought to get it through.[1]

A little sociability during the past week, twice among Arabs, an Iraqi Bedu servant of Domvile, this Kipling-like person that I told you of, and the son of the Sheikh of Hebron, whose uncle[2] has been standing for the mayoralty of Hebron, and the nephew said gently to me as we were leaving supper that he knew that the English always settled appointments by rules and not by influence, but if his uncle's name happened to crop up in the course of conversation with the HC he would be very grateful if I would just mention that I knew him and thought him a very charming, reliable and honest fellow. I said that that would be rather difficult as I had never met him. He said that that would be arranged. Luckily I don't suppose it will, but I think it makes friendship easier if one does not appear to be incorruptible – which is one of the things that Englishmen make such a fuss of, the most fuss being made by those who are mentally most corrupt, whose minds are rotten with prejudice and dishonest thinking.

I was most excited to find myself in W. Temple's preface,[3] quite undeservedly, but nice publicity. I have written to him. It may not be very professional but I think it great which is more than most professional philosophers have any hope of being, both great breadth and great seriousness of thinking.

[1]The saddle was to form a large and unlikely item in Helen Sutherland's luggage.

[2]Sheikh Mohamed Ali al-Jabiri succeeded in becoming mayor of Hebron and retaining the post for many years.

[3]The Gifford Lectures by William Temple, Archbishop of York, *Nature, Man and God*, thanked T and two others in the preface for 'very numerous suggestions for the clarification of statement and, in some material instances, of thought'.

TO ECH
13 NOVEMBER 1934

GOVERNMENT HOUSE
JERUSALEM

Night is all at odds with morning, which is which.

I must write to you since it is upwards of five in the morning (in the best sense of the word 'upwards', when one doesn't know for certain whether it means 'more than' or 'less than'). It is years since I have worked so late – not since the old Manchester days – and I really have been working too, not simple working (sic), with a wink and a nudge and a guffaw. It has been fairly hack work and therefore not mentally fatiguing in the way that John Stuart Mill, read at the same hour of the morning, used to be – simply getting HE's papers ready for his return tomorrow ('tomorrow' in a conventional sense of 'after I have been to bed', actually in about 5 hours time), and trying, like a foolish virgin who has been standing idle all day in the market place and hired at the eleventh hour to trim my lamp in order to see to unbury the talent which my master gave me before travelling to a far country in the hope that on his return he will find me neither an unjust steward nor a Prodigal Son. (Fill in references: that might be a good question for one of Cheese's[1] divinity papers.) I must say I am thankful to be back in luxury again.

From Home to Home
Though you may roam,
It is one of those old-fashioned fallacies
To suppose that Homes are nicer than Pleasures and
  Palaces.

Forgive this scintillating letter – you will admit that I rarely do it – it probably comes of writing on an empty stomach. Or else it is the wretched mosquito that has been humming round me and biting every now and then, which takes the place of the ancient gadfly and stings me to wit. I find it hard to decide whether I hate mosquitoes or moths more – the pain of being bitten or the misery of having a great woolly body bumping up against one's flesh.

One day when I feel maudlin I shall write to you about your future – but not now. I am so bureaucratized that I would almost advise you to go into the Treasury.

I spent this morning looking at the lovely Dome of the Rock with a Moslem youth[2] who knows all about it – of good family (4th cousin of the Mufti) so the sheikhs toadied to him – also schools hidden away in alleys and hovels and courts of the time of Salah-ed-din Ibn Ayub and the Mamluks. We will see them all pray Heaven.

[1]G.C. Vassall, master at the Dragon School, thus affectionately known by all. For many boys an introducer to literature and the English language and a humanizer of divinity.
[2]Possibly Musa Husseini, later to be a graduate of the universities of London, Bonn and El-Azhar. Executed for his involvement in the assassination of King Abdullah.

TO DFH   GOVERNMENT HOUSE
19 NOVEMBER 1934   JERUSALEM

Yesterday was a full day – the opening Meet in the morning, attended by HE – my pony much too full of beans but jumping like an angel, or an ostrich perhaps is a truer simile. Then I had to hurry back, much too late, for an evening walk with Norman Bentwich, Haji's friend, who wrote the book that I read on the boat on the way here. A dullish dinner party of soldiers – during which I went to sleep but was forgiven.

TO DFH   GOVERNMENT HOUSE
25 NOVEMBER 1934   JERUSALEM
                                          SUNDAY

This Private Secretarial existence cuts the marrow out of the day and leisure is whittled down to nothing. I do unreservedly thank God that I shall expire in ten days or so: the game is very much not worth the candle. HE is lovable still but the tryingness of the life and my unsuitability for it become daily plainer. May God keep the new Private Secretary in good health and odour, that I be never called upon again.

From the point of view of seeing Aunt Helen it is particularly a nuisance. Today is Sunday but we have not worshipped because our Benedictines are at 9 and we felt that it might be rude to miss quarter-to-nine breakfast; so even Sunday gets eaten into. In the end we spent the morning seeing sights, seeing them quite pleasantly with this nice old boy – old Etonian old boy – Sir Reginald Hoare,[1] Envoy Extraordinary and Minister Plenipotentiary at Teheran – a beautiful thing to be – very gentle and humble, as frightened of being late for a meal with HE as we – the blue-eyed scholarly restrained quietly humorous sort of old Etonian. He says he never had any memory and therefore when the other fellows had to learn 40 lines of Virgil he was always given 12 lines of English. He and Aunt Helen get on quietly and pleasantly.

But it is all laid on too thick – no time to sit back and breathe: dinner parties every night – last night 6 couple of Jews, the night before 6 couple of nobs. It is a strain I am afraid for her and a bore for me, since the result is that we seldom get the peaceful times together which we would like. Yesterday was best and we had a good walk together for three hours or so after lunch – down towards the Dead Sea, a little way out into the wilderness, on the edge of which Government House perches. Even then we were harassed by thoughts of being unpunctual for tea, as indeed we were. Aunt Helen battles nobly in conversation with HE, and wins usually in the end and makes him laugh; but he is a testing sort of person. It is clear really that this was not the perfect plan – though *afterwards* (which is always a poor substitute for *now*) it may be nice to think of having met so many nobs. At present we have both a definite feeling of *embarras de noblesse* and think what fun it would have been in the cold ill-victualled Austrian Hospice waited on by nuns and not by scarlet-sashed Soudanis marshalled by a splendid British butler.

Tomorrow should be more peaceful for then HE goes to Amman for the day when Abdullah's son is married with a lot of fuss and food. The inside of the day at any rate will be ours.

---

[1]Sir Reginald Hoare. Minister in Teheran 1931–34. A post that was later to be occupied with great distinction by Haji Bullard (see p.76).

TO DFH   AUSTRIAN HOSPICE
9 DECEMBER 1934   JERUSALEM

I have just been re-reading your last two letters and looking out of the window into the garden, the dark green slightly swaying cypresses and the jolly bright green lettuces, and wishing that I loved lettuces more as diet, they look so pretty as vegetation. I rejoice to be back here and at peace, cold though it is and loathsome though the only means of getting warmer – a great black stinking petrol stove like a cockroach – is. Its warmth is all pretence, it simply sends out little darting red flames like the backcloth to the puppet show of *Faust* that Teddy and I saw at Salzburg, or the fireplace in *Hunker Munker*. I seem for the moment to have lost my power of revelling in the cold which I used to have or pretend to have after dinner in the drawing room at Bamburgh.

I rather wonder about this winter, whether I shall move somewhere warmer and equally peaceful; the Fast I thought of as possible, but that is rather more expensive than I think would be justified and anyway hotels are loathsome places to live in, exposed to the regular toadying greetings of the staff and the insolent stares of the other visitors at every entrance and departure. It is a question whether central heating is a joy that outweighs the beautiful but chilly love of nuns. When I left Government House finally yesterday evening I still hadn't decided the question and felt very like a waif launched out into the world uncertain where I was going to sleep that night. I feared that I might find myself back again on the steps of GH but in the end drifted here more from failure to decide on anywhere else than positive desire to be here. But they were all very beautiful and welcoming, full of Grüss Gotts and Wie geht's, and the Bishop thank God is off to Cyprus confirming the churches, so that there is a feeling of greater levity in the air. The nuns' eyes are bright and the Vice-Rector sings his sentimental songs after dinner louder and less guiltily, and the Fastest Nun of All joins in and gently hums the *Lorelei*.

The only thing that makes me not wholly contented with the place is that the gap where my teeth were is still sore (I am told by the dentist whom I trust that that is as it should be and that it is all going on very nicely indeed) and that makes me pine for comfort more. I don't want to be told that it's stringy boiled beef or nothing, but to be cajoled into tempting my delicate gums with the softest of creamy soufflés. That used to happen at GH, but it is really a joy to be finished with that. The awful dinner parties became more of a strain as we gradually sank from the sometimes interesting quality to duller and duller plebeians. There is some glamour about the Chief Justice[1] and his beautiful gentle wife, but scarlet and unhappy Mr and Mrs Fourth-in-the-Post-Office was a trial – wouldn't have been probably if one had been feeling in normal health and could have got the first troublesome effort over.

Now that I have left GH I can love it, but I am thankful to be safe from it and feel this peace to read and write and think and look out of the window is almost too blessed to be lasting. May Heaven inspire my successor to give satisfaction. I had a lovely walk with HE yesterday afternoon before I left – a thing he enjoys but rarely does. We walked down the hill into the wilderness towards the Dead Sea. A wonderful and windy Northumbrian afternoon, with patches of untrustworthy windswept sun alternating with fierce rain or dark purple cloud heaps like God on Sinai wheeling on one overhead and then retiring without pouncing in rain upon one. I felt rather like Fool to Lear, that great man, old, having possessed power and a palace, now without either out in the storm: 'Come in Nunkle, Come in out of the storm.' Or like those medieval kings who chose to wander disguised as humble men among their peasants to get their reactions to recent pieces of legislation. He made me stop and ask the Arabs whom we met what they were doing and when they began ploughing and many difficult questions which I didn't really know how to translate but pretended to. After one of these questionings HE not looking where he was going fell backwards into a pit, which I felt even more Learlike, or even a little Biblical. I rescued him out of it but felt that if I had been a really good bodyguard he should never have fallen into it.

We found his caddie too which was romantic, living in a cot in a tiny village on the spur of a hill. It felt like discovering the home of a gnome that one has often asked the way to and discovers at last by accident having lost one's way in a forest.

Perhaps it was simply that as dark began to come and the crimson light to die off the Transjordan hills the evening began to take on a Hans Andersen-like feeling.

Met and liked Norman Bentwich again. John Richmond returned, much profounder after England and Austria, had dinner with him last night and he talked extremely sympathetically till eleven about Communism. An affectionate parting with HE, and with Perowne – saw him off to Malta alas yesterday.

[1]Sir Michael McDonnell. In June 1939 a large section of old Jaffa was blown up by army engineers, ostensibly as part of a town-planning scheme but in fact to provide easier access for the troops. An Arab resident petitioned, and in due course the Chief Justice delivered a judgement in which he said: 'The petitioner has done a public service in exposing what I am bound to call a singularly disingenuous lack of moral courage displayed by the Administration in the whole matter.' This endeared him more to the Arabs than to the Colonial Office, and a few months later his resignation was announced.

TO DFH   CHEZ BOWMAN
23 DECEMBER 1934

It is half-past ten on Sunday evening and dear Humphrey has just gone up to bed, after an effort to send me too – nominally for my own good, but I am sure a great deal more for his peace of mind as householder. He is one of those unfortunate people who dream of lights left on and windows left shut or open (whichever their windows should never be) and housemaids seduced and their favourite china smashed – you remember Aunt Helen and me and Brian MacKenna[1] long ago. He has done his best to send me to bed, both with friendly advice and by cruelly turning out the stove. He would have opened the window too but he knew that I would only shut it again as soon as his back was turned.

But I can't force myself to go to bed at half-past ten at my time of life – and Bowman is really being extremely gentle about it – gently obstructive though. The last difficulty which he put in my way was to tell me that there was neither pen nor ink in the house as he and his wife always used fountain pens (which apparently they didn't lend to their visitors). So that for the second week in succession I am afraid you will have a smudgy letter. Forgive it.

It is happy to be here – even with the temporal pain of stovelessness. I love Bowman, and his flow of conversation is very easy to live with. His deeply ingrained Tory and Etonian prejudices are tempered by his affectionateness. I don't try and argue with him – indeed it fills all one's time simply listening to him – and he has this wonderful dramatic sense which makes all his stories beautiful and comic even when there is no particular point to them. He makes one see clearly by his dramatizations the sort of life which went on here immediately after the end of the war – all the odd army flotsam that drank and embezzled and swaggered and drove about all day in Government cars which nobody ever knew who paid for.

(Monday) The air is full of bells. I curse myself for not having worshipped anywhere yesterday. I feel in consequence sinful this morning – a feeling increased by having fallen asleep last night with the window shut and the light on. Tonight HE has beautifully asked me to dine with him. I shall go on to the Latin service at the Church of the Nativity afterwards, with the new young High Church private secretary.[2]

I have met one more admirable person – an architect called Hubbard[3] – young handsome and revolutionary. He ran away from Rome when he was Rome Scholar (what Nicolete was, but he in architecture) because he loathed the work that he was made to do – forced to measure imperial monuments when what he loved was Byzantine churches – and is now about to marry a girl who quarrelled with the British School in general and was turned out and I gather ran away after him.

[1]Brian MacKenna. Oxford friend of T's. Later judge in the Queen's Bench Division of the High Court.

[2]Ralph Poston. In 1956, when Director of the Near East Arab Broadcasting Station in Cyprus, was put, quite illegally, under house arrest for refusing to broadcast the rubbish wished on it by Bernard Fergusson, in charge of psychological warfare for the ill-fated Suez expedition. Subsequently ordained.

[3]Pierce Hubbard. Later partner with Austen Harrison in an architectural firm which built in Malta and England.

TO ECH
30 DECEMBER 1934

AUSTRIAN HOSPICE
JERUSALEM
SUNDAY

[Refers to his paternal grandmother, who had just died at her home in Cornwall, aged ninety-three.]

It is one of these necessary but lamentable ends, lamentable but not tragic, like the end of autumn, grief at the complete conclusion of a period that was bound to be concluded and could probably not be concluded at any juster time. But the conclusion is bitter – the 'worlds of wanwood leafmeal lie' that in spite of Hopkins I don't think that one gets much more enured to in maturity, unless one's spirit is Roman. Imperial Rome I mean, not Papal. I am glad by the way that her funeral was on the day of the feast of Thomas, Bishop and Martyr. The introit for today I was reading I think on the day when I got the telegram about her death, the day of her death that is I think, and it is the magnificent one which David has done a lovely engraving of, full of cows and caves and stars, which he gave me a copy of and which I like an ass in an enthusiastic moment gave to a quite unworthy person. You know it I expect – 'Dum medium silentium tenerent omnia, et nox in suo cursu medium iter haberet, omnipotens sermo tuus, Domine, de caelis a regalibus sedibus venit.' It was a wild moonlight night with clouds being swept across the moon in streams which that verse of the psalm fitted.

At lunch I had a less tedious conversation than usual with the Catholic Bishop who keeps this miserable tavern. We discussed the Presbyterian Church. He was shocked to learn that the High Commissioner, as an elder, administered the sacrament. I comforted him by saying that it only happened three times a year if then. But the Bishop was obviously sound in objecting that the High Commissioner is quite out of touch with Saint Peter, and therefore any sacrament administered by him is invalid and inefficacious. The new Private Secretary has twice refused to go to the Scotch Church with HE, so we may have the fine spectacle of a Private Secretary being driven into the wilderness for his religious convictions. I hope not.

1935

This was the year the British Government, led by MacDonald and after June by Baldwin, embarked on a policy of appeasing the dictators which, at this stage at any rate, enjoyed the solid backing of public opinion. In June Britain signed a naval agreement with Germany. In April MacDonald and Laval, the French Prime Minister, met Mussolini at Stresa and set up a so-called 'Stresa Front' which was supposed to prevent breaches of the international order. Six months later Italian armies invaded Abyssinia. The League of Nations proved incapable of action. Sir Samuel Hoare, the British Foreign Secretary, and Laval concocted an ingenious plan which would have given Mussolini almost all he wanted except the glory of military conquest, but this proving too clever by half Hoare was obliged to resign.

International events had their repercussions in Palestine. The year saw by far the highest level of Jewish immigration ever reached before the creation of the state of Israel – 62,000 legal entries. The Zionist Congress, meeting in Lucerne, demanded that the expansion of the National Home should be still more speeded up. A building boom was one consequence of the influx of new capital, but as before benefiting the towns not the countryside, where there was increased unemployment. Arab anxieties mounted, and in the autumn the six Arab parties, most of them little more than personal fiefdoms, took the unprecedented step of co-operating in an approach to the government. (In this they were probably encouraged by the success of similar tactics in Egypt and Syria.) They asked the High Commissioner to forward to London their three-point demand: for a democratic government (which would of course have produced an Arab majority); a ban on further land sales to the Jews; and the total stoppage of Jewish immigration.

TO DFH   AUSTRIAN HOSPICE
[6 JANUARY] 1935   JERUSALEM
                                          EPIPHANY SUNDAY

I sit in slight gloom, having recently bathed myself and

dressed myself carefully in my best dinner jacket (I have only one – my dinner jacket and my best trousers, anyhow) and gone in a motor car out to dinner with a middle-aged woman of whom I am fond, to be told sternly that the dinner was yesterday and that she had a very nice one with turkey and good company and that now she is going out to supper herself. So I came rather wretchedly and ashamedly, after the sort of apologizings which you can imagine, back to these ginger biscuits – which even though an extremely superior kind which I have just bought (Romary's – I recommend them – to Teddy especially for cold winter nights) are not like the hot meat dinner for which I had been all day happily preparing myself. What makes it all so stupid is that after what I suppose must have been my (I should like to think, but can't honestly, that it was *her*) initial mistake about the day I was extremely careful about the invitation, writing it down first on a sheet of foolscap and then in a great diary with which the office had provided me, and which, I had thought, was going to revolutionize my life as regards method – but so far obviously it hasn't. It is not worth dwelling on – she will forgive or has forgiven me, and I trust will ask me again. But it makes one almost despair if all the trouble which one takes to keep an appointment should be thwarted by the imbecility of hearing 'Saturday' as 'Sunday'.

While I think of it – absolutely trivial – but might I have some more Lady's nibs. I think that I have run out – some pinched or lost but mostly used. This is an inflexible beast. Do you have to use each nib a bit first so as to avoid duty – a bore if you do?

I have been reading *Resurrection* – began it and read a lot last night and a little this afternoon. I'm glad to be reading a novel again and glad that it's Tolstoy – a lovely heroine, and it's wonderful how Tolstoy can make her appear lovely by always speaking of her eyes as squinting – 'her dark slightly squinting eyes filled with tears'; it really makes her much more beautiful, don't you think? And a very good picture of Easter midnight Mass – 'All was beautiful; but above all Katusha, in her white dress, blue sash, and the red bow on her black head, her eyes beaming with rapture.' Very clear isn't she?

The happiest thing of last week was a walk which I took on

New Year's Day down to Jericho. It was a beautiful firm morning, still and sparkling, the sunshine liquid in rooms, like clear water. I had said that I would walk there with Iliffe, but he with foolish geniality had asked about eight other people, so I told them that I had work to do and came on two hours behind them. An admirable walk down the gorges, by an easy path across the wilderness. It was sunset while I was still on the hill above Jericho – a glorious one, prolonging itself through different kinds of colour and gradations of brightness. I sang songs and thought upon Zion, that is to say Bamburgh and our blessed past, as I walked a little footsore the last few dull kilometres into Jericho itself.

Garstang was warm though I had not seen him for almost two years, and I'm afraid had spoken ill of him on almost every occasion I had of speaking of him at all. He gave me a good supper and I was thankful for it and slept in John Richmond's bed in the little house by the spring which had belonged to me, while he like a good host slept on the floor on a mattress. And I came back here early in the morning, by car, but a beautiful short walk with the newly risen sun first. Now I have pledged myself to take a half or 2/3 day off with Bowman tomorrow and eat sandwiches on the Hill of Temptation, just above Jericho – a lazy and happy plan, but I ought to be working. He shamed me by telling me that tomorrow is a public holiday for Epiphany. I believe it is, but a person as humble as I I don't feel ought to pay attention to Feste which his office doesn't acknowledge. It is all very well for the Head of a Department. Anyhow I must go for I have broken faith too often with him to dare to do such a thing again – rather flout the office. I'll read *Resurrection* in the sun on top of the hill. This morning to the Dormition for Mass – good: I not so much so.

TO RHH   [AUSTRIAN HOSPICE
20/21 JANUARY 1934[5]   JERUSALEM]
                                             SUNDAY NIGHT

It is rather late on a moony night: I have just had a bath at a Maryish[1] sort of hour, I hope without disturbing the household – such household as there is. The ill-used

Czechish and bearded Vice-Rector is the only person I think who lives within a hundred yards of the bathroom. The nuns I have come to the conclusion don't sleep in rooms at all but just disappear into the earth like rabbits as soon as it gets dark.

I shall truly postpone it [income-tax] as little longer as I possibly can – and try to finish it before Aunt Helen comes on Saturday. I have the flattering embarrassment of our being again both asked to Government House for some of the time – beautiful of HE, and fleshpots are always a temptation, so is pomp (though one more quickly loses one's appetite for that). But I think that I will refuse in advance for both of us. I have consulted with the ADC and he thinks that I may. But when asked, orally, by HE I could make no proper oral reply, except thanks, and certainly couldn't put my reasons for thinking it better not to come, though quite honourable ones, into words. I think that we shall be happier in this simplicity, though I don't know what Aunt Helen will do about the cold at night or the badness of breakfast in the morning. I must get her some Lapsang Souchong I think – or the nearest approach to it that you can get in the bazaars of Jerusalem.

I had a not very good day hunting yesterday – very heavy underfoot so that every step which the horse took was an effort, but lovely spring weather, the very early shoots of corn smelling sweet, and the first red anemone. The beautiful sight of this rich early green vegetation against the rich red earth. The earth is tipsy with rain this winter – far above the average – which ought to mean a good year for farmers, or a bumper crop at any rate, which isn't unfortunately the same thing.

As my pony had been lately lame I stopped at three and sat on a grassy bank just outside Ramle and learned Arabic words for a couple of hours, watching the animal market in front where townspeople and villagers and Beduin were mixed – huge cattle and new-born kids moving in and out among them, all in the sun with green meadows round them and a white town, ornamented with conventional minarets and palm trees, behind them.

I picked up quite a pleasant young man who likes wine and agrees nine times out of ten with what one says, and brought him back to dinner – where the Heurtleys[2] were. You know of them – British School at Athens – Carr B and Haji are both links – though we have fortunately got beyond the stage of conversation when you have to refer more often than is natural to the links. I gave them some of Aunt Helen's claret and my own sherry and they liked both, and it washed the taste of the Austrian Hospice food out of their mouths. I talked too much – but it is too late to help that. I think one always does with a semi-sympathetic audience.

Now it is a bright and beautiful morning. I wish I were in the country. My Transjordan journey is put off and off owing to the mysteriousness of the people who have the power about giving me the leave that I ask for. I want it as soon as possible – a couple of days with Aunt Helen and a ten days' journey would be beautiful. These last few days I have had to be half a PS too – not easy – except that I always like to be in the know, and this has been a rather interesting week to be in the know of – appointment of a Mayor of Jerusalem.[3] I'll tell you about it next time. Also I like being in the company of HE. But it means a rush and rushes are horrid. The gardener who is going to take this letter to the post is itching (literally itching) to be off. So I had better finish. The riding gloves and white waistcoat reached me and are beautiful.

[1] Mary Jameson (see p.67) had the reputation of keeping eccentric hours for going to her bed and rising from it.

[2] W.A. Heurtley. Museum Librarian.

[3] Ragheb Bey Nashashibi, Mayor of Jerusalem for many years, was unseated by Hussein Khalidi, who enjoyed the backing of the Mufti.

TO DFH   AUSTRIAN HOSPICE
27 JANUARY 1935   JERUSALEM

After lunch we went to this village – Ain Karim – where the pleasant runaway architect that I told you of lives, on the side of the hills about 4 miles from Jerusalem, among cypresses, and looked at a house. Though not perfect I think I shall take it, for it would be so much more satisfactory than continuing hospice life. In matters of this kind I think the only thing to do perhaps is to act on intuition. I could easily reason myself into living in this hospice for ever, in pure laziness.

The imperfections of this house we saw are partly an old

Greek nun who wants – indeed I think insists – to go on living in one of the bedrooms; a rather rheumy old creature – had it been a Latin nun of the kind that keep this hospice or Sister Matilda I would have welcomed her and damned the scandal. As it is I think I must try to buy her out. It is true country – a pleasant garden – a long view over a great basin of a valley planted with olive trees. I will discuss it all carefully with Aunt Helen and decide before she goes. She will be so good in saying how many spoons and things one ought to have. She has very strong views, too, which I think she has expressed to you, about a stove.

TO DFH   HOTEL FAST
3 FEBRUARY 1935   JERUSALEM

Then [tomorrow] I go to Transjordan on my long-planned journey, with, I hope, Sheikh Mithqal[1] – but that is all still a little in the air. It is difficult to make plans with people in another country in another language. As a result I have hardly made any, except indefinitely through the plump and friendly Arab Private Secretary, son-in-law of the Transjordan Chief Minister, the latter of whom I am at this moment trying to telephone to – another intermediary. I don't look forward to my telephone call when I get it. I am bad over distances and bad in foreign languages over the telephone, and this will be a conversation of both. My plan is to start if possible from Kerak and ride south along the ridge of the hills between the Ghor (the valley which joins up the Dead Sea to that little finger of the Red Sea which runs up to Aqaba) and the railway line, by Shaubak, Bosra, Petra, Maan, the Wadi Rumm, and eventually touch where the old railway line to Mecca used to be before Lawrence blew it up at Mudawwara – that is near the frontier of Saudi Arabia. Of course it is very likely indeed that I won't ever get as far. One difficulty is likely to be that if Sheikh Mithqal comes he is likely to have his horses at his home, near Amman, which might mean about three days much duller riding from Amman south to Kerak first, and there is not very much time since I have only got 12 days leave and have used almost 3 of them already. But I hope that difficulty will be overcome somehow, and I gather that they won't mind my taking a day or two's extra leave if necessary. Indeed with all this rain one may well get stuck somewhere as far as returning by car is concerned. But in spite of the wet I don't think that there would be much point in putting the journey off, I was about to say. Now however (four hours later) I have met some officers from Transjordan and talked to a man there by telephone and they all say that it would be hopeless to try and ride there now – all the tracks impassable even for horses. So that this much boasted journey will have to be put off again and I will go back to normal work tomorrow. I am going to be allowed to do that and postpone this journey until whenever it's dry.

It is a very windy, buffeting early morning, but the rain has stopped. I want to tell you a little more about Aunt Helen's visit, though she will have told it all to you herself and more fully than I do. She bore the hospice beautifully and managed through love to withstand discomfort. She also managed to persuade the sisters to cook better – which was a wonderful act. I don't think she quite bullied them, but gently hectored them, into frying potatoes in butter, making fruit salads from fresh grapefruit, oranges and pears, cutting out many of the horrible meat entrée courses, and above all giving us *Wienische Kaffee mit Schlag* instead of the loathsome tepid Turkish coffee which the nuns themselves, when pressed, admitted that they hated. To these dinners, improved with good wine – much of it Aunt Helen's too – it was possible to invite people without shame, and that was pleasant. Though I regret on reflection that the people whom I asked were all English, though all nice English.

Our journey to Galilee began on Thursday afternoon in pouring and miserable rain – the whole country was hidden by it – but it was exciting enough to have escaped together from Jerusalem, without knowing where we would arrive or sleep that night, for us to be able to bear the rain. We actually lay in another Austrian Hospice at Nazareth, kept by the monks of Saint John of God, one very red in the face and wide in the body, the jolly-friar sort, but he was not so very jolly to begin with – a little stern, but gradually he mellowed – and a tall, gentle, bearded monk with a melancholy mouth waited on us at dinner, which we made gay with two-thirds of a bottle of hock that had not been finished the night before and I brought with me.

Aunt Helen enjoyed both the monks and the hospice and was charmed by the austerity of it, which in a less religious house she could have thought discomfort – an austere teacupful of hot water in the early morning and a pretty austere WC. But the coffee was admirable, and orange and lemon trees held up their fruit just under our windows. We were shown round the Holy Places of Nazareth by a rather benighted Franciscan, Brother John, who annoyed Aunt Helen by not believing in the Virgin's fountain because it was not a matter of faith, and contradicting her statement that the Virgin and Our Lord went there for water by saying in any case only the Virgin went there. It all shows how dangerous it is to mention Protestant sites (the Virgin's fountain she had got out of George Adam Smith[2]) to Catholic priests.

From time to time during that day the sun shone, which was lovely, particularly because almost unhoped for, and we could snatch at the periods of sun and use them thankfully. It was sunny, though extremely windy and the mud clogged our boots and made us slow, when we climbed the Horns of Hattin – the Crusader battlefield that David Jones loved but never visited. We reached the nearest horn where Reginald of Kerak made his last stand against Saladin and the wind there was tremendous, but it was beautiful to look down over the grey lake and Transjordan dark grey in thunderclouds behind, and the broad plateau of the battleground to the south, and mountains mixed with dark clouds stretching into Syria in the north. There was a pleasant goatherd whom we chatted to – and we sheltered behind a rock from the wind with him and his son.

[1]Mithqal Pasha el-Faid, Sheikh of the large and important Beni Sakhr tribe.
[2]*The Historical Geography of the Holy Land* by the Very Reverend George Adam Smith. First published in 1896 and often reprinted.

TO RHH   AUSTRIAN HOSPICE
11 FEBRUARY 1935

This will again be only a rather short letter I'm afraid, as all yesterday was taken up by a visit to archaeologists at a place called Tell Duweir, in the foothills to the west of Hebron, just at the point where the hills meet the plain. I had been there two years ago with the Richmonds, but yesterday it was far lovelier than then, breathing spring, green meadows, grass and young corn smelling almost as sweet as English fields in May, wet red earth and sprigs of vetch crops beginning, every now and then a red anemone. They were extremely pleasant and hospitable hosts too – the leader is a man called Starkey[1] who used to be a draper and looks it and is as a result charming; and they are all pleasant and friendly people.

I went down there with Starkey late on Saturday night – found a fire in the bedroom prepared for me – that standard kept itself up with early morning tea and cream to my porridge. I spent the morning with Starkey going round the dig, and thanked God that whatever I was I was not an archaeologist, charming though they all were and happy though the actual life obviously is, and much though I should love to live always in the country and in the company of Arabs. Yet the actual digging is even duller than I had remembered it; so much that is purely mechanical, putting up lines and trucks and chutes and clearing ground for dumps, so many of the things which have to be done being things that only bright boys can do. Even when I consider the Secretariat dullest (as I have been during most of last week) I remember that I never have considered it as dull as I used to consider digging.

The particular reason for the dullness of the work of the last week was that as there have been floods again after all the heavy rain of last weekend, particularly bad in Nablus and the district round where 24 people altogether were drowned, mostly Beduin, and a terrible loss of property and many houses tumbled down, I had to keep getting the reports from the Heads of Departments and District Commissioners dealing with the matter. That doesn't sound dull, but it is hateful I think to get and compile second-hand information, leave out some bits as not fit for the public, put a general *Times*-like self-complacent gloss over the whole thing, turn it into pompous official language, and then see it in the paper next day as an official statement, when for all you know half of it may be lies owing to the difficulty of hearing what one's seniors say over the telephone and the impossibility of making them repeat it more than a certain number of times –

or if not actually lies certainly not a complete picture of the facts.

Granted that that is what both history and journalism are, yet that is at any rate their function, but my function is not. This is not a matter of much importance, but it has reminded me that I want as soon as possible to be in a district, where one is or ought to be a factor in the events of the district and not only an observer and recorder, but perhaps the latter is what one is fated to be. From time to time I suggest such a transfer to my superiors, but I am pretty sure that they will keep me here for another year at any rate, and I have therefore bought the house which I told you of, and hope to move in in a fortnight or so. It will mean having a little furniture made – a table or two and a chair or two and a cupboard. It is in fact furnished but so foully that I have got the old woman to turn most of it out. The cost is only £30 for the year so that I shall not be involved in any great expense. The local carpenter will make the few necessaries cheaply; the Russian woman who will cook and tidy, will I am told cook and tidy cheaply. I went out to see it again on Friday and loved it. I shall travel by bus normally, on foot when there is time, and by car in emergencies, but I shall try to avoid emergencies.

[1] J.L. Starkey. Excavating at the biblical city of Lachish. Murdered on 10 January 1938 by a band of armed Arabs on his way to attend the opening of the new museum in Jerusalem, financed by Rockefeller, architected by Austen Harrison and adorned with sculptured reliefs by Eric Gill.

TO DFH   JERUSALEM
17 FEBRUARY [1935]   SUNDAY

Forgive pencil. I write in the Fast Hotel where I have come for a supper of bread and cheese and coffee. It is a cold and lovely evening, with the moon now full or almost so and high up in the sky. Very beautiful to walk through the old city on these nights – all the domes and arches and half-arches and trailing narrow streets with their architectural deficiencies obliterated and only the beauty of their strangeness.

I think it was stupid to come here, even for so simple a meal, and for two such good purposes as writing to you and keeping myself awake by drinking coffee. But there are people in a bar talking nonsense to the barman and that is disturbing. I think I had better cut this hotel out of my life finally now that the cottage is actually becoming a fact – it is both expensive and spiritually corrupting. But since Aunt Helen went I have only once been able to face dinner at the hospice, and then I found that the old bishop was even duller than I had remembered him. A harridan called Mrs Stewart Erskine, staying in the hospice, has unfortunately begun to be kind to me and invited me up to her room to what she called China tea yesterday – not really China at all – but there were chocolate biscuits, which almost made up for over an hour's tedious conversation about Palestine. She is strongly and ignorantly pro-Arab and is writing a book to say so.[1] She prides herself on being the only person who has spoken his mind frankly to HE about the political situation. Actually HE has to listen almost nightly to some guest or other explaining the political situation to him frankly, from the pro-Arab point of view.

Nothing of very much consequence during the week – a good deal of it work, perhaps a rather large proportion of it interesting. Then on Tuesday I went over to Ain Karim and saw my music master and my dancing master. It became fearfully Chekhovian in that they both began moving furniture that I didn't want (most of it that is) out of the house, with the sad old woman there in the middle of it. It felt like an execution (the bloodless kind) and I the bailiff. She was very mopy, but is staying on, if she wants, in one room till the end of March. But I hope this arrangement, which involves practically living in sin as well as in discomfort, will not go on for long. I don't suppose I shall move in for another week at any rate.

The cottage will be hardly furnished at all – a few pieces of absolutely vital expenditure, like a cupboard and a dining-room table made out of a rather jolly reddish hard sort of wood, unvarnished; nothing else but wine, icons and books. That ought to make a beautiful bareness. I had meant to go hunting today but since the ground is heavy from rain, and my horse's cut only recently healed from the over-reach, which I may or may not have spoken to you about in other letters, the experts thought that it wouldn't be sensible, so I simply rode in a high wind in this bright sun for a couple of hours through the orange groves. Here the Arabs do seem to be becoming a slave population – Beduins in tents near the Jewish colonies doing their dirtiest work. John Richmond I saw this evening and I think he will come riding in the Transjordan with me when I go, that will be when he has done with Garstang, the 7th of March or so.

O yes, and one other thing, I have met a very faint pale quite pleasant person, Keeper of an Anglican retreat and rather worn as a result of it, like a flame rather blue at the best of times which has almost gone out – recommended me by Aunt Violet.[2] I go with her to Hebron tomorrow. She is said to be a friend of Evelyn Underhill's so I suspect her of being a mystic. She says that she has no fire in her room here which makes me almost sure of it. Only great inward warmth could keep me without a fire in Jerusalem.

I would like to cut my expenditure down to £300 a year, though at present I seem pretty far from it. Anyhow I will draw no more on my home account (it has been un-businesslike of me to use both so casually) except that I want gradually to pay off Blackwell, Adamson and Bradbury – I think still about £60 in all.

[1]Mrs Erskine was a prolific author and embarrassing champion of the Arabs. Among her books were biographies of King Feisal of Iraq and King Alphonso XIII of Spain, *Palestine of the Arabs* and *Beautiful Women in History and Art*.

[2]L.V. Holdsworth (Hodgkin). Author of *A Book of Quaker Saints* and many other works.

TO DFH   AIN KARIM
31 MARCH 1935

This has been a rather stirring week – too full of people and work for peace but for once none the worse for that. I have been having for lunch today Furness[1] again and his niece, staying in Jerusalem with him, whom I like, and the pleasant fat old genial Chief Justice and his beautiful but almost too gently spoken to be intelligible wife whom Aunt Helen very much liked. They enjoyed it I think as they stayed till four, sitting and talking in the garden, not one of Michail's[2] most admirable lunches but not offensive.

I agree with what you say in your letter that one must to begin with not expect a new cook to bear many fruits. The fruits that he does bear anyhow are good ones, and their monotony is probably a good deal due to the lack of amenities in the kitchen (e.g. so far he has no table) and not merely to the monotony of his mind. But a cookery book or two would be a great help for both of us, say Lady Jekyll and *French Cooking for English Homes*. I could easily get one or two of the simpler recipes translated into Arabic for him. I find it impossible to guess offhand how even the simplest things are cooked – Zabaglione for instance which ought to be easy enough – and he is not very good at guessing at the meaning of my rather hopeless descriptions.

[1](Sir) Robin Furness. Press Officer for the Government of Palestine 1934–36. Seconded to Jerusalem, which he loathed, from Cairo, which he loved, and where he had been Oriental Secretary at the Embassy. Later Professor of English at Fuad I University. Published translations from the Greek Anthology. His niece, Diana, an artist, captured T's heart for a while.

[2]T's servant. An Orthodox Christian from Bethlehem, easy-going and affectionate, and a good plain cook, he surveyed with bewildered amusement the irregularities of the Ain Karim household. When he married, T became godfather to his first child, baptized in the Church of the Nativity. I met him again in 1945, and found he was working as a nurse in a lunatic asylum ('the mads', he called them) for which his Ain Karim training had no doubt prepared him.

TO ECH   [AIN KARIM]
(N.D. EARLY 1935?)

On Wednesday we start for the Decapolis – I, John Richmond and a pack of Popish priests – really wise and charming Dominicans – who keep their white suits cleaner than one would have imagined possible among the dustiest antiquities. I sit writing to you exquisitely dressed, in my dark blue chaste suit, with my gay blue sleeveless shirt (you can't of course see that it's sleeveless – but I have the novelist's privilege of telling you things you can't see) and my golden loony tie that Lucy gave me – the last of the loonies.[1] I think I look a little like a pale Jim Ede – I hope I do.

I have a dead crocus in my button-hole. I have been having lunch at Government House that is why. I was asked because the Governor, Allenby, the Secretary of State for the

Colonies and the King and Queen of the Belgians were all out to lunch. Those are the sort of terms I am on with Government House – not thought tidy enough to meet the older ones. The day drifted off into Arabic lessons – in the sun here being told the story of Snow White and Rose Red by Nastasya. It's very exciting, I haven't heard it for years. We had to leave off half-way through, and won't be able to finish it for a fortnight – sickening. Well old fellow I really must stop now – Cheerio (I have to teach Nastasya not to say Cheerio – it's strange what awful words even the nicest people pick up).

[1]Ties knitted by an old woman in a cottage near Rock, but no real evidence of her insanity.

TO DFH   AIN KARIM
8 APRIL 1935

[Re. his birthday]

I got hold of your (and Cookie's – thank and bless her for it) good rich cake from the parcel post that day, and began it at supper. At supper I had a rum but good assortment – the Hubbards (the young handsome architect and his wife, the Rome runaways), Ann Richmond, and Andrews[1] (a very good Australian, middle-aged, about the best administrator in the country). We ate the cake, and otherwise it wasn't a bad dinner. But it is better to be alone, or with some of the very few friends. No, that is a misexpressed sentiment. I do like at least 90% of the people that I invite here. Only it is a lovely place to be alone in also – these early birds and the smell of may and other blossoms still, great purple lords and irises almost beginning. You will love it – if I am still here when you come.

I had a good talk about Catholicism and the conversion of England with Heurtley – Haji's friend, archaeologist, who was in Greece, Ithaca, two nights ago – if such talks are good. But I think probably that unless I am a Catholic admiration of Catholicism isn't much good – a waste of spirit. At present I am a bad Anglican (bad in that I attend seldom and won't subscribe to a new hideous concrete church for the native branches in Haifa, besides being sinful), and pretend to be a good Catholic. I must talk to Teddy about this – and of course you. But I am increasingly thinking how useless are these unpractised beliefs – just so much empty conversation. The shadow of Rudin[2] again.

[1]Lewis Andrews. Acting District Commissioner for the newly created Galilee District. Murdered by Arab gunmen on 21 September 1937 as he was leaving the Anglican church in Nazareth. Shouted, 'Run for it; they've got us', to Pirie-Gordon, who was just behind and escaped.

[2]Ineffectual revolutionary Turgenev character in novel of the same name.

TO DFH   AIN KARIM
14 APRIL [1935]   PALM SUNDAY

An undistinguished week: indeed I have done nothing at all good or interesting except manage to live more in Ain Karim and less in Jerusalem. That is wholly good, and I begin to feel more a member of the village than I did, gradually getting to know the people and to be able to smile less indiscriminately, I mean to know more who I am smiling at. Today for the first time I spent an entire Sunday here, not touching Jerusalem, and have done nothing but see two friends eat two ample meals walk a very little distance and try to finish this story that I spoke of.

The beauty of the place is extraordinary. I get tired of hearing that except from people that I really love – but the flowers and scents now are glorious; anemones over but poppies which I love more are flowering in great patches and masses on the sides of paths and hills; lords are still beautiful, irises just beginning, and a lovely gentle yellow flower like a mixture of a marsh-mallow and a rockrose and a tall primrose has spread about the place. The air especially at night is rich with may and orange blossom and other flowering tree scents that I don't know the names of. When you add this rather more than half moon which makes the village look like a white bruise on yellow skin and shows more clearly all the symmetrical ridges of olive terraces circling like contour lines round the hills – I don't know what happens; that was a stupid way to begin this sentence – I think I was going to end that the beauty becomes almost painful, but that isn't really true.

I do pray that you will see it all, though in a way I should like to think that I should be out of the Secretariat by the time you come – ? this autumn – but again I should like you to see it all flowering and so would you. I have a lot of quite good garden flowers in petrol tins too under the white arch that acts as a sort of porch to my front door. People say put them into earthenware pots, and they certainly would look much nicer so, but I am lazy and am growing used to the look of even these disgusting tins as part of my home.

I have at last stopped being too lazy to put my books into the shelf, but the bookcase doesn't really suit the room, too urban. I had it in the Austrian Hospice you know and it is stained. The rest of the furniture in this room, two tables and two not very arm chairs are plain wood which I love more and which better suits the plainness of the blueish white wall and roof and stone doors. I think it is very Quakerly. My Hodgkin aunts would love it; I wish that they could see it. Perhaps Aunt Violet might actually think of coming, though Aunt Lily would bear the discomfort better, not that there is any discomfort, but the sort of simplicity which the nicely brought up would feel was discomfort; you would I am afraid, though you would bear it.

Michail is preparing supper, the sun has just set. I have two architects coming – Harrison, the friend of Gill's who has built everything good almost that has been built in this country, and the Hubbards, my neighbours. Michail is making the second of his two puddings – Spanish Bread. Did I tell you that I had found out that that extremely innocent pudding is really, both in name and flavour, a corruption of sponge cake? He has got hold of some chocolate powder, and has I think with great beauty of nature and imagination written in chocolate over the white fluff with which the cake is covered 'Evviva Mister Hodgkin'. The idea is wholly his – I only told him how to spell the words. The language is because he was brought up in a Catholic school I suppose: anyhow it is difficult to write in Arabic characters on a cake I should think.

I went to Low Mass this morning – a rather short and rollicking service: I ought to have gone at eight instead of at seven for they were having their real Palm Sunday celebration then. I saw children of prominent parishioners carrying

wands of branches stuck with flowers down to the church. I
hadn't till reading some of the missal prayers thought of it as
Olive as well as Palm Sunday – more real to think of,
especially here where the village and hills and valley are all
thick in olive trees.

Dues, qui dispersa congregas et congregata conservas: qui
populis obviam Jesu ramos portantibus benedixisti: be-
nedic etiam hos ramos palmae et olivae quos tui famuli ad
honorem nominis tui fideliter suscipiunt; ut in quemcum-
que locum introducti fuerint tuam benedictionem habita-
tores loci illius consequantur . . .

These guests will soon be coming. I suppose for their sakes I
ought to wash my hands.

O one other pleasant thing last week, a dinner with a man
called Tom Williams,[1] member for the Don Valley, the most
sensible Labour politician that I've ever met, not that I've met
many – sensible about his party and its weaknesses and
tolerant of my assertive ignorance, brought out here on a
Jews' propaganda expedition.

[1]Tom Williams had been MP for the Don Valley since 1922.

TO DFH
22 APRIL 1935

AUSTRIAN HOSPICE
MONDAY

I have let the Easter weekend slip through my fingers –
Friday I went to the Benedictines – a very good Mass there –
extremely spectacular but simple too, and the congregation
part of the ceremony, which they aren't always. The kissing
of the cross is one of the rites which does that – gives the laity
a feeling of unity with the clergy, and with one another. All
wore black vestments. Almost the best part was the long
reading of the account of the passion and crucifixion in, I
think, Saint John. The Abbot sat on a chair just beside the
altar while the celebrating priests sat on the altar steps – a
beautifully natural-looking form – as though sitting in the
open air.

It was a day full of watching religious ceremony, for in the afternoon I watched the Moslems going down to Nebi Musa (by the Dead Sea – they feast there nominally in memory of Moses – a great plateau among hills) – beautiful beating of skin drums and cymbals, pipe playing and dancing, ten young men in a row swinging and bowing, old men vaguely swinging, coloured flags of the Moslem towns and the Sheikhs sitting on horses at the back. A beautifully hot day. I walked downhill a little of the way with the procession when they had come out of the Old City, and then sat down on a piece of wall and watched them go past.

Then Saturday and yesterday I spent between working and visiting Mrs Antonius and enjoying the company of her child,[1] who has lately become very favourable to me – and Katy Antonius I find now the most sympathetic and friendly person to be with of people in Jerusalem, and her home the pleasantest to be in. They gave me a chocolate egg.

[1]Soraya Antonius, only child of George and Katy. Educated at Cheltenham Ladies College, like her mother, and the Slade, she returned to the Middle East and devoted her life to the cause of the Palestinians.

TO RHH   AIN KARIM
29 APRIL 1935   MONDAY

On Saturday night, the eve of the Orthodox Easter, I went to the church of our Russian nuns here at about midnight. I remembered from two years ago the Russian Easter service – besides it comes into *Resurrection*, do you remember, Book I chapter 15, one of the best in the book. This was admirable and simple, though it lasted for about four hours (I slipped out and slept for a couple of hours in the middle) it seemed to consist almost all the time of the priest with his long loose hair and silver ?cope going round the church and saying to every group of nuns 'Christos forcriss'. (I am not sure of the spelling of that second word: you and Teddy will put it straight for me: the meaning is anyhow clear; I wish I knew even a mouthful of Russian; it is a glorious language to listen to.)

From time to time too we walked in a line round the church and kissed the priest's crucifix and were given these beautiful bright painted eggs and white wax beaded ones, and

little things to eat. As a visitor I was given far more than I
deserved of everything and came away with about half a
dozen eggs. Then at about one we all began to kiss one
another, at least I was left out of that, my own stupid
embarrassment probably, the beautiful Abbess I think would
have let me kiss her had I tried to. But we all said 'Christos
forcriss' to one another and answered something else –
beautiful to see the nuns kissing, their faces lit by the candles
burning on the tall cylindrical iced cakes. (I go on writing in
the not yet started bus. I am afraid that this letter won't catch
today's airmail. I have been rather stupid and missed the bus
that I had meant to catch. An odd sight in this bus – a small
boy, about 6 years old, dressed in Franciscan habit,
pretending to drive. Perhaps in this monastic town Franciscan habits are what sailor-suits are with us.)

I haven't yet told you of the end of my midnight Mass with
the Russians – their fine old faces kissing one another in the
candlelight – and all this wonderful mixture of eating and
praying – always a good mixture. At half-past three we went
with all our presents of eggs and cakes outside into the
refectory and broke our fast – mine hardly worth breaking
I'm afraid – and ate great squares of sweet bread full of
raisins, feast bread, and cheese and eggs, our painted ones,
and bitter fish (?anchovies). I sat in the place of honour on the
priest's right, opposite the Abbess, but neither could talk
anything but Russian, except that the Abbess had one or two
gentle words of English. So most of my conversation was, less
interestingly, with Sophia, my so to speak landlady. But I
smiled constantly at the Abbess.

One other thing last week was my walk on Monday to Nebi
Musa, where the Moslems feast for a week and worship
Moses. I don't think the Moses part is fearfully serious, but it
was pleasant and medieval – like the May Field rather I
imagine or any annual gathering of the people – the Mufti
and his sheikhs at home to anyone who likes to come. On the
day that I was there there must have been about two or three
thousand people there – every sort and degree – townspeople, fellahin and Bedus. I got among the townspeople
rather – a fruit merchant with a husky voice whom I
happened to know – less fun than to have been among the
other sorts, but it was pleasant to recognize acquaintances,

masters of cafés and so forth, and see how different they were in their own atmosphere – who were leaders and who slaves. It was a good walk down there too – about five hours over the hills, through a great flock of storks – arriving a little before sunset to see them racing their horses in the dust. The place itself lies among low hills just above the north end of the Dead Sea – a great many-domed hostel, full of courtyards.

I have been reading Great Claus and Little Claus – a horrible story. How can you have read it to me and I enjoyed it when I was so young? I remembered it as something gay – but there are three murders, two attempted murders and one natural death in it, and the murderers of Little Claus are made to appear in an altogether praiseworthy light.

TO DFH   AIN KARIM
6 MAY 1935   MONDAY

I'm afraid that again my Sunday letter has turned into a Monday one – almost Tuesday in fact. I am ashamed to write on so vulgar a day as Jubilee Day, though it is also (I see from Aunt Helen's missal) the day of S. Joannis Ap. & Ev. which is a better festival. I didn't have to participate in any of the functions as you'd imagined: though a public holiday that didn't mean much as I had work to do.

The flower of the British went on to the roof of the Secretariat with the consular corps in tail-coats, with selected priests in B. habits, and some loyal Jews (I didn't see if there were any loyal Arabs) and cheered from there. I stayed in my office and could see the soldiers and some tars and mounted Arabs (the very expensive kind that only the most fastidious children with soldiers get given them, when they are already sated with every kind of Zouave and Spahi and Indian Prince and Ambulance set) and dozens of evil-looking armoured cars.

What was most beautiful was all the line of grey city-walls black and white along the top with people, mostly Arabs, town and country ones – as if to see Quintus Arrius go by and not the High Commissioner. (He was in national dress, I suppose, inspecting the troops; I didn't see him.) There is something splendidly eternal about the people of Palestine you feel they'll stay on being much the same (individually even if their society is better) when all these blustering soldiers and officials (the soldiers don't bluster – only the officers – but they are the instruments through which the civilian power is able to assert itself) and policemen who drive back the crowds against the wall for the soldiers to go by have been turned out of the country. Shepherds will go on playing pipes when all the brass bands are scrapped, and wearing Palestinian clothes when all the tail-coats have been destroyed by moths. This sounds sentimental as I write it. It is any rate not to be interpreted as a pro-Arab and anti-Jew sentiment. I have fallen asleep in the middle of the last sentence.

TO DFH   AIN KARIM

12 MAY 1935   SUNDAY

It seems strange to be writing in ink – I have got used to a typewriter. But tonight I didn't like the look of it – besides John Richmond is in bed and probably either he would be disturbed or I would have to do it in my bedroom. The rooms are so close together that what the eye doesn't see the heart is continually grieving after. He is anyhow awake I now discover from the sounds of the spray with which he is trying to drive off the insects – one of the few bothers in this house, but they would be in any house. Moths I have managed to reduce to a few lonely strays, but sandflies seem to come through all the cracks and to be born with flit-proof lungs and though their bites are usually gone by next morning they are infuriating at the time.

Today is the anniversary of our goodbye at Southampton, as I expect you have been remembering too – a very appropriate Gospel for the day – 'Modicum, et jam non videbitis me: et iterum modicum et videbitis me ... Et vos igitur nunc quidem tristitiam habetis, iterum autem videbo vos, et gaudebit cor vestrum: et gaudium vestrum nemo tollet a vobis' ... and the good simile about the woman when she has borne a child – at the time I thought of it in connection with Aunt Nelly[1] principally, meaning to write to her – now I think of it for us and for Aunt Margaret. But it is a good comforting passage for anybody, after a rather fearful Fascist Epistle – Servi, subditi estote in omni timore dominis, non tantum bonis et modestis, sed etiam dyscolis!

I had to go into Jerusalem this morning unfortunately to work so went to the Dormition, the Benedictines, again. They had a beautifully rich way of pronouncing Mo'-dicum, holding up the whole sentence to make a great deep sound out of the first syllable. Other than that I have really not done anything today, not getting back here till about three and so losing more than half the day as far as enjoying this place is concerned – read a very little Arabic – walked with John at about sunset – the valley with these beautiful concentric circles of olive trees growing up round the hills, the barley still green (just outside the walls of Jerusalem, walking back from the Dormition, it was golden and some of it cut), running along the terraces like water in channels.

Now again next morning – I am trying to eat my breakfast with one hand and to write to you with the other. Last night finished with having the Hubbards and Domvile and Chad (long a) his Iraqi Bedu servant – the last I'm afraid rather bored as the conversation became general and political. Domvile is an imperialist by conviction, the Hubbards are not and will not even keep up British prestige in Jerusalem by wearing the right sort of trousers and hats – which wounds the feelings of Bowman as well as Domvile. It was one of those rather hopeless conversations – just saving itself from becoming a regular argument. We only just avoided discussing whether Kipling was more immortal than Lawrence – as Domvile swore he was. Now I sit in the café having missed both bus and post – forgive me. I am afraid all my letters are becoming irregular nowadays, partly from this pleasantly unpunctual country life. By pushing we've just caught a bus.

[1]Ellen, sister of RHH and widow of Carr Bosanquet, who had died on Easter Day. Margaret Jameson's only son, Andrew, had died on April 17, his eighteenth birthday, the year before.

TO DFH   AIN KARIM
26 MAY 1935   SUNDAY

It is really Monday morning early – I went to bed quite early but I have been woken by sandflies: I have shot them down with my flit-gun, but am now feeling wakeful and don't yet want to go back to bed simply to see whether I shall be bitten or not. I had meant to write to you at sunrise tomorrow (today) but I'll at least begin now. It is just after moonrise, a very shrunk-looking violet moon, quite hot still, and by day very hot – enough to make walking quite an effort and to make me more inclined than ever to fall asleep in the middle of the day.

In fact I always do now – on my bed in the Austrian Hospice, that's a great comfort to have, a small room on the top floor, just above my old one, the one Gill's daughter Joanna used to have. They let me sleep there whenever I want day and night – a bother for them I'm afraid since I'm very irregular and often don't know till the last minute whether I want to sleep in Jerusalem or not. But they are always gentle and welcoming. I have a different sister now, the one who looked after Aunt Helen, not the plump and laughing Sister Gottburger – she the most beautiful of all – but we still meet on the stairs and say Grüss Gott, and sometimes launch out on a few sentences of bolder conversation.

Did I tell you – I'm not sure that I didn't – a joke that the Vice Rector made – the simple bearded Czech? I was trying to explain to him that I wanted to have a room in the Austrian Hospice to sleep in from time to time. He said 'Will you want meals here too?' I said, 'No, I only want a *pied à terre*': he said 'What, only pommes de terre?' I then tried to explain to him by saying Fuss im Erd, but it doesn't seem to be a German metaphor. It was silly of me to have tried French though, a dangerous language.

The days go by without being full of very much. I read depressingly little, and scraps of several things – I have not time reserved unfortunately – so pieces of the day dribble on into other pieces and work dribbles out over all of it.

Sometimes there are pleasant talks in the evenings with people – e.g. on Thursday in a Jewish Kosher sausage shop with a young woman called Diana Furness, niece of the Press Officer here, him I think I've spoken of, a pleasant and gallant rather devilish old rake – she an admirable person, here on a visit. Instead of turning one out at midnight as a

British restaurant would have done the family began to have their own last meal in the front of the shop – a beautiful black-haired old man in a small black cap, his wife and grown-up children, and then to take off their boots, collars and ties, in a sociable not a hinting way.

I've been out into the garden – it's going to be another hot day, already warm though only a quarter-past six – surprising how high the sun is up at so early an hour. My horse it is true that I haven't ridden for more than a couple of months, which is lazy of me: I could and should have hacked it. Now it is being brought up to Jerusalem, and Poston (the Private Secretary) going to pay for half (at least half) the cost of its stabling. He will ride it, and so will I when I can get a chance. The hour's drive, there and back, was what chiefly prevented me before – far and not always easy to get lifts. Now I shall really try to begin again – it's good for me as you say.

Yesterday to High Mass in honour of the canonization of Blessed More and Blessed Fisher – it got one two days' indulgence, but I don't suppose that applies to black Protestant sheep that creep into the fold.

TO DFH   AIN KARIM
4 JUNE 1935

I am feeling very pink about the face and crimson about the nose and scorched about the neck, having spent the last two days in a rather hot mad-dogs-n-Englishmen sort of walk with John Richmond.

For once I had two days on end free – this Government which hardly observes days like Good Friday and Ascension Day, though nominally holidays, does regard the King's birthday as a feast which is too sacred to be interfered with by work; so not having had a walk lately it seemed a good plan.

It wasn't an altogether successful walk though pleasant to look back upon. We have decided that we set out too casually on these journeys, and that if we organized them rather better beforehand we would have less to try to begin organizing them in the middle. This time for instance we had decided to walk from Nablus down to the Wadi Fara' to a place called Jiftlik, at the edge of the Jordan valley; then next day on down the Jordan Valley to Jericho. Actually we had to sleep 8 kilometres short of Jiftlik the first night, having not started from Nablus till ten in the morning and so missed the cool part of the day. Another disadvantage was that John started out with a stomach-ache which not only made it difficult for him to eat but made him not interested in buying food – you know how difficult it is to buy food when the other person says that he won't eat anything, whatever you buy. I got some bread, black olives and fresh black figs in the market at Nablus – much too much of all of them. The only really intelligent thing that we had bought was a water bottle, and it would have been more intelligent to buy two of them since it was very thirsty walking and, though there was a river running near us all the way down the valley, we as far as possible avoided drinking out of it, except at its source.

The best parts of the walk were as usual the drinks – first out of the silver bucket which the Greek priest lets down into Jacob's Well at Shechem – pleasant to be there again and think of the other two times that I'd been there – first with the Gills in the sun a year ago and then with Aunt Helen in the rain in January. The next was where a stream crossed the road, just near the source – a beautiful green strip on each side – apples and figs and other kinds of fruit trees. We sat in the shade for an hour then, having drunk and washed in the stream, quite clean.

Then when we moved on from that resting place the walk got steadily less comfortable – shoes and heat and thirst all at once. We cursed and had difficulty about drinking out of the water bottle at hourly intervals. It was a very good valley – more a gorge than anything – deep and rocky with this bright green stream running through the middle of it, full of rich pink tamarisks. (The last half-dozen lines were, as you can guess, written just before falling asleep – it's now the Austrian Hospice and a hot summer's afternoon.) At about six though we found a small ruined-looking house beside the road, just when we were thinking how wretched it would be to have to go any further. They told us there that Jiftlik, where we had meant to go that night, was two hours off, so that excused us from trying to get further that night. We were beautifully entertained by an Arab from the Yemen and his friends, who varied between one and half a dozen.

We supped off liban and bread and milk, which he mixed for us saying the whole time that it wasn't good enough and only Bedu food. Beautiful to rest spread out on the ground and to see the stars come out and for half an hour the young crescent moon – it must have been its first night. We slept comfortably on the roof – a cool wind – very tricky climbing up to it by a shaking ladder whose steps were two feet apart.

Next day was less good walking. John's foot became gradually blistered. I persuaded him not to go back the way we had come but to go along the Jordan valley as far as this Roman fortress, now nothing but wrecks of banana groves, called Phasaebis. It was of course a good deal hotter there and his blisters made the last 10 kilometres miserable for him – the air is so heavy down there – although there was every now and then a jolly breath of cooling breeze to drink in. But I was quite glad that we didn't try to get to Jericho on foot, but rested among the blackamoors who looked after the perished banana groves, drinking cool spring water in the shade till at about two a motor came and fetched us back to Jericho and Jerusalem.

[Undated (first page missing)]

The night before last I came in at one from chatting quietly with Jews in a café – Billig,[1] the nice Professor of Oriental Languages at the Hebrew University – and found the door locked against me – the front door, not the outer garden door. So being on principle opposed to beating people (except my parents) up on such occasions, and knowing that I can sleep always anywhere and under any circumstances, I lay down like Jacob, putting my coat under my head for a pillow, and a mat under my thigh for softness, and slept in the full moon. Not very well though, as there was a wedding being celebrated very noisily just over the way, and it was surprisingly cold in only a waistcoat.

[1]'Billig's murder was a tragic example of the insanity prevailing in this country: the most harmless, likeable person one could wish in this land of hatred' (George Antonius in a letter to T, 23 August 1936).

TO ECH
[probably June 1935, when ECH had been offered a job
tutoring the children of a wealthy Bombay industrialist]

It should be a good place to watch events from – a pinnacle
on one of the flying buttresses of the imperialist stage of
capitalism and not a niche on its façade. This tutoring of the
Begums of Oude seems to be ideal from that point of view.
India is obviously more important evidence for the nature of
British Imperialism than any other country, and a year or two
there would give you at any rate enough material for a good
superficial judgement – which is all one can hope to get to
begin with. All this is obscure because it is written in a hurry
on a hot afternoon. What I principally mean is that I think
you'd agree that what is most necessary is to decide one's
attitude to society – to this and to Communism. Until one has
done that in no job can one have security of tenure, nor, if
one foresees quite soon the breaking up of the system on
which all the careers one might take depend, can one possibly
be careerist. One can only be experimental.

TO DFH   AIN KARIM
17 JUNE 1935   MONDAY

Various things have been happening, nothing definite, yet if I
don't talk about them you aren't having as complete a picture
of what is going on as I want you to have. That is the worst of
weekly letters, though I think they are a good thing and I
almost always love writing them. But they become historical
and objective rather, and people like Mary or Aunt Helen
that I write about once in three months to probably get a truer
in one way picture since there's no continuity and I only try to
talk out of a mood. If we always told one another about
moods one would always have to explain next week how one
had got rid of the one of the week before; not that we don't
tell one another a lot of what's momentary. (A good moon
tonight: two days past the full, I think. The village looks
yellow and bright; there is the sound of a woman wailing for
her demon lover coming from it.)
   One of the things is that Diana Furness who I think I've

spoken of once or twice vaguely went back to England on Saturday. She'd been here for the last two and a half months, a painter, a professional but doesn't make a living by it. I have a painting that she did while she was here, an interior, indeed the interior of my sitting room in a manner of speaking. I mean that she looked at my sitting room and then went home and painted the picture. You would say it was rather like Ben Nicholson I think: that ought to help you to visualize it better. She is about my age, the niece of the Press Officer – infinitely more living and beautiful and a better friend than anyone else in this country – only Katy Antonius comparable.

But like the Bailiff's daughter of Islington she was coy, or rather often unresponsive, and when we met at any rate in company we tended to argue, often about things that neither of us cared tuppence about, you know the awful way in which one does. We didn't meet very often and for the last ten days she was here I didn't see her at all, though she was staying then with Katy and ill, or at least mildly so. It was only by accident that I saw her to say goodbye. Then only thanks to Katy that I said goodbye in friendship and didn't end with a quarrel.

Ever since she has gone I have been realizing how horribly self-centred my love for people is. Here, with nobody apart from those two and John that I am really fond of, it has become more so and I more dried up, I'm afraid. But this has woken me up, I pray for long if not for good. It is a thing that people are always saying and not new, but it is new to me, or anyhow I have never felt it as clearly and illuminatingly as I did on Saturday, and do still though of course more faintly, that one must love people simply as themselves, not for the satisfaction to be got out of them or out of knowing them. I saw what a tremendous amount of self-love was included in what I thought was love for all the people that I am fond of. This is very bare but you will understand – I wanted to tell you however sketchily what was, is, in my mind.

TO DFH   JERUSALEM
[UNDATED]   WEDNESDAY

I am here tonight because guests took me back after supper. I have left some work unfinished and want to get at it early tomorrow morning, before Nurock might come and finish it for me, I hope by 7 o'clock. This is the hospice room. It is beautiful to be able to come and go so freely with a bed always there, food if I want it and a Grüss Gott and no questions asked from the nuns – the sort of way that people live in *News from Nowhere* – should live in the future. The guests were Catholics, friends of John's, he an orientalist and a wit – she beautiful and lively – but not sympathetic really; also a young man transferred, after 4 years in Uganda, to the Secretariat – nice, simple and interesting. But no chance to talk about Uganda tonight.

TO DFH   HAIFA
7 JULY 1935   SUNDAY

Good wise letters have arrived from both of you which I won't try to answer now. I certainly won't do anything immediate – it was stupid of me not to have made that clear in my first letter. I think we must certainly have chances to talk first whether on my leave – or better when, if, I hope when, you are here in the autumn. Don't mind about old Samuel[1] saying don't come before March. November is jolly good though there are no flowers – not as good as March and April I admit but a very pleasant month for travelling about in.

A procession has just gone by in front of the window – Arab Catholics, peasants, beating skin-drums and singing. They have been doing that ever since eight in the morning and it's now half-past four. I am not sure quite what the ceremony was, whether Baptism, Circumcision or Confirmation, but it was something to do with the children. They looked about five most of them, so more the right age for circumcision than for any of the other ceremonies. The word the Arab I asked about it used means 'a vowing to God', which is non-committal. But from the tune they were singing it might have been a Moslem wedding. Kinglake would be rather scornful about such enthusiastic Christians. Wonderful to have kept at it with their wives and children all day – they walked off carrying their children on their shoulders or swinging them along holding their hands.

Outside streams of cars of new pilgrims are arriving. They are going to displace me – I was given an ultimatum yesterday by the Carmelite Director, and another one this morning by a very unpleasant Arab butler. They are perfectly within their rights as they have a rule – I think a very stupid one – that one mustn't stay more than three days in the hospice. I have so far stayed six and thought that by obtuseness I could stay out the whole three weeks or so that I shall be in Haifa. But I've failed. I mean to write something bitter in the Visitors' Book – my only revenge for being turned out on a Sunday afternoon to find a fresh roof to my head. Of course with more prudence I would have looked for a home yesterday, but it is the sort of thing one does put off, and I hoped that when the Director saw me in Mass this morning he might give me a 10 days indulgence to let me stay, but he hasn't.

It is beautiful on this promontory, with sea on three sides and the lighthouse part of the hospice swinging beams of light round all night – the harbour and the town below, this afternoon full of sailing vessels with their sails furled and a few small white sails, and sand and sea on the other side and falling rocky ground in between. That is what I have out of my bedroom window, with now and then a train on the railway line which runs along beside the sea.

I think Daddy is right in saying that a summer in Jerusalem probably stretches one's nerves, but I don't think that has influenced my judgement much. The chief question seems to be whether it is good to go on doing work which one believes is not of any use to people, or for how long it is worth while doing it in order to be sure in one's own mind that one is not judging its lack of usefulness rashly. I agree that one must be sure of that. I am quite willing to go on for two or three more years in order to have more grounds for certainty. I must stop occupying this writing room which is filling with American pilgrims eager to describe the view and the journey to their parents and children and husbands and wives at the writing table that I am occupying. 'Our devotions are at 6.30 on one of the Terraces.' From that remark I guess them to be Protestants of a rather left-wing and open-air sort.

---

[1]Sir Herbert Samuel. First High Commissioner for Palestine (1920–25). Honorary Fellow of Balliol, 1935. Viscount, 1937.

I have been wanting to write to you all day but have put it off until now. You remember this Crusader castle where I spent a weekend with HE about a year ago. He was up here, and very generously and friendlily invited me for these two nights. I shall get up at 6 tomorrow (or say I will), ride with Poston the PS, and then go back to Haifa at half-past eight.

It has been happy to be here – it's beautiful to have castle and rocks and sea and long sandy beach again. I have read very little, bathed four times (my back is even a little pink from the sun, but no more than pink), and we have had pleasant conversations – about Crusades, poetry, the war, drink, English agriculture and other things. He has been very lively and good company – pleasant to have no one else but Poston. I find I can talk easily with HE even on subjects that we would disagree on, but I don't feel ashamed of not forcing matters to a disagreement. It seems better to be easy with people that one's fond of when one knows that dispute will not get anything done of any use to anyone.

(I am going on writing this in an eating-house in Haifa – Monday night.) I have been talking to the proprietor. He laid his hand on mine and, having asked me my income and my age – I told him the truth about both, Sie mussen *erden* he said – an siebzehn, achtzehn jahren kann man erden, aber an funf und zwanzig muss man. I agreed. (Teddy will put the German straight.) I have had many beautiful letters from you – my last two have been dry I know.

I am living now in rooms that I have borrowed from this man Pirie-Gordon[1] whose place I am taking. They are free, not too far from the town, and full of Victorian novels – Marryat and that sort rather, smelling very strongly of binding. I hope to stay at least another week and if possible a fortnight – enormously much better than the Secretariat. If this sort of work could be made to continue it would give a different aspect to all that I said in my letter about a career. Don't think that *that* letter makes any difference to your coming here in November – it makes it all the more necessary and to be longed for. The thing that makes the difference, chiefly, between this life and the Secretariat, is that here one is compelled to deal with people – poor Arabs wanting not to be turned out of an antiquity site (Athlit Castle), workers wanting to build houses, men living in tin huts wanting to sell melons but refused licences by the public health people. One of the abominable things about this town is that I think going on for 10,000 people can't afford to live in houses (there are not nearly enough and the rents are very high) and live in these miserable huts made out of old petrol tins mostly, spread all over the sandhills to the north end of the town. And as the land is from time to time needed for town-planning schemes or government or industrial buildings, so the people living in the huts get evicted and driven further away from the town and their work – if they have any.

This is a scrappy letter in return for all your lovely ones. I am now falling asleep on the balcony where a jolly cool wind blows from the sea which beats near by. My jolly friendly landlady is an Egyptian I think but called, unEgyptianly, Mrs Birch. I hope we shall have better luck with one another than in past relationships with landladies. She seems more affectionate than any in the past. She has offered me brioches for breakfast tomorrow which is a good gesture.

[1]Christopher Pirie-Gordon. Then in the Palestine Government service, later in the Trucial States and Yemen, and ended as Consul-General in Florence.

TO ECH   AIN KARIM
25 AUGUST 1935

I didn't send you a telegram today wishing you a very happy birthday. I had one written in the Post Office at lunchtime today and had borrowed the money to pay for it and then I thought that this is unpardonable extravagance and romantic-ism. With the streets full of beggars and Europe possibly about to go to war there seemed something hysterical and out of place about expressing my love and blessings in a telegram. You understand, I think. Telegrams, and even more cables, seem to belong to the romanticist period of our lives which is past: they don't fit in with attempting to be realist.

On the other hand I was very anxious to communicate with you, feeling in close communication with you. Perhaps all the less need to communicate. But I have all day felt particularly anxious to see you – that is to say my normal lacking of your company has energized itself as a positive missing of it: you know the feeling as well as I do. It happens fairly rarely when absent for a long time from people one loves since one hardens up – but every now and then the clouds open and one sees the green and fertile plain that one has left and notices how far up the bloody mountain one has gone and how far one has got to go and how hard it is raining and how wet and exhausted and hungry one is (metaphor, as you may have guessed, from climbing that small mountain, whatever its name was, opposite Patsch). I had meant to write to you earlier in the day but Bulos el 'Araj ('Paul the Lame' to translate – that makes him sound like a medieval Bohemian King, which he is far from being: he is actually a Christian Arab, a friend from Jericho, the first person to be kind to me in this country) has been here for most of the day.

I do believe that there is no such thing as international morality or that conceptions of justice have any effect on one nation's treatment of another. From the little I have seen of governing I should say that national self-interest is the only sort of motive that ever determines national policy (national self-interest being, in bourgeois nations, the interest of the ruling class, the dividend-owning and dividend-controlling class), though individuals administering the policy may be determined by other motives if they are exceptionally high-minded and strong-willed people: e.g. this High Commissioner does certainly act out of a sense of obligation, but that doesn't have any effect on the broad lines of national policy, in this country or elsewhere.

I enclose a poem – not a very good one – called 'On First Dipping into Lawrence's *Seven Pillars of Wisdom*': its only virtue is that it was spontaneous. It is very crude. [It is. It begins:

When the next war comes, Arabs,
You shall not be made the instruments of imperialist
    aggression

and continues for twenty-four Whitmanesque lines.]

It is particularly bad because it apes a manner of expression which isn't really my own. There is a horrible danger of going too quickly and using the jargon of a kind of Communism that one hasn't yet experienced and in which one doesn't believe – which probably damages such true belief in Communism as one has got. Don't you agree?

My lamp is bubbling and going out. Half-past two. Goodnight.

TO ECH   HEBRON
28 SEPTEMBER 1935

The office is already beginning to stink of warlike preparations, and soldiers and air officers are beginning to rattle their sabres and enjoy the smell of work after 17 years with nothing to do but fill in forms and fine their men and go to cocktail parties. I had a dinner two nights ago with Domvile, an Air Force intelligence officer, and a friend of his, a military attaché from the legation at Jedda. It was a hopeless conversation – I both drank and talked too much. It is an unpleasant feeling to argue with people with whom you have no basis of agreement. As you said of David Jones, what is pleasantest is agreement upon essentials; failing that one must have understanding of the other person's essentials. Domvile and the dude from Jedda and I had not. We were talking of course of war. They quoted Saint Crispin's day at me when I said that affection for England was to me pleasure in Shakespeare and green fields and not loyalty to the national Government.

I am sitting now in a Beduin tent resting after the first day of a 3 days' journey between Hebron and the Dead Sea – this completely desolate country with only a few Bedu camps here and there in hollows, hens and chickens keep coming in under one corner of the tent and going out under another. We have just drunk coffee – 3 cups and then you refuse – also some tea which Salim Husseini, the effendi (in the technical sense, not the contemptuous sense in which English administrators like to use it) who is travelling with me made on his Primus, with Ali, who I have hopelessly tried to draw on this page – he is very handsome. The only true thing about the picture is the largeness and blackness of his eyes, with very white whites – wild like Steerforth's – a narrow and hollow face, and a devilish and shifting smile. It is bad to drift like this into Lawrence-like idealization of the Bedu, but their manners are beautiful and their jokes, what I can understand of them, good, and so is their appreciation of what they can understand of mine. Any faults they have are, I think, only the result of poverty. The more I see – I have so far seen very little – of the laws of this country working the more I agree with the Marxist principle that the purpose of political power is principally to maintain class ascendancy and retain class privileges.

TO ECH   AIN KARIM
21 OCTOBER 1935

I do not include the mention of a fellowship [at All Souls] for you in my prayers, as I did for a First, for I do think it would be extremely difficult for you to live in that Social Reformist atmosphere (at best, and at worst *The Times*, the *Round Table* and Sir John Simon) without becoming partly infected by it. I should have been worse corrupted than you would be – but the atmosphere of Rowse[1] and Berlin (personally lovable though he is) would I think reduce one gradually to a state of cynical intellectual acquiescence in social evil. That is why I think this time in a colonial society is probably a good thing for me; one sees bourgeois rule and society and culture in a much truer light than one would through the port-wine-coloured spectacle of All Souls.

As Derek once said to me and I may already have repeated to you, the dominant tone of the mind of the bourgeoisie is really the *Daily Express* and not the *Manchester Guardian*, and the sooner one realizes it the better. Possibly you could learn to live a pariah's life like Goronwy Rees. But more and more I find it hopeless to try to maintain any sort of intercourse with people who are absolutely opposed however socially nice; one either sells oneself or produces friction, with me usually the former; that apart from its moral badness is a waste of time.

I shall be disappointed if you do get an All-Souler in that it is likely to postpone your coming here; if you do not come before the end of November I shall be inclined to give up living in Ain Karim, partly because it absorbs two hours a day travelling to and fro, partly because I think Sitt Sophia, my landlady who I have imprisoned in a cabin down below, will want to move into this house by the time the cold weather comes.

I spent a rather futile evening last night trying to make an old woman's flesh creep. The old woman is Miss Carey:[2] she lives in my village and is truly good to the villagers. I am sorry to say though that she firmly believes that the whole of the British Empire mandates, Crown Colonies, Self-Governing Dominions and all are bound together by mystical and invisible chains, I mean bonds, which run between them and the Royal Family. I offered to lend her Fox on *British Colonial Imperialism* who might make her see other and less mystical bonds, but she wouldn't borrow it. It is horrible how many genuinely decent-feeling people are perfect material for Fascism if their brains are weak.

I must stop writing to you and get dressed. Now England will have a general election and another thundering majority for a Government more nationalist than the last with the battle cry of sanctions, in which the Labour Party will join and drown their own thin pipes about unemployment and so forth. I do not see anything except imperialist war that will drive the English working class to Socialism, and only then as a reaction after having plunged into the war (or been plunged) and fought in it, most of them. This time it seems from what Derek tells me that the Communists will support (though try at the same time to use for their own purposes, capture control of it for the working class) a so-called League of Nations war to protect the territorial integrity of Russia and France against Fascism. But what if the working class doesn't get control of it? I should have thought the answer is that it will get control of them and instead of the war becoming a Socialist instrument they will become again imperialist instruments. I do not understand how Communists make out, if they do make out, that the interests of Russia are always indentical with the interests of the working class in other countries.

[1]A.L. Rowse, Isaiah Berlin and Goronwy Rees were all Fellows of All Souls.
[2]An elderly Englishwoman who had built a sort of shrine on a hill above Ain Karim,

where Christians, Moslems and Jews were supposed to meet and be reconciled, but didn't and weren't.

TO ECH   AIN KARIM
8 NOVEMBER 1935
[Planning for ECH to come to Palestine]

There are plenty of good boats I think from Constanza to Haifa if you like the idea of that route; I think it would be interesting. Avoid British boats because of the company; if you want to study the imperialist outlook you will have plenty of opportunities here and needn't begin on the journey. One factor is that Katy Antonius has suggested my coming to Cairo with her at the end of this month or beginning of next. Of course I should only go if you came too, but it might be possible to fit it in with your arrival if you arrived at Port Said. If not we could go down together later. It is of course all dependent on my being able to get a few days' leave to which I am not really entitled. She would be an ideal person to be with in a strange foreign town from every point of view. I have told her that we shall both go there with her if it can be managed. The chief advantages other than her company would be (1) interesting people, (2) good mosques. I don't think you could regard it as useful for your work; one has rather to avoid the tendency which I fell into horribly of regarding everything from riding round Byzantine churches to tea-parties with Jews as useful to one's work. But you will know better.

One other thing: books. Will you if you have time invest about £5 to £10 in left-wing literature, as you think best, partly for me but principally for the clerks here; I want to start a shelf of such books which they may read. Will you also bring and read yourself on the journey, if you haven't read it already, Dutt's *Fascism and Social Revolution*, very good. Derek sent it to me but I want a spare copy to lend to people. I think Fox has recently written a well-reviewed book about Marxism and the capitalist crisis. Any books about imperial history which you can pick up I should be grateful for, even from a bourgeois standpoint.

I must do some more work and then go back to Ain Karim. [Letter completed in the Secretariat.] A good sunny day;

tomorrow is Saint Crispin's day;[1] there is a great quarrel going on between civilians and air force about who is to sit closer to the Union Jack.

[1]Not exactly. Presumably refers to Remembrance Day celebrations.

Soon after my arrival in Palestine in November 1935 T took three weeks' leave during which he planned for us to see parts of Transjordan and, if possible, St Catherine's monastery in Sinai. We hired three horses, five donkeys and five muleteers, one to look after each beast, from the village of Yatta, south of Hebron, and set off from the Manger Square in Bethlehem on 18 December. We came down to the Dead Sea at Ain Jiddi, then an uninhabited spring of pure water (there was no road or even track along the west shore of the Dead Sea in those days), went round the southern end of the Sea, past Jebel Usdum (Sodom) and the Palestine Potash Company's works, into the semi-tropical Ghor and up to Kerak. There we spent our first night under a roof, that of an Irish priest in the Italian hospital, other nights having been spent in Bedu tents or in the open.

In Kerak we were joined by Prudence Pelham, who had turned up in Jerusalem shortly before I did. She had gone on from art schools in London and Paris to work at Pigotts with Eric Gill – the only female apprentice, I think, he ever had – learning stone-carving and lettering. There she met David Jones, and they became devoted friends. 'To my mind,' René Hague wrote in Dai Greatcoat, *a collection of David Jones's letters, 'this friendship was the most important personal relationship in David's life.' She had come to Palestine with no special aim in view except to travel, and David had told her to look Thomas up, which she did. That she was a very remarkable person will, I hope, emerge from these letters.*

From Kerak we rode to Shobek (where it snowed), Petra and Maan, where we were guests of the mayor – that is to say, entertained to dinner and accommodated on the roof of his house. The next day we took a taxi with him to Akaba, being passed on to the mayor of that place, still a cluster of little houses on the sea shore, whose inhabitants lived off fishing and smuggling. A pencil note in Prudence's handwriting:

We arrived at Akabah in half darkness between the setting of the sun and the rising moon – but it was still twilight enough for us to see the half ruinous village built along the narrow dark blue tongue of sea and the dark cluster of date palms round the village. Crowds of little boys and a tall fine old man – ? the mayor – welcomed us with the usual politeness and more than usual kindness, and we went with him and his sons through the white-walled haram into his house. It was the nicest Arab house we had seen – square, whitewashed scrubbed floor with long white mattresses round the walls. There was nothing in it besides ourselves, a coffee-pot and a painted tin trunk. Gradually the family increased and the room was soon full of people. We were melted with happiness and our words were sugared with the thought of a second hog sleep and feed. It was decided that I should sleep at the police post and de-louse myself in privacy, but not till after supper.

We hired three camels and two guides and set off for the monastery. It was cold by day and very cold by night. Prudence had malaria off and on, and on the first night out I developed jaundice (this ought to have been easy to diagnose from the colour of my eyes and urine, but never having come into contact with this complaint we referred to it vaguely as a fever). We had no tent, and only extra jerseys to put on at night. T had an abba *(cloak) and I a* farwa *(sheepskin coat). Prudence had a sleeping-bag, and chivalrously let me use it when my temperature was higher than hers.*

The middle of the Sinai peninsula in the depth of winter is not an exciting place. It is a bare plateau of hills and wadis *with no vegetation. As far as I can remember, in all the eight days we spent there we saw nobody. We lit a fire each evening when we camped and went to sleep tolerably warm, but by dawn the fire had long gone out and we woke extremely cold. The food we had was largely flour, from which we made Arab bread, tins of bully beef and dates. This is not a diet to attract the sick. We reached St Catherine's monastery at sunset, after the gates had been shut, but shouted pleas to a monk on the high wall secured our entry, though of course guides and camels had to stay outside.*

I fear I have not made this four weeks' journey (including nearly a week in the monastery) sound particularly attractive, but there was much to enjoy. T was all the time in his element. As I wrote to my parents from Cairo:

For four weeks he has enjoyed and mildly exercised dictatorial powers. It is perfectly true to say that he has done absolutely everything on this journey and that Prudence and I have only made complaints or made weak suggestions when they were too late to be of any use. He has made the decisions, made the plans, seen the objections, met them, talked to everyone whether guides or hosts, done the quarrelling, bargaining, thanking, rewarding, interrogating, reprimanding and exhorting. He has also done physically five times as much as either of us and he alone has not been ill. His lassitude seems to be very closely linked to his occupation – in Jerusalem where he is doubtful about the utility and interest of the work he is occupied in he is sleepy and not so energetic, but released from the formality of being a government official and among the Arabs he is far more active and energetic than most people. As we drooped his vitality increased, until at Sinai, while I spent almost all my time on my bed and Prudence sat in the sun, Thomas was talking with the Greek monks, attending their four a.m. service, and was preparing if necessary to make a forced march on camel to fetch a car to transport the enervated bodies of his companions back to civilization.

One Sinai picture in particular sticks in my mind. The three camels are plodding mournfully in line under a leaden sky, T's leading, while the two guides march by their sides, occasionally giving them a prod with a stick which produces angry grunts, or starting up a mournful ditty. T has sat himself back to front on his saddle and is reading aloud in an effort to cheer up his lacklustre companions. The book he is reading from is a volume of Gibbon's Decline and Fall of the Roman Empire.

TO DFH   KERAK
23 DECEMBER 1935   MONDAY

This is no letter. I am ashamed of not having written anything yet – I must send some word now – and we are trying to get off as soon as possible, and I am sitting in the seat of the chief constable of Kerak whose work will be interfered with as long as I stay here. The trouble is that these days are so short we travel all the time that there is light, practically, and when we arrive there is no daylight for writing in. We sup by firelight, listen sometimes to someone playing music on pipes, and then sleep. It has been a good journey so far. I think Teddy is happy – beautiful to have him to travel with again – mostly beautiful country. The people we travel with and the people we meet are good. These generalities are no good.

Prudence has turned up – yesterday, recovered from her fever. It's nice to have her too. I hope she enjoys staying with this nice Catholic priest from Liverpool again. I truly will write you a proper letter, at latest in 5 days' time when we hope to be in Petra. Then we hope, if money and time make it possible, to get to Aqaba and Sinai. All safe I promise you. We are very well in body.

TO RHH AND DFH
[DECEMBER 1935]

I haven't written to you the long proper letter that I want to. I am ashamed. There have been times when I might at least have begun to but have failed. Now it is Petra and we are starting this morning to go southwards to Rumm and Aqaba. Two camels are roaring in the stable waiting for Teddy and me. Mohammed and Ali (the two Beduin we started out with) and Shaikh Suleiman, the owner of the smartest camel, are sitting round the fire making tea. Prudence is in bed a few yards off: she has brought a bed of her own which she pitches beside us when we sleep beside the fire in whatever cave, tent or bit of open country we sleep in. She has malaria now – or rather had yesterday – which is wretched for her: she says she is all right today and wants to start. I trust that she truly is. We don't want to stay in Petra. We don't very much like the place, and it is expensive since we can't well avoid having sophisticated 4-course meals at the table of the man who lets us sleep in this cave – not only us but our followers. The two Beduin, and now the owners of the camels and some of their friends and relations, eat at our expense, or would if we stayed longer. It is like paying for the upkeep of a mercenary army that you've hired when you can't fight because of the rains.

It is being a beautiful journey still. With God's help I will write it all to you properly. We travelled from Kerak down towards the Dead Sea at the south end – stayed with a sheikh whose bedding turned out to have been bug-ridden and gave Prudence bites which she has been suffering from ever since. It was a lovely great arched room that we slept in and ate bread and mutton. Next day we stopped and (you will be glad to hear) washed our bodies clean at a spring – got rid of a good deal of old dirt by stripping naked – it was a most beautiful spring with palm trees going up beside it. We slept in the Wadi Araba, south from the Dead Sea, a tropical sort of country, full of camels grazing among bushes and houses of mud thatched with leaves – African-looking we thought. Next day we began to climb back again into the hills. A Bedu boy from the Howeitat was with us and sang to us as we walked – a most beautiful tune – short but complete and repeating itself verse after verse.

The day before had been Christmas Day – not noticeably except that we gave one or two presents to each other. Teddy got a belt from Prudence, white wool with leather straps. We had singing and dancing on that evening too – a wild fertility sort of dance and song from some of them, and a raiding song: a good entertainment which went on till we fell asleep. One song invented as it went along about us, praising our noble qualities.

I finish this letter eating good bread – like pancakes – thin and damp and brown on the outside. Mohammed, the most loved of the two Bedus who have come with us from Jerusalem, has just been asked if he has had any bread yet and has given his usual answer that as long as he has us to look at there is no such thing as hunger for him. We must load and start. Forgive this letter being again so short and bald and bad.

We went up a valley to Shobek from the Araba – the Crusader castle – very cold and high up – slept one night in the cold on the mountains with Bedus and another night beautifully and with a room to ourselves in a room like a bedroom at the keep in the tower at Shobek – belongs to the police. I finish from the back of a camel.

1936

This was to be in every sense the worst year yet. In April German troops marched into the demilitarized Rhineland, and Britain and France made no effort to stop this breach of the Versailles Treaty or the accelerated pace of German rearmament. The Spanish Civil War erupted in July, and soon the Franco forces were receiving massive assistance from Italy and some from Germany, which modest backing for the Republicans from Russia and the much publicized International Brigade did little to counterbalance.

In January the Palestine Arab leaders received an answer to the three-point demand they had put forward in November – a democratic government, no more land sales to the Jews, and a complete stoppage of Jewish immigration. On the first point they were referred to the proposals for a Legislative Council, which the Zionists had rejected at their Lucerne Congress the previous summer and on which the Arabs were still undecided. Further land legislation was promised, but the Arabs were told categorically that 'there can be no question of the total stoppage of Jewish immigration'. They were once again invited to send a delegation to London for discussions.

The Arabs agreed to do this, but before it could arrive a debate in both Houses of Parliament had killed the idea of a Legislative Council stone dead. The Arabs not surprisingly saw this as yet another example of the overwhelming influence exercised by the Zionists and their sympathizers in the London corridors of power (just as later they were to dominate the corridors of power in Washington).

Arab exasperation slid inevitably into violence. In April a general strike was declared and an Arab Higher Committee of ten men was set up under the presidency of the Mufti and with all parties represented on it. Armed bands began operating in the hills, aiming their attacks mainly at the railways, telephones and other communications. Troop reinforcements were sent in and martial law declared.

Thanks to the intervention of the Emir Abdullah and other Arab rulers the strike was called off after six months, but only after a great loss of life and much hardship. The Peel Commission was set up and in July 1937 reported, recommending the partition of Palestine into Arab and Jewish states with a

151

small continuing area of mandated territory including Jerusalem and Bethlehem and a corridor to the sea at Jaffa. The report was accepted by the British Government, and by the Zionists on condition that the boundaries of the proposed Jewish state were enlarged, but rejected by the Arabs. Violence resumed. The rebellion became general, leading on to the St James's Palace Conference of January 1939 and the White Paper which restricted Jewish immigration to 75,000 over a five-year period, after which it would depend on Arab acquiescence. Then came the war.

TO DFH   SINAI MONASTERY
12 JANUARY [1936]

We are sitting in the sun waiting for breakfast: it will, I think, be omelette, brown toast and jam, persimmon and grapes: a good sort of breakfast. We are being treated very well – increasingly well. The monks have generously forgiven our forbidding outsides – dirt squalor poverty beards – and treat us with great hospitality. They are even going to let us pay for our entertainment by cheque. As usually happens with Teddy and me, we are short of money. Stupid always to misjudge. However this hasn't yet landed us in any major difficulty – thanks to God and not to us.

I shall be probably two days late back at the office – but I have wired to them saying this and apologizing. This is the third day of our visit here: it's beautiful to be so idle after having been fairly strenuous. The food too is very good – there is no one here but us. We are asked twice a day by the kind Arab cook what we want for our next meal – so far we have eaten splendid meals, the two last centring round (i) roast chicken and roast potatoes (ii) tomato soup, full of rice, into which I emptied the contents of lightly boiled eggs – very feeding.

Teddy unfortunately enjoys none of this. He is sick every now and then and off his food. It is a great bore for him as he was very much looking forward to nice food – he and Prudence planning meals ahead. But ever since he arrived he's been a bit sick – the cause we don't know – I should think probably the cold on the journey (it was foully cold always at night – when it was worst we kept a fire going all night – there was always plenty of wood, luckily) and then the monotony of the food – variations on the theme: bread, bully beef, sardines, dates, halva (the sweetmeat I sent you 3 years ago for Christmas) and Gamardin (a product of apricots, like sweet brown paper – the women in the Jebel Druze, Prudence says, boil it and spread it on their faces as a cosmetic) – had something to do with it.

I was a fool not to have got hold of better provisions before we started. I don't mind a lot of that sort of dry food, but Teddy and Prudence both I think need fresh vegetables and fruit much more than I do. If I'd been more sensible I would have bought at least potatoes and eggs before we started. But you know how it is. One starts off in a hurry and is improvident. I hope neither of them will suffer for long as a result. Prudence seems practically restored I think. Teddy I hope will be as soon as he gets back into warmth and the right sort of food. He and Prudence then think of going on to Cairo for a bit – a good plan I think. The Antoniuses will be there and will be good to them – they'll stay in some cheap hotel – look at mosques. Better for Teddy to get his whole holiday over at once and then settle down to work, and a pity not to see Cairo. I wish I could too.

I haven't properly explained why I am going to be 2 days late in getting back to Jerusalem. Partly it was ordinary miscalculations: we naturally travelled slower than I reckoned – took 8 days over the journey instead of 6. Partly it was the difficulty of getting a car here. It takes 3 days for it to arrive – a messenger has to post over the hill to the nearest telegraph office. All this I should, of course, have found out about beforehand and reckoned on, but I didn't. Now I can only hope the Government will excuse me. I imagine it will.

It has been a pleasant idle three days in this monastery. I am ashamed of myself for not having climbed Moses' mountain. Neither Teddy nor Prudence were in a climbing mood and I was too weak-willed to go and climb on my own. It would have taken a day to go up and down. On the other hand, although I've seen a good deal of the inside of this monastery I don't feel that I know at all really how the monks spend their lives or what they exist for. The particular monk who looks after us – and I suppose all visitors – is a rebel, as far as I can make out, talking very ineffective halting Greek to him. He hopes to get away to Jerusalem in the spring to stay with the monks of the Holy Sepulchre and seems to think that that may be a way of escape, whether into the world or only into a new monastery I don't know: I think into the world. He was the son of a carpenter in the Island of Zakynthos and worked at carpentry. As far as I could understand he would like to work with his hands again. He says that the monastery usually gives people work as far as possible contrary to their tastes. The inactivity which the job of attending on visitors involves him in obviously bores him: he is very fidgety.

I wish I could talk to him properly. I stutter over every word, and usually in the end can't remember it and have to begin the sentence in another way. [Letter continued in Suez.] On the last evening when we talked with him he said that he thought the life of monk might have been all right in the old days but was now almost impossible. He also said that the two things which he wanted most were money and to travel. He was very good to us – sitting most of the time silently with us, fidgeting. On the last evening he invited Prudence and me to his room (Teddy was lying down on his bed as by then the sun had set and it was cold.) We were given some sort of liquor – like grape ferment with a scented purple syrup that looked like methylated spirits and tasted like rose-leaves – walnuts and almonds and strawberry jam in a spoon. We asked him how he kept warm in the winter in his miserably cold room. He showed us one of the white woollen vests that he wore, looking like string, made for him by his mother in Zakynthos. I showed him, in return, the green jumper which I was wearing, knitted for me by my mother in England. A good bond. I hope I may meet him again in Jerusalem.

Suez doesn't seem to be so nice a town as I at first thought it would be. We eat and bath well in this Greek hotel called the Windsor. But Prudence and my look at night-life last night was unsuccessful. We found only a very bad circus where a fat girl revolved with a thin boy on a trapeze, and a donkey was bullied by clowns. Today I shall go to Kantara [crossed out]. On second thoughts I shan't. We'll all go to Cairo together and I'll go a bust on an aeroplane to Jerusalem tomorrow. I shall be able to see the Antoniuses, and Teddy will probably go to a doctor. He is much better – eating boiled

154

fish and tangerines. But probably it would be better to see a doctor to be on the safe side.

[Undated fragment; perhaps associated with previous letter]

Yesterday I went in the early morning – just before dawn – they were praying in a very small sort of Lady Chapel dedicated to Moses – the place where God told him to take off his shoes as this was holy ground. The floor carpeted and all the walls covered with icons, most of them old and beautiful. It was a beautifully informal service, very free and easy. The Abbot leant against one side wall, six priests and myself against the wall opposite the altar. The two youngest and least bearded priests leant against the other side wall and gave the responses – no acolyte business. When the celebrating priest put on a new coat to celebrate in he got it and put it on himself. The Abbot came up to the altar and took his piece of the sacrament. The other monks were given theirs at the end of the service and went out eating. I went again this morning early, but being a Sunday the service was held in the body of the church and was more elaborate.

The sun is up now and I am sitting basking in it. It is a beautiful monastery, like a very haphazard town stuck within the walls of a fortress. The walls look old – medieval the bottom of them at any rate – with stone earthworks stuck later on the top. A path runs round the top of the wall within its thickness – every now and then there are platforms with little cannons pointing out of slits – rather like the Bamburgh ones, but much smaller cannons. Presumably you didn't need big ones to keep off Beduin.

It's odd to think of this little island of wealth and fertility going on existing in the middle of starving and hostile Beduin. Now the Beduin are kept off without cannons – what Locke called the change from the state of nature to the state of civil society. The monks gain, but the Beduin don't, from the state of civil society. The monastery distributes bread to Beduin who come for it – twice a week 5 small loaves per family I think is what they get. Besides, the Archimandrite who is also librarian strolls in the morning up and down his roof, distributing largess, dates and nuts, dropping them into the pavement below for the children. The result is that there is always a swarm of Beduin hanging about in the courtyard, waiting or hoping to get something given them.

TO ECH AND PP   JERUSALEM
16 JANUARY [1936]

It is very unpleasant to be back. The place is like a tomb – or like purgatory. Everyone seems miserable and oneself impotent to help – the streets full of beggars and Beduin hanging about looking for work, looking bedraggled – the Secretariat full of madmen, men hopelessly wanting jobs for themselves or their relations, clerks bullied and underpaid, British Government servants bullying and overpaid, comfortably enjoying their separate life and parties and jokes. It is like returning to a nightmare which has been interrupted by a pleasant dream.

Partly my feeling is simply dislike of work after idleness – and a great deal the missing of both your companies, and regret that that lovely journey is over – but it does partly arise from the nature of the work. But all this there'll be opportunities to talk about. I always used to regret complaining letters I wrote at the beginning of every term. This is too much that sort of letter . . .

One nice thing was the greenness of the country between Ramle and Jerusalem yesterday. All the crops and trees looking bright after the rain the day before – the olive trees in particular – all the trees looking like spring. Another was a great flock of turkeys going up the steps of the convent of the Sisters of Zion. The women typists were the friendliest people to meet again. They are the most human people in that office: they seem to stand up against the withering air of the Secretariat more effectively than the men – keep their independence more.

I wish I had asked you more about your jaundice on the telephone this morning. I hope it isn't giving you trouble and that you are really recovering from it. The doctor will give you better advice than I can and Prudence will see that you eat the right things – brandy and bread and milk.

TO DFH   AIN KARIM
20 JANUARY [1936]

I am again ashamed about writing. I have been back in
Jerusalem five days and have put off writing until now. I
meant to write a short letter as soon as I arrived, to say I had
arrived safe, and found half-a-dozen beautiful letters from
you both – to make up for the dearth during the last month. I
wish I had, I put it off until Sunday, yesterday, instead. Then
though I had the whole of yesterday free I didn't sit down to
writing to you. I put it off till after supper and read the *Seven
Pillars of Wisdom* instead. You know how one does: not that I
enjoy reading the 7 Pillars more than writing to you – I don't
– but that it is less effort almost always to pick up a book and
read than to pick up a sheet of paper and write.

Then the Hubbards came to supper – I had asked them to
come – they stayed till nearly 12, Frances Hubbard and I
having a barren talk about Communism, spoilt by my
ignorance and dogmatism and her pig-headedness. It is a
horrible wasted empty feeling to have tried and failed to bully
someone into believing something that he won't believe. It is
a real mental bust arguing don't you think? I thought I had
got better about it. With Prudence and Teddy there were no
arguments, thank Heaven. It is a very true truism that one
always argues from weakness about subjects that one doesn't
completely (or at all) understand.

Not much news worth telling, I think. I left Teddy and
Prudence together in that racy-sounding hotel the Hôtel de
Paris in Cairo. I don't expect they'll be here for another week.
They enjoy one another's company a great deal – I enjoy
theirs and wish I was back there with them. Horrid to return
to Jerusalem after so good a journey. I miss them both very
much, especially since Katy Antonius is in Egypt and not
here. Harrison has given me the Webbs' book on Russia
which I want very much to read – and have begun to read.
That is the pleasantest thing that has happened today. It has
been what in England one would call a raw day – that is to say
one's hands turn pink and cold when one goes out. It has
rained a good bit too. A good joke in the bus coming home:
one Arab, rather drunk, was talking about how bad he
thought it for Moslem women to follow European fashions in

clothes and shouted, waving his arms, 'God and the prophet Mohammed commanded that women shouldn't go about uncovered.' Then the bus driver, a very wise man, said 'Shut up: God and the prophet Mahommed commanded that men shouldn't be drunk on the bus.'

TO ECH   AIN KARIM
23 JANUARY [1936]

I am ashamed of yesterday morning's telephone conversation. I can't manage that bloody instrument. It gives me no feeling of being in contact with you. I shall give up using it from now on. I shall I swear I shall. I have suddinley oranged to be a quite different tipe of Humans nacher from Now On, it is curuous but i have, which if any thing come in my Parth i say Be Cair full it is william P. taplow on the Up Traque. as i am not quite the tipe of clarse you thort i was i am not Quite so easy dornted as you appears to of Thort.[1]

Letters are a better way of communicating I think. I loved yours, written in the Brasserie Restaurant Finish (?fucking-finish).[2] I got it yesterday soon after I'd finished (that word dogs my trackque) talking to you. It was a great comfort to have. The world seems full of rubbish about George V. Even the Arab Nationalist papers join in with the rest in saying what a splendid chap he was, instead of talking about him rationally as the figure-head of the Government that oppresses them. There was a funny remark in an account written in the *Palestine Post* by Weizman, the Zionist leader, of his interview with the King after the Balfour Declaration. They talked about the Russian Revolution and George said to Weizmann, 'I always told Nicholas that he ought to take more interest in his subjects, but he never would take my advice.'

The dawn is just breaking; the sun is on the tops of the hills but not on me yet. This is not to show off how early I get up; in fact I'm afraid I've been too lazy to go to bed. I need your good influences; you nicely say you need mine. I wish you would both come back then. Then I might go to bed at the right time and you might spend less money on shirts and cinemas. But I should think from most points of view Cairo must be a much pleasanter town to be in than Jerusalem. So though I want you to come back I shan't be surprised if you stay. I suppose I might eventually be able to starve you out, like Parliament and Charles the First, by not voting you any supplies, to spend on your mistresses (I'm afraid I have mixed him up with Charles the Second). Give my love to Katy whenever you see her. It is beautiful of you to have bought me a present. I excite myself wondering what it is. I have nothing for you, though I keep meaning to go into the suq to look for a new knife for Prudence. There are a lot of pink almond trees in blossom; in between the grey rocks all the country is green. Flowers are beginning to come out; birds are singing rather more than they did. It feels like spring in Ain Karim; in the office it is bloody cold and the man I work with is twenty times as Spartan as I am; he likes to work with all the doors and windows open, though in other respects a nice man.

[1]This is 'Taplow language'. *Private Opinions of a British Blue-jacket*, 'edited' by Hamish Maclaren, became a cult book in Gill-Hague-Jones circles and beyond. This was the sort of language in which the supposed diary of William P. Taplow was written.

[2]Hamid Sharari Pasha, Mayor of Maan, informed us over dinner that he had been taught some English by RAF officers from a nearby camp. Would he tell us, we asked him, what he had learned? He obliged: 'Good morning, how are you, Happy Christmas, hubble-bubble, fucking fool, finish!' with a fine dismissive clap of the hands.

TO ECH   [HAIFA][1]
19 APRIL [1936]

I had lunch with the wife of the Acting District Commissioner. She said: 'Of course it makes it much more interesting living in this country if one knows Arabic. It's such fun to listen to the conversation of the Arabs one meets in the street, and would you believe it, 99% of the time they are talking about money – just money. They hardly know how to talk of anything else. Mustn't it be dull?'

Now, would you believe it? it's awfully funny ·
How natives have nothing to talk of but *money*.
Such materialists are they they don't give a cuss
For the world of the *spirit* which fascinates us.

Do come soon – you and Prudence.

¹T had at last, but much too late, achieved his aim of being posted to a district, but it simply meant that he exchanged one office for another and lost the refuge of his Ain Karim house.

TO RHH   DISTRICT COMMISSIONER'S OFFICE
23 APRIL [1936]   HAIFA

You will have read in the papers of these accursed riots. For the present it seems as if the killing of Jews by Arabs and of Arabs by police has left off, which is a comfort, and the unrest has taken the form of what looks as if it may become a prolonged general strike among Arabs. That is a better way of putting pressure on the Government, I think, though it is bound to involve a lot of suffering for the workers and shopkeepers who strike. At present the strike is not complete. Most of the Arab shops all over the country are shut, except foodshops, restaurants and cafés. The port is working here, but at Jaffa I think work has stopped. The railways are still working, but there isn't much road communication between the large towns – Jewish cars and lorries move mostly under convoy.

The idea of the Arabs organizing the strike is that it should follow the lines of the recent one in Damascus, which lasted 7 weeks and succeeded in getting all the Syrian demands granted. The attacks on Jews were spontaneous and were, I think, simply the occasion for the Arab leaders to put into effect their plan of organized opposition to the Government – when people's feelings were suitable for it. The work of receiving, dictating, writing down and passing on telephone reports about what is happening is very unpleasant – these bare police accounts written in hackneyed terms don't give me any idea of what is really happening, and I am too tired and lazy to try to find people in the town to tell me what is happening at night when my work is finished.

I'm writing in the beautiful garden of this German Hospice, beds full of pale purple scabiouses and snapdragons and marigolds, all planted very thickly. I had a good refreshing after-dinner nap. It's very hot and enervating now – a Sirocco, I think: the temperature is 85 and the air is oppressive.

I met here 2 days ago a nice man called D'Avigdor Goldsmit[1] who'd been at Balliol with me – a friend of Derek's, like me converted by him to Socialism but more recently. Otherwise since Sunday I've been in the office most of the time. I've sent my resignation and letter to HE in at last.

[1](Sir) Henry D'Avigdor-Goldsmit was after the war to become a Conservative MP and Minister for Housing.

TO ECH   DISTRICT COMMISSIONER'S OFFICE
[MAY 1936]   NORTHERN DISTRICT
                                            HAIFA
                                       TUESDAY

I sent off my resignation this morning. Glad to have it off my chest especially with these bloody riots on. I wish I was out of this hypocritical business – police and troops and meaningless reports about crowds and excitement and demonstrations – talk and telephoning – people hanging about and being kept waiting about for no reason. It gives me a pain in the head. As far as I can see the troubles are likely to go on for some time and to get worse rather than better. They have called a general strike here tomorrow for an indefinite period. The same thing I gather is happening in Nablus and probably will happen in most towns. As Sir Arthur Wauchope remarked in a telegram yesterday to Mr J.H. Thomas,[1] 'the situation appears to be developing along the lines of the recent situation in Syria' – that is to say an organized strike to be continued until the Arab demands for:

(1) stopping Jewish immigration
(2) stopping sale of land to Jews
(3) responsible government

are granted, or the Government can repress them.

A strike, I suppose, is always likely to produce demonstrations, dispersions of crowds, baton charges, etc. But I hope they'll concentrate on the struggle against the Government and not kill any more Jews. This may mean that you'll be stuck at Ain Karim and I here for God knows how long. The Syrian strike went on for 7 weeks. You could probably get through tomorrow if you thought it worth while – but that would mean leaving Prudence: no point in bringing her here now, I think, even if she wanted to come. Much worse to be stuck in Haifa than in Ain Karim (very nice to be stuck in Ain Karim). If things go on as they are now I shouldn't be able to see either her or you much ... At present you could get through by train but not by road. But the railway workers may strike with the rest tomorrow. In that case I don't know how you'd come. Consult Furness who must be as well informed as anybody. Telephone again some time.

I am in the middle of eating two enormous very good cheese sandwiches – wearing your tie, Prudence's blue braces, my mother's green shirt and my father's grey suit – in a pleasant Jew café in the middle of the town. I am fair fed up with this sickening so-call whitemans burdin. A sergeant gave me some beer in the office last night. A girl has just gone past with her hair done in 8 long tight ringlets – very fetching. I am still hungry – I shall buy some chocolate. I do not cease to miss you both.

[1]Colonial Secretary.

TO ECH[1]
19 MAY [1936]

HOUSE OF BUTRUS THE POTTER, ALONG THE BEACH AN HOUR'S RIDE ON A FAST HORSE SOUTH OF THE SEAPORT OF HAIFA IN THE KINGDOM OF JERUSALEM.

The truth is that what little will I ever had has become petrified in the last week or two. Living with Prudence as you know is rather like drifting down a beautiful reach of the river in a punt on a hot summer's afternoon. One is little inclined to exert oneself. Not that I mean to call her responsible for my not having exerted myself. That has mainly been due to my own demoralization arising out of contempt for my impotence to do anything about these repressions or even to know much about them or about the effect that the strike is having on people. Just being a wheel, well I can't avoid saying it, a cog, in the repressive machine – spending as little of the day in the office as possible and as much of it as possible at home with Prudence. For a few days I thought I had better go away now to an Arab village, I thought of Athlit, without waiting for my 2 months to expire – follow the policy of Hitler and Mussolini of the *fait accompli*. Until Sunday I gradually became more bothered about this and rather hysterical and very much wished that you were here to give me your advice. Prudence's advice was of course to go if I wanted to go. In the end, on Sunday, I decided that 2 months wasn't worth making so much fuss about, and annoying people who had treated me well like our father and HE and that going away now would probably turn out to be simply a dramatic attempt of my feeble will to exert itself and wouldn't produce any particular advantages.

Prudence's passion now is to go to the Jebel Ansariya in Syria, having found from reading *Tancred* that Astarte is worshipped there. I am tempted to go with her but don't see how I could. I hope there is no risk in her going back to Ain Karim alone – if she does go. Jerusalem seems to be full of horrible promiscuous shooting now. You read in the papers probably that that nice Austrian engineer from the Austrian Hospice who used to be silent and morose all day but tipsy and conversational and jolly at nights was shot dead in the street at 8 in the morning, wearing a tarbouche – thought to be Jewish reprisals for the three Jews shot in the cinema a day or two before. Such useless killing – which seems always to get the most harmless and innocent people. If only they aimed at a District Commissioner or two.[2] Indiscriminate killing can't do them any good, whereas I suppose discriminate might.

I had a horrible dream last night about Arab terrorists who went round the streets splitting Britishers down the skulls with axes like what's his name in *Crime and Punishment*. As they struck they shouted *audha b'illah min ash-shaitan ar-rajim* – the *shaitan* being the particular Britisher whom they were splitting. The last man they had done in was a very nice gentle Social-Democrat – a sort of Warden Adams[3] – I had a *tête-à-tête* supper with his widow. I knew it was going to be my turn next. It was not the idea of being killed but the idea of being killed with an axe that terrified me. As a result partly of this too exciting dream I am more than usually inert and sleepy this morning.

The strike seems to be going on with determination. The villagers, who are losing badly by not selling their produce in the towns (I'm told Tireh – the big village south of Carmel – is losing LP100 a day), seem to be determined not to give in. As far as one can see the movement is out of the hands of the leaders and in the hands of the people: that may be too much of a generalization and my only evidence is hearsay. So far the Government seems not to have made any effort to force people to pay taxes or to seize their property for non-payment. The Jews are dissatisfied with what they consider the Government's insufficiently repressive measures – although there are now over 800 Arabs under arrest, hundreds of shot-guns supplied to Jewish settlements, collective punishments applied to a number of tribes and villages. Telephone wire cutting and attempts to blow up the line are the commonest forms which spontaneous opposition to the Government takes at present: but all these isolated acts I think only annoy the Government and don't have any effect on its will.

I have much more to say to you but had better get this letter off now. El hamdulillah – I have been brought tea and 3 ginger biscuits by the prettiest stenographer. I feel revived. Did Prudence tell you about our wanderings in the desert of Haifa before we reached the promised land of Khayat beach – how, after leaving the Carmel German Hospice, she slept successive nights in Hubbard's bed, the Windsor Hotel, and the District Commissioner's office. I began to write you a letter from there at 6 in the morning while Prudence slept between two green baize tablecloths torn off the tables of Bailey and Pirie-Gordon, but like a fool lost it.

[1] By now on his way back to England by boat.

[2] They did, two years later killing the man T had called 'the best administrator in the country' (see p.121).

[3] W.G.S. Adams. Warden of All Souls 1933–45.

TO RHH AND DFH   DISTRICT COMMISSIONER'S OFFICE
28 MAY [1936]   HAIFA

I feel a pig and more than a pig for not having written to you for 10 days, and the letter which I wrote to you 10 days ago was only an apology for a letter, with a promise of another letter soon. The reason for my not having written has been that I have been trying all this time to decide whether I ought to leave the Government straight away, in view of the manner in which it was dealing with the disturbances, or whether I ought to stick to my undertaking and stay in the Government until I was replaced. When I wrote that last letter I was in the middle of trying to decide. I then decided that things were not yet bad enough – the Government repressions were not severe enough – for me to be justified in going. Last week however various new things happened – new repressive measures on the part of the Government which made me decide that I was justified in going. That was on Sunday. So I wrote letters to the Chief Secretary, HE and Max Nurock asking to be allowed to resign at once, and explaining why. I mean to enclose a copy of my letter to the Chief Secretary which puts my reasons as plainly as I can put them.

I hope that you won't dislike what I have done. I don't see that my staying on here would be to anyone's advantage. I think it is clear that the strike and disturbances will go on for some time longer. While they are on, the ordinary work of administration is reduced almost to nothing – it takes up not more than an hour a day of my time. The rest of the work is War Office work. It will not be difficult for Bailey[1] to get hold of a man to do that instead of me since the work of many Government departments is held up owing to the strike. Indeed he has already got hold, or is about to get hold, of a man called Sulman,[2] a Land Settlement Officer, to do my work. But in any case I don't think it would be possible to go on working for the Government now, even if I were much more necessary than I am. But you I expect will look at the thing partly from HE's point of view, and therefore will be reassured, I hope, by knowing that the Government will be no worse off by my going than by my staying – and I will certainly be better off.

It will be a great relief to be out of the mockery of having to pretend that I want the Government to win and the Arabs to be beaten, which runs through all my work. I saw Bailey yesterday – told him that I wanted to go now – and gave him my letter to the Chief Secretary. He sent it on with a note saying that he had no objection to my going. So I hope they will release me in a day or two. Bailey was kind – I don't like him as a man but I find it impossible to resist kindness. Instead of the argument which I thought we might have he edged us off on to what he considered common ground, and talked about what a pity it was that the Arabs had such bad leaders. I'm grateful to him for not putting any obstacle in the way of my going and for having avoided giving me executive work to do in these disturbances.

I don't want to come back to England for 2 or 3 months at any rate – apart from the happiness of seeing you and a few others. I have rather an Albionphobia, which I read yesterday that Byron also had – Prudence also has it – a dread of going back to England – Lawrence had it too of course. I expect it's common. But I think also that I may be able to do some good by staying on in Syria for a bit, write something about these disturbances and try and get some newspaper to publish it, through Derek or Sigle, to counteract the Zionist propaganda which floods all the press – and perhaps see enough of Syria to write something about that too. I shall go first to Baldwin if he's there, then with his help find, if possible, a village to settle down in for a bit, as I had previously planned to do in Palestine. I expect I shall be back towards the end of the summer.

Palestine is no good for her [Prudence] to live in with this struggle going on which limits all one's movements and in which one can take no part – though it's unpleasant to feel that one is running away from it while it is suffering – though one's presence can do no good. Like having an ill person whom one can do nothing for.

[1] M. Bailey OBE. Assistant District Commissioner.
[2] A Druse from Kfar Seif near Acre.

PP TO ECH   SPINNIES BREAKFAST BAR
11 MAY [1936]   7.15

Katie would be shocked & you I think would not be entirely approving if you had seen us this night: I disguised as a billiard table, sleeping between 2 layers of green baize on the floor of Thomas' office. Your parents would have had rather a fit – although Thomas, Lysander-like, lay far off in the passage. And Pirie-Gordon if he had arrived 5 minutes sooner or we had left 5 minutes later, would have felt that all he had come to regard as the Decencies of Life had been thrown to the winds! Even so I got caught in the lavatory – thousands of chaps suddenly arrived, all of them suffering presumably from dioreah, and posted themselves outside the door. I stamped with a masculine stamp. Strange to say we eventually got out unobserved. I had meant to sleep in the district C's own office in sympathy with Civil Disobedience. But it stank.

Thomas has gone back to the office where he can sleep legitimately. I think of you with envy, having the run of *all* those first class soffas [in the boat back to England].

PP TO ECH   [BEIT BUTRUS]
12 MAY [1936]

It seems miraculous that we should be here in this pottery – properly installed and subsisting entirely on buns within a stone's throw of the sea. You cannot conceive how excited I am. I shall make pots & live here for ever. It costs £1 each a month. We have two excellent stone-floored rooms – one with a balcony. There are 6 puppies & two little girls, Bugger I have dropped my cigarette down my neck & it has burnt a couple of holes in my nise chest. It is sickening that these nice things didn't happen before you went away. I don't see how you could have resisted this nice place & this sea.

Wednesday I've just had lunch with Butrus & Sitt Dora to whom the house belongs. We sat upon the ground & eat in the usual way with greece running up to your elbows. Dora is beautiful – large, opulent, handsome & sensual. She roles about invitingly after a meal. She also plucks her eyebrows & has plucked mine, in spite of my protests, to a thin surprised arch. She has a spotted dress but no draws, red-frilled or otherwise.

I found a dead stork just at the edge of the sea. It was beautiful with its legs stretched out straight behind it & its neck curved pathetically back over its body. I wonder why it died just like that at the edge of the sea? And I saw *13 tanks* slinking up the road in single file – a new kind, they looked like mangy animals, like hyenas – very horrid. And an airoplane flying so low it nearly hit me on the head. I wonder what it is all about? Thomas is allmost decided to run away from the office instead of waiting another two months. I encourage him in this. He looks iller & iller every day. He thinks he will go to some village where they will never think of looking for him. I hope he will. Haiffer is of the *devil* & what is the point of keeping this contract anyway?

PP TO ECH   [JERUSALEM]
1 JUNE [1936]

It is a lot later than I meant it to be – but you don't get any peace these days – everything seems getting worse & people fiercer. I do not blame them. It is really horrible to see the tired, *satisfied* faces of Pirie Gordon & Co after they've beaten up some unfortunate village with the help of 2 or 3 platoons.

I went once too often to the well & got peppered by a shotgun – I really couldn't believe the man was shooting at me! He was an awfully bad shot.

Well as a result of the 'General Unrest' I've come to Cuds[1] & to get my luggage – there seems no hope of getting started on the Black Watch [an inscription she had been commissioned to do by Wauchope] so I shall go to Syria. It is nasty here, there is a curfeu at 7.0.

I've been staying with Peake[2] for 3 days. All the schoolboys in Es Salt rebelled and beat up some police (!) & openly dified the Emir & said they wouldn't be good. So everybody thought there was going to be a riot and they wouldn't let me out of the house. I saw the Mayor of Ma'an sitting in a caffé as I drove past in Glubb's car we shrieked at each other & waved & I was soundly ticked off & not allowed to get out & have a coffee with him. So now I've come back.

I'm in the Fast & the curfeu has rung & it's bloody ruin to stay here (I forgot to say I touched Peake for £25!) even so, it's ruin & I don't like these pale grey journalists like disembodied spirits in horn rimmed glasses.

P.S. I hear that Thomas & I have been denounced in Haifa for identifying ourselves with the felahin! I don't know what this means. I've no idea what address to give you, don't think I shall be at Ain K for long and I don't know where I shall go in Syria. I should think c/o Thomas would be safest and I'll keep in touch with him. I do wish he'd leave that sod of an office – he looks so ill.

Emile[3] tells me he has heard from a Jewish typist in the office at Haifa, whom he knows, that Thomas is known among the typists as 'Sweetness', isn't that nice?

[1]El-Quds. The Arabic name (the holy place) for Jerusalem.
[2]Colonel F.G. Peake, Peake Pasha, raised the Arab Legion, the Jordanian army, in 1923, and commanded it till April 1939, when he was succeeded by Glubb Pasha.
[3]Emile Marmorstein. St Paul's School and St John's College, Cambridge. Orthodox and strongly anti-Zionist Jew. Author of *Heaven at Bay: The Jewish Kulturkampf in the Holy Land* and many scholarly articles.

TO ECH   HOUSE OF BUTRUS [ATHLIT]
1 JUNE [1936]

Just back from Khayat beach refreshed by a talk, a cup of coffee and 2 cigarettes with a very sensible man – that is to say he thinks the same as I do on all the subjects which we talked about – that Russia was probably the happiest country to live in, that Zionism gives us a pain in the neck, that the arrogance of most Englishmen in their colonies was unbearable – like a deep draught of beer to a thirsty man our conversation was. He is a Viennese Jew, the manager of Khayat beach – the café part of it. You probably know him – used to be head waiter at the German Restaurant. If there were only more chaps like him.

Then I walked back along the beach – planning to write this short letter to you. The moon is the shape of a pear drop, and reflected in the wet sand where the sea has just been looks like the shine on a very highly polished mahogany table. I feel lonely without Prudence. Back I hope on Wednesday when Katy also comes here on her way to Jugo-Slavia. George I saw today on his way back to Jerusalem from Stamboul. It was a relief to talk to him – tell him how bloody things were here and how I had now got out of the

Government and ask his advice about what to do next. My present chief cause of uncertainty is that I want if possible to stay on for a few days to visit some of these villages where the military have been let loose. I've given up any idea of staying on in a village for any length of time here, partly out of sense of duty to HE and principally because I gather from George that I should be bound to be detected and reported by some Government spy in whatever village I went to, which would mean little prospect of ever being allowed to come back or even of going to Syria. Syria and Palestine apparently have an arrangement to swop lists of undesirables. Partly also because I want to get one or two articles finished and sent off as soon as possible. The ignorant and distorted stuff one reads makes one sick.

How are you dear Teddy? I miss you very much. Like Adam living alone doesn't suit me. Tomorrow or the next day will I imagine be my last day in the office. It will be pleasant to serve Stephano for a bit instead of Prospero. Hey day, freedom; hey day freedom. Ban ban Ca-Caliban. Get a new master, have a new man.

You would have enjoyed supper here tonight, eaten just after sunset on the roof. Snails – which they ate (Sitt Dora and her beautiful daughters, Habub and Haiyat) at a terrific rate. I was given hard boiled eggs as they know I am no snail-eater. I told them my brother enjoyed snails.

PP TO ECH   AIN KARIM
3 JUNE [1936]

The few men of the village who can read, hold rival circles in the caffés – reading out the newspapers – since the strike the village seems so tremendously full of people I never saw before. Mahomed Shit has joined the CID – Mahomed shit. Nothing happens during the day which makes the nights & the shooting seem nightmairish & unreal. Late at night there seem always to be shootings usually far away on the hills and sometimes near. You see tanks creeping about up on Miss Cari's new road – I hate this most.

I hear 70 out of 80 Arab Police in the Jerusalem district have resigned and on the 14 June all Arab police all over the country will strike. 6 of the northern municipalities have struck and all Arab officials gov. officers etc are reported to be going to resign. 3 more battalions have arrived from Egypt & Martial Law according to Emile is imminent. What makes me almost angrier than anything is the attitude of these socalled Jew socialists who talk like reactionaries of the time of the Indian Mutiny. After all *who* introduced strikes as a political weapon into this country I would be obliged to know?

There's some shooting going on outside, and I think if you will excuse me, I will go to bed & get under the bed clothes.

PP TO ECH   BEIT BUTRUS
6? 7? 8? JUNE [1936]   MONDAY

This is ... secondly to cover Thomas's article which he asked me to send you. I have corrected the spelling mistakes! I like 'Hooligan Allenby & Bandit Lawrence' *very* much, in fact I think it's excellent, the whole thing. Thomas is still in Jeneen. I went with him last night & we stayed in Rashaad Shaur's brother's house – it was nice but Rashaad Shaur's brother addresses you as if you were the Albert Hall & a mass meeting at that, & it isn't much fun for *you* because you never get your turn. Still the food was jolly good & the sheets were white & smooth ...

I'm not going to bother you with accounts of what is going on here because I'm sure Thomas has told you – anyway the subject sickens you till your back teeth are awash. It's a bloody WAR alright in so far as the civil chaps make no attempt to control or administer anything any more but leave it to the local Colonel & his Loyals to beat up the village & loot & destroy the houses. Many people are up in the hills, armed, and I gather it will get very hot as soon as the moon light goes – thank Christ she is bright & white & round as a mellon at the moment.

I'm going to Sidon tomorrow or the day after – Thomas is going to Nablus when he gets back from Jeneen & then on to Syria I think ... Did you meet Shaur when you were in Haifa? He's a very sinister young man with a rich care & two riffals – we believe he is the Black Hand of Nablus, itself.

PP TO ECH   HOUSE OF BUTRUS THE POTTER
15 JUNE '38 [1936]

It seems a long time since we heard anything of you. How are
you? Mabsoud? Thomas has gone off to Syria – told to get
out within two days – literally 'seen off' by the Police. Very
nice too – for him I mean. We have all been weeping to see
him go, Dora, Haboob & Haiyat, & then we sat on the floor &
made tea & Dora beat the drum & shook her mountainous
breasts & I washed my shirt & the table cloth & mournfully
swept up Thomas' fleas & shook them out of the window.

The sea is still nice & good to be near even tho' everything
gets daily bloodier. Have you seen the new emergency
regulations? anyway here they are. Yes ma, capital punishment for snipping a tellegraph wire! Who is this intelligent
Galligha[1] who asks questions about the Palestine D's?

[1]Presumably Willie Gallacher, the only Communist MP (see p.184).

PP TO ECH
18 JUNE [1936]

Thomas left me a legacy of Palestine Posts – the whole bunch
since the beginning of the strike – Gawd! they don't half
make a wonderful anthology of nonsense. I hope you admire
our restrained letter to Manchester G. I wanted to have some
blood & thunder & fuck in it but Thomas wouldn't allow it.

I am still very much shadowed & suspected by the police,
curse their religion – it makes me feel like a sneak-thief &
not, as I should have prefered, Matta Hari!

TO DFH   HOTEL PHOENICIA
16 JUNE [1936]   SIDON

I have left Haifa at last – left it yesterday. I have not heard
from you for a week through my own fault – your letters will
have been going to Beirut. I have written to Baldwin asking
him to send them here.

You had said that you were troubled that I might do
something rash or unwise, being wretched on account of

having to work for the Government through these disturbances. I hope you don't consider what I have done rash and
unwise – asking to leave the Government immediately. It
seems to me the most sensible thing to have done in the
circumstances, and George Antonius, who has much clearer
practical judgement than I have, agreed with me. If I hadn't
left then I think that I should have left now with these new
emergency regulations imposing the death penalty for many
offences (shooting at the police or troops or interfering with
Government communications), and giving the High Commissioner power to destroy villages the inhabitants of which
have 'aided or abetted any offence involving violence or
intimidation'. The Government is coming steadily nearer to
making open war on the Arabs: I don't want to have anything
to do with any of the Government's wars – least of all against
the Arabs. I hope that you are not bothering about that. I feel
great relief at being out of the Government. The Government is probably relieved too that I am out of it. But I agree
with what you said in a general way – that your love for me
and mine for you are different in kind, since what I *do* matters
much more deeply to you than what you do matters to me. On
the other hand I can only do the things that I decide to do –
although in deciding what to do I want to think how what I
do will affect you. Obviously my selfishness and lack of
imagination prevent me from thinking nearly enough how
what I do will affect you (or anyone else).

But the thinking how an action of mine will affect you
ought to come before making a decision. If it does, then you
wouldn't want me to change my decision in order to please
you. You wouldn't for instance have wanted me to stay in the
Government to please you, would you? (Damn. I wish we
could talk. It is late at night. My brain is not too clear, and
what I am trying to say keeps forming itself in such an
abstract way that it sounds brutal.)

I'm reading Lawrence's *The Rainbow* now – a beautiful
book. Have you read it? I think you would enjoy it. I am
continuing this letter next day. I have just finished a good
breakfast of bread, olives and coffee, which I was watched
eating by a new acquaintance called Hassan Effendi Zain,
whose brother was, I think, the President of the Lebanese
Republic.[1] He doesn't look at all a president himself – wears

a white wedding waistcoat and European jacket over an Arab skirt. I was sitting in a café beside the sea yesterday evening when I was told that this important chap had asked me to supper – he apparently always likes to ask strangers to supper. He has a very nice house beside the sea – a big room with a beamed ceiling where I had supper: a good supper of salt fish, cucumber, bread and apricots stewed with some aromatic flavouring. He talks very little – didn't even sit and talk to me while I supped. He wanted me to stay the night and had made up a bed for me but I refused – wanting to get back and write this letter. I thought he was cross, but he can hardly be that as he arrived here at half-past seven when I was just up and asked me to supper again tonight. He asked me what I would like for supper and then chose for me a vegetable I hate called Bāmieh. I don't think it exists in England – green, like a bean but bigger. He's not easy to talk to, and would probably have been prepared to stay here till supper time, but kindly went when I said I had work to do.

I like this town. There are fine remains of a Crusader fort on an island across about a hundred yards of sea, and I believe nice mosques though I haven't seen any yet. I visited yesterday evening a beautiful Turkish cloister, now used as a convent school – a kind reverend mother, who took me round, avoiding the schoolgirls. I wish we had come here together – it must lie about due west of Nabatiyeh – that Shiite village we went through where the horses were dressed up and the boys stripped half naked on the way to Belfort. The hills slope down gradually behind. Opposite I have tried to draw the proprietor, but it is a very bad picture. He really looks rather like William II of Germany as an old man – much more dignified than in my picture.

They are very attentive to me and the beds are very clean. I hope soon to get some writing done. I posted yesterday a very moderate letter to the *Manchester Guardian* about these disturbances – tried to express it in the sort of way that they would have sympathy with. But I fear they won't publish it – too long for one thing; they are too keen on Zionism for another. This room is just above a narrow street: nice street noises come up – people selling things – cabs going past with jingling bells – every now and then a policeman blowing his whistle at the traffic when a bicycle gets off-side.

¹The Zain family were Shias, so related to the Speaker of Parliament, not the President.

TO ECH   [SIDON?]
[? JUNE 1936]

[First page missing]

[. . .] that I have obtained it [refers to material for an article he was writing] is not due to any privileges which I have obtained as a Government servant, but simply to my having talked to the people I've come across, whom I might have had a similar chance of talking to if I'd never been a Government servant. All the same, while I argue this case, I realize that I am being casuistical. I have been, as a Government servant, in an exceptionally good position for talking to people (Arabs I'm thinking of) and hearing about events through them. Still I don't regard this as privileged information. I have been carefully through my article and cut out anything in it that might have had my Government experience as its origin.

As regards my personal obligation to people in the Government – HE and Nurock – I think that that is personal, and that there is nothing in the article personally offensive to them. It is imperialist policy that I am attacking, not its executors. But there again one can't be too cut-and-dried. In attacking imperialist policy one is of course also in a way attacking its executors.

I can see that this article – because of its anti-imperialist point of view more than because of anything it actually says – is likely to be regarded by any friends I have in the Government as a betrayal. After all I have served the Government and taken its money for the last two years. If it were not for this war between the Government and the Arabs it would obviously be better not to write about Palestine at present. But there is this war and all the weapons, guns, soldiers, prisons, concentration camps, press, etc., are in the Government's hands, and are being, I think, brutally used. That makes it seem necessary to use the small weapon that I can use on the side of the Arabs – who seem to me to have clearly right on their side in this struggle, which is why I am going to go ahead with the publication of this article.

Sigle asked me if I wanted the article to be published under my name. My instinct was to say Yes since I knew the Government and probably other people who came across it would realize it was mine. Therefore since there would be no advantage in dishonesty it would be better to be honest. But thinking it over I thought our parents would rather it was anonymous since it would then attract less attention, especially among those of our relatives who enjoy pouncing on shocking things we do and annoying our parents about them. So I have asked Sigle to let it appear without my name and with the note: 'The author of this article has lived in/been closely acquainted with Palestine for the last/some three years.' I hope she will be able to manage that.

There is a strong and unpleasant feeling of hostility in this town. Wherever I go I hear shouts or whispers of 'Yahoudi'. Boys follow me carrying sticks: so far they haven't used them. Even when one gets talking to people and they are friendly, there is an undercurrent of hostility. The strike in Palestine has meant a lot of loss here, and it's a poor town anyway. That is the main reason for the hostility I think. Trade between the Lebanon and Palestine seems to have stopped altogether. Sailors who would normally be working shipping melons from Palestine and taking them on to Beirut are out of work. The same with motor drivers who would normally be taking vegetables into Palestine. They (the people of Sidon) have orders from the Strike Committee in Palestine not to let through any lorries carrying food to Palestine (presumably to Jews). So whenever a lorry comes they stop it, break it, and destroy or take off for themselves whatever it contains. The young men and children do this – the police apparently hardly interfere. They beat up four lorries yesterday, and had a sympathetic strike here and in Tripoli on the same day. Naturally therefore they don't like me, thinking me a Jew.

But however inevitable this hostility is it is bloody. One has a faint idea how bloody it must be for Jews in Palestine. Not that that gives me sympathy for Zionism, but for the victims of Zionism both Jews and Arabs who are forced to grow up in this bloody Nazi sort of atmosphere in which hate and hostility is looked upon as the only praiseworthy attitude. It makes one feel like despairing of politics altogether and relapsing into a sort of Tolstoyan pacifism – which I expect I shall end in relapsing into anyway – conflict is so altogether hateful – these miserable children brought up to go round the streets shouting Yahoudi and singing national songs and breaking up lorries full of food with hatchets.

TO DFH
10 JULY [1936]

C/O BALDWIN
BRITISH CONSULATE
BEIRUT
SATURDAY

It has been very nice to get your letters, and to know that you don't mind as much as I was afraid you would about the article. It is of course propagandist and quite unconstructive, but at the time when I wrote it I felt that the only thing to do was to meet propaganda with propaganda. Now I feel that less – being further from the centre of things one gets cooler. I agree that one ought to be able to answer the questions which ordinary sensible people are likely to ask. I'll try to think about that more. But when I have finished writing the article which I am trying to write now (and which is taking much longer than I had hoped – I had meant to send it off today, but it isn't finished yet), I shall give up writing about Palestine for a bit. It's a bad thing to become a one-subject man. Which is one reason why I am glad that I am coming back from Palestine: it is in some ways so very particular a problem. Possibly I shall understand it better after having been in Europe for a bit. At any rate I shall be glad to be less out of touch with Europe. Teddy says that the gloom of the prospect of war hangs over everyone in England.

Baldwin is very kind. He shows no sign of wanting me to go away. I don't want to go until this article is finished. It is too hot to be a very good place for writing in, but not hot enough to be uncomfortable. His garden is beautiful – full of great sunflowers and frangipanes and those great crimson flowered shrubs that were growing wild in the valley going up from the Jordan to Amman – what are they called? They seem to be being watered all day and are therefore as tall and thick as a jungle.

As for going back to Jerusalem, I don't want to do that now – though eventually I shall have to. But I don't see any reason to think that Palestine will be in any less miserable a state in a month or two's time than now. You can't just repress national rebellion with quantities of troops. But I suppose they may stifle it for a bit.

TO ECH   C/O BALDWIN
12 JULY [1936]   BEIRUT
                                                              SUNDAY

I am sending you the MS of an article about the Palestine debate – I don't know what you think of it. I think it is

    too long
    too discursive
    too propagandist
    based on too little experience (especially about landless
       Arabs and Arab workers).

However it is vigorous in style and has a good many facts in it, and I hope you will be able to find some paper to take it – possibly the *Labour Monthly* again, which Sigle said would like to have something about landless Arabs. Will you see her about it? Perhaps better have it typed first. It is rather messy – a good deal owing to my having usually been sweating when I wrote it and having sweated on to the pages. However Beirut sweat may add to the eventual interest of the MS.

    Baldwin by the way tells me that his Consulate have had instructions from Jerusalem not to give me a visa for Palestine if I apply for one.[1] So I am banished. Banishéd.[2] It is a nuisance. I don't know the reason. But I seemed to be very much under suspicion the last fortnight when I stayed in Palestine after having resigned – and Prudence after I left. She was followed in the streets of Haifa and her room at the pottery was searched every day when she was out by a British detective. She drew scurrilous pictures and stuck them on the wall for him. Apparently it was thought that I hadn't really left the country and by keeping an eye on Prudence they would eventually find me – like watching Flora Macdonald in the hope of catching bonnie Chairlie.

    Don't tell our parents about my banishment. I'm not sure that it doesn't make things easier. It gives me less reason to feel a sense of obligation to HE in what I write. I suppose really a complete breach with HE and my other friends or ex-friends of the Government is inevitable and it is stupid to try to plaster it up. They must all think that I have behaved disgracefully. Possibly Nurock alone is tolerant enough to remain on friendly terms. Anyhow I hope that the High Commissioner will go to Ain Karim and pack my boxes if he won't let me come to Palestine to pack them myself.

[1]Extract from a letter to Thomas by R. de C. Baldwin, Consul-General in Beirut, dated 28 July 1936, containing sensible worldly advice which it was now too late for T to follow:

As to your query about the advisability of committing yourself to statements of opinion known to be distasteful to authority – well, it seems to me to resolve itself into a question of expediency. If one is in the House of Rimmon, one should be prepared to do a certain amount of bowing down, or else to be kicked out. If you are ready to be kicked out, well and good; but if you want to stay a bit longer in the House, for God's sake do a bit of bowing. It seems common sense. We are apt to forget that outside England, France and the Scandinavians and Switzerland there is *no* country till you get to America on the other side of the world where free speech is permitted. I am all against kicking against the pricks unless I have made previous dispositions in the event of the pricks kicking against me.

[2]Cf. *Romeo and Juliet*, Act III, Scene 2:

Tybalt is dead, and Romeo banishéd:
That banishéd, that one word banishéd,
Hath slain ten thousand Tybalts.

TO DFH   ALEPPO
8 AUGUST [1936]

I don't give you an address to write to here as in two or three days I expect I shall be going from here: I am not certain where I shall be after that, but I think I shall try to settle in some Druse village in the Lebanon where it will be cool enough to write.

My boils (which are carbuncles) are much recovered. But they are a great nuisance to dress every day. I suppose it is good for me to be forced to do it – but it is all the same a bore. I ought to be doing it at this moment (it is now 8 in the morning) but have put off the tiresome business in order to write to you. I have very good ointment which opens and heals them quickly – also tablets to purify my blood. As you remember they have a generally enervating effect on one – reduce one's energy. As a result I have been very inactive here. It's hot too which makes one inclined to inactivity. Walking round the suqs with Prudence or visiting mosques with her – going to a café in the evening with this charming nationalist doctor that George Antonius introduced us to, called Keyyali,[1] reading Tourneur's *The Atheist's Tragedy*, dressing my boils, and being compelled to talk to M. Balith the stupid egotistical brother of the owner of this house, who is present at every meal and to whom conversation has to be made in French, about fills the day. I sleep a good deal – at night on the roof, which is very pleasant and cool. There has been a moon these last few nights but it's waning quickly now.

[1]Dr Abdel Rahman Kayyali. Leading Syrian politician and eminent author.

TO DFH
21 AUGUST [1936]

HOTEL D'AMERIQUE
PLACES DES CANONS
BEYROUTH
LEBANON

As for my furniture I had a letter from Sophia two months ago asking if she might keep it as some of hers had got damaged by being stored below and I replied saying yes. I have had another letter from her saying that my other possessions are safe with her. She didn't say that she was embarrassed by them, so I don't suppose she is. However I have now written to Michail asking him to pack for me and put the luggage into the hands of Thos. Cook's.

As you probably gathered from Poston's letter I am not allowed to return to Palestine. I found that out from Baldwin when I got here. I didn't tell you as I thought it would distress you to know it. I gather, also from Poston's letter, that the reason for this was the favourable comments made about my resignation in the Arab Press. It seems to me to be an insufficient reason. I also think that the Government should have told me this before I left Palestine. As it was I left meaning to come back and pack in a month or two. I admit that it would have been the best plan to have gone to

Jerusalem and pack as soon as I resigned. Actually I stayed in Haifa for 10 days, chiefly in order to finish the article I was writing, and didn't foresee that then there would be this ban on my re-entry into Palestine. However it is only to be expected from this military dictatorship. I got a kind letter from Mrs Bowman, forwarded by you from England, who I have asked to see that Michail packs up and to do what she can to find him a job.

I don't think that I could make social work a permanent work, for reasons which I'll try to think out and explain to you when we meet. But, immediately, I think I had better take this few weeks' teaching course in an elementary school which begins on Sept. 14th. I have had another letter from Sir Percy Nunn[1] saying that I can do that without committing myself to going on with the whole year's teaching course. Having made the proposal myself I had better stick to it. While in London I can find out more about teaching and my suitability or unsuitability for it. Don't let the unsettledness of my future worry you. It seems to have these unsettled periods. I expect it will settle down again soon after I come back to England – for a bit at any rate.

[1]Sir Percy Nunn, Professor of Education at the University of London.

Thomas came back to England in September 1936, in poor health and pretty miserable spirits. He was now twenty-six, had tried two professions, archaeology and government service, and failed in both of them. Most of his contemporaries seeemed set on careers which suited them; several were married. He had no prospects and no income. It is not surprising that he should have clung tenaciously to the one absolute he now had in his life – the Communist Party. I have added one or two letters written from this period (he had lodgings for a while in Holford Square, King's Cross, which he liked because Lenin had lived there before him). Getting people like Willie Gallacher and Jamal Husseini to meet each other was not going to change the course of history, but it gave Thomas the feeling that he was doing something useful, as, in a small way, did selling the Daily Worker *on street corners.*

For a short time Thomas taught in a primary school, but was not much good at it. Thanks to Lionel Hale, now literary editor of the News-Chronicle, *he reviewed novels for that paper. He addressed meetings about Palestine and wrote articles, the first of which is given in Appendix II. Two things rescued him from this depressing situation – he returned to Cleator*

Moor in Cumberland to work for the Friends' Unemployment Committee, where he had already been briefly in 1933/4, and in adult education found an occupation which he enjoyed, did extremely well, and which in one form or another was to occupy the rest of his working life. And in December 1937 he married Dorothy Crowfoot.

Thomas never went back to the Middle East, except very briefly, but what he had learned in Palestine about colonialism, the Arabic language, and Islam was to stand him in good stead when, after the war, he became immersed in the history and problems of Africa and, later, of South-east Asia. He died in Greece on 25 March 1982, and was buried in the Peloponnese village of Tolo, near Nauphlia.

TO ECH   [ROCK HALL]
[? NOVEMBER 1936]

Clearly with democracy crashing and the Labour Party allowing it to crash it is the political aspect of a job that is the most important. I'm inclined to be suspicious of applying for this university job as I know what makes me inclined to accept it is that it would give me, from many points of view, immediate personal gratification.

Damn these decisions.

It is beautiful to be here – pheasants running across the grass – brown leaves which Hall [head gardener] sweeps up into a pile – Northumberland voices. All the emotions which I didn't have on getting back to England 2 months ago I have now. Rather melancholy to be in a place so saturated with the past. Rock and Bamburgh are as much England to me as Ain Karim and the Dead Sea are Palestine. I'm glad the Communist Party allows me to be sentimental about England nowadays (see an article in this month's *Labour Monthly*). I wish you were here too and we could go for a walk together.

TO ECH   32 HOLFORD SQUARE
8 OCTOBER [1936]   LONDON WCI

I have indeed shaved my beard[1] and by my capitulation have brought one day nearer the overthrowing of democracy and the establishment of a Tory dictatorship under which the right of free beards, like every other democratic right, will be trampled underfoot. However £50 will I hope go to the Spanish workers as the price of my shame.

This week began in a good proletarian way. I went with Diana Furness to Aldgate and helped to bar Mosley's way – then marched to Shoreditch Town Hall singing the *Internationale* and a good catch, new to me:

> Mosley and Fascism – what are they for?
> Murder and buggery, hunger and war.

Both accurate and inspiring, don't you think. On Monday I talked about Palestine to the Wood Green Branch of the CP, and met a jolly Scotsman who is propaganda agent in London for the Catalan Government. He told me how they'd found an image of Christ with buttocks which swung open and were found to be full of pesetas belonging to the priests.

---

[1] 'T came back to England with a tawny beard. Though small, it so distressed his mother that she promised him £50 if he would shave it off.

TO ECH   48 CLARENDON ROAD
15 JULY 1937   LONDON WI I

I am pretty sleepy having got back at 2 a.m. last night from a meeting of Jewish comrades in Stoke Newington where we drafted a statement on Palestine to submit to the Politbureau (?Harry Pollittbureau) of the CP.

The meeting with Gallacher was fairly satisfactory, I think. Jamal spoke well and was conciliatory.[1] He was clearly surprised and pleased to find, listening to Rennap,[2] that a Jew could be as downright anti-imperialist about Palestine as he was. Also he was impressed with Gallacher's good sense. I think that the meeting had at least the good result of establishing cordial relations between Jamal and the Extreme Left (Jew and Gentile). It also gave Gallacher some material. But what is clearly needed is that the Arab struggle against Partition should have wider support among the left than simply among the CP. Pritt,[3] I hope, is going now to arrange a meeting of the Palestine Committee of the Labour Party, at which Jamal and Rennap will speak. If that comes off it should be useful.

[1]Willie Gallacher, the Communist MP, and Jamal Husseini of the Arab Higher Committee, were far from natural allies, in spite of T's conviction that they ought to be. I recall a dinner at Jamal Husseini's house during which he explained that the Bolshevik Revolution was all the work of Jewry. T had a hard time maintaining that it wasn't, but that if it had been that would have been something Jewry could be proud of.

[2]Ivan Rennap. Member of the Communist Party, author of pamphlets and a book *Anti-Semitism and the Jewish Question*.

[3]D.N. Pritt MP, KC. Fellow-travelling Labour politician and prolific propagandist.

Appendix I

I have been unable to trace a copy of Thomas's letter of resignation, but give the Chief Secretary's letter in answer to it, and his answer to that letter, in which he asks to be allowed to leave the service immediately instead of after a two months' interval, as he had originally agreed.

I also give the two letters sent to him by Wauchope at this time. These seem to me to show a quite extraordinary degree of tolerance. As Thomas said in his Antonius Lecture, 'that he should have written as he did shows better than anything else what a nice man he was'.

TO TLH FROM THE CHIEF SECRETARY[1]

	CHIEF SECRETARY'S OFFICE
25 MAY 1936	JERUSALEM
	PALESTINE

Sir,

I am directed by the High Commissioner to acknowledge the receipt of your letter of the 10th May, with regard to your resignation from the public service in Palestine, and to inform you that His Excellency has noted with satisfaction your statement of willingness to remain in the Service until arrangements for the arrival of your successor have been made.

The High Commissioner has been in telegraphic communication with the Secretary of State as to the appointment of a successor and he has been informed that it is preferred to postpone the selection of a British Cadet Officer until August next, when the field of candidates is larger and likely to yield the best selection.

In order, however, to meet your wish that the termination

of your services should not be avoidably delayed, His Excellency has telegraphed to the Secretary of State requesting that an officer already serving in one of the Oversea Dependencies be appointed to take your place in Palestine.

The result of that request will be made known to you as soon as the Secretary of State's reply is received.

So far as concerns your application for local leave and for permission to spend some time, after leaving the Service, in Palestine or Transjordan, I am to say that the High Commissioner would prefer to defer a decision until normal conditions have been restored in the country in view of the very great pressure of work upon all officers of the District Administration.

[1]J. Harthorn Hall.

TO THE CHIEF SECRETARY
[LATE MAY OR EARLY JUNE 1936]
Confidential

I acknowledge with thanks the receipt of your letter N70/9 of the 25th May 1936, with regard to my resignation from the public service of Palestine.

In my letter of the 10th May I undertook to remain in the public service until arrangements for the arrival of my successor had been made. Since that date, however, the situation in Palestine has changed and I regret that I now find it necessary to go back on my undertaking.

I do not wish to impose on you a statement of my political opinions, which must appear to you to be controversial, but some such statement is necessary as an explanation of my decision not to adhere to my previous undertaking.

In the last two weeks the Arab strike has been intensified. So have the measures which the Government has taken to break the strike and to repress disturbance. The situation appears to have developed into an armed struggle between the Government's police and military forces and the Arabs. In this struggle I am unwilling to take the part which as a Government official I am obliged to take. The struggle is, as I judge, the result of the Government's refusal to grant the three principal demands of the Arabs, which demands I consider reasonable. I am therefore obliged to regard the Government as primarily responsible for these disturbances and have no sympathy with the action which the Government is taking to repress the disturbances, however necessary they may be from the Government's point of view to restore order; from my point of view I do not wish for a restoration of order which is obtained by force of arms and without satisfaction of Arab demands. The greater the degree of force used by the Government the less possible it becomes for me to obey the instructions of the Government. Since, however, I had undertaken to remain in the Government service until my successor was appointed I had no alternative but to remain as long as it was possible to do so. So long as the Government's attitude to the Arabs was mainly defensive I thought it possible to remain, and to do the work which I was told to do, however personally repugnant. Now, however, that the Government, as it appears to me, has taken up the offensive against the Arabs, to participate in the Government's repressive measures (which constitutes by far the greater part of my work) is not only repugnant but impossible. By impossible I mean, I suppose, morally impossible. In speaking of the Government's offensive against the Arabs I am thinking principally of the increasing participation of the military in the Government's repressive activities; of the breaking down of civil liberty (of which the wholesale deportations of political leaders and the forcible prevention of municipal councillors from attending the meeting at Ramallah are instances); and of the punitive raids against villages carried out by police or troops or both. Particular instances of the Government's offensive against which I wish to protest are the expedition of police and military against Zub village in the Acre sub-district and the seizure of its property, and the expedition against Kafr Kanna in the Nazareth sub-district which resulted in the shooting of an Arab girl.

Since the work of the Government consists in participating in the activities which I have described I regret that I am not able to continue to do the work of Government. In these circumstances I consider it preferable, from the Government's point of view as well as my own, to leave the Government immediately rather than to remain in its service, in discharge of a formal obligation, avoiding as far as possible performing the duties which the Government lays upon me. I can see no advantage to be gained by my remaining in Government service and avoiding doing the Government's work while in receipt of the Government's pay.

I am grateful for the consideration which HE has shown in telegraphing to the Secretary of State requesting that an officer already serving in one of the Oversea Dependencies should be appointed to take my place in Palestine, in order to meet my wish that the termination of my services should not be avoidably delayed. But this fact does not seem to me to make it possible to act otherwise than as I have decided. I am sorry for the inconvenience which this decision is likely to entail for HE and for yourself.

I note that the High Commissioner prefers that a decision should be deferred on the question of my application for permission to spend some time, after leaving the Service, in Palestine or Transjordan, until normal conditions have been restored in the country. For the present I propose to stay some time in Syria or the Lebanon. My semi-permanent address will be: c/o R. de C. Baldwin Esq., British Consulate, Beirut.

TO TLH FROM ARTHUR WAUCHOPE   GOVERNMENT HOUSE
27 MAY 1936   JERUSALEM

My dear Thomas,

I gather from Nurock that you are now anxious to resign and leave the service without delay.

In your earlier letter you said you were willing to leave it to Govt. to decide when your resignation should take effect, and I had hoped you would continue your duties till your successor arrived.

I gather now you feel you cannot serve Govt. usefully any longer. You will appreciate the fact that by leaving Govt. when Administrative work is greatly increased by the first duty of all Government in all capitalistic states, namely the maintenance of good order, you embarrass Govt. and throw extra work on your colleagues.

However, if you tell the CS that you feel you can no longer

perform your duties with any real advantage to Govt., I shall accept the fact and your resignation.

I agree with you that differences in political opinion need not interfere with friendship, and I hope very much you and I will meet again when we are both living under happier conditions than either of us are at present.

There is of necessity much sadness for you and for me; but that is unimportant compared to the general affliction throughout the country today; and that again is less important than the suffering and bitterness that I fear will continue tomorrow. I feel I have more chance of lessening this by serving within Government, you feel the opposite. That difference though acute need not end friendship or regard.

I write in haste, but I wanted you to understand my position just as you have made clear to me your position.

29 MAY
PS Your letter to me & CS now arrived. I waited to post mine till they did arrive.

Your request to leave Gov. service will at once be granted.

Let me know if you are coming to Jerusalem before you go if you'd like to meet.

TO TLH FROM ARTHUR WAUCHOPE GOVERNMENT HOUSE
31 MAY 1936 JERUSALEM

My dear Thomas,

In this wicked world it is difficult to live outside the capitalist system.

I do not know if you feel drawn to the Society of Friends – as you know, they have decided to work within the C system.

For the last 6 years I have been interested in their work of assisting people to go back to the land.

The only 2 schemes I know worked on a non-capitalist basis are certain Jew settlements here – the 2 young ones mentioned on p. 4 of enclosed pamphlet. I thought it might interest you. Please return it.

I look back on the months you worked with me here with nothing but pleasure and memory of happy hours. Bless you my dear Thomas – a French woman once said of me Arthur, coeur de chrystal. I do not deserve that. I believe you do.

Appendix II

Thomas's first excursion into political journalism was the article in the Labour Monthly *for July 1936 given here. He must have sent a copy of the article to his successor as Private Secretary to Wauchope, Ralph Poston, on whom had fallen the responsibility for clearing up after Thomas's expulsion, and the letter this evoked is given also. It is further evidence that Thomas was at this time in an angry and irrational mood. Had he ever seriously supposed that in the prevailing conditions he would be allowed to stay in a Palestinian village to observe the impact on it of the 'disturbances'? Did he seriously think that the High Commissioner's Private Secretary would be willing to donate the money raised by the sale of his horse to the Arab strike fund? Did he seriously imagine that any High Commissioner, let alone Wauchope whose character he knew so well, would decide off his own bat to stop Jewish immigration and 'grant the country a reasonable measure of independence'? Or were these just the splenetic reaction of someone facing for the first time the injustices of the world and the impotence of individual efforts to right them?*

THE EVENTS IN PALESTINE

By BRITISH RESIDENT[1]

In most accounts of the Palestine disturbances which I have read in the English press, even in those sections of the press which do not normally blatantly champion imperial interests, the picture drawn has been one of Arab hooligans and bandits, hired with Italian gold (or

---

[1]The writer of this article has lived in and been closely acquainted with Palestine for some years.

German or Russian, according to the particular political point of view), instigated by self-interested Arab politicians ('effendis'), attacking the lives and property of peace-loving Jews, whose only object is to develop the country economically in the interests of the Arabs, while the British Government, anxious only to do the decent thing by both Arab and Jew, tries with a gentle hand (too gentle, that friend of oppressed races, *The Times*, thinks) to restore order.

This picture, if it were true, would be unintelligible: which is a good *a priori* reason for believing that the picture is untrue.

The three main falsehoods which seem to recur in almost every account of these disturbances are: (i) that the disturbances have no political justification; (ii) that they are the result of instigation; (iii) that the Government uses gentle methods to repress them.

I

Articles about the disturbances appearing in the press always leave out their political background altogether; the disturbances are represented as occurring in a political vacuum. What is their real context? The Palestine Arabs, who were induced to desert from the Turks to the British during the last war with promises of freedom, have for the last eighteen years endured an undiluted British autocracy. The whole legislative and executive power in Palestine is concentrated in the hands of a British High Commissioner who carries out the instructions of the British Cabinet. The latter is nominally responsible to the Permanent Mandates Commission of the League of Nations, which exercises a largely fictitious supervision over the administration of the Palestine Mandate. Like other mandated territories, Palestine is for all practical purposes (except from a tariff point of view) a Crown Colony. There is no vestige of self-government, less even than in the most backward African colonies. There is no contesting the fact that all the really responsible posts are held not by the Palestinians themselves (whether Arabs or Jews) but by Englishmen. A legislative council of the normal colonial 'concealed official majority' type was offered by the British and refused by the Arabs in 1922, and again proposed and withdrawn in 1929. A legislative council of similar type was offered by the present High Commissioner in December of last year. This council was to be composed on a community basis and to consist of five official members, eleven nominated unofficial members (three Moslems, four Jews, two Christians and two 'Commercial') and twelve elected members (eight Moslems, three Jews and one Christian): the Christians would presumably be Arab Christians. If the relative weights of the British and Zionist elements and of the Arab element are compared (this would be likely to be the actual line of cleavage over any major political issue), it is clear that the British and pro-British forces (five officials, seven Jews and two 'Commercials') would, with the casting vote of the senior official member, be stronger than the forces representing Arab interests (eleven Moslems and three Arab Christians), even at the most favourable estimate. The council would moreover be rendered finally clawless by the fact that money bills, the annual budget and the twice-yearly labour immigration schedules would be outside its scope, and that the High Commissioner would have emergency powers to pass legislation without the council's consent and to postpone the holding of elections for more than twelve months after the council's dissolution. The effect of the establishment of this council would be that British colonial policy might sometimes be impeded but could never be actually thwarted. The institution of such puppet councils is favoured by the British Government, as they are powerless to harm British interests and at the same time provide a useful safety valve for anti-imperialist feeling. Such a piece of machinery would be useless either to carry on the struggle for ultimate Arab independence or to realize their day-to-day needs.

What the Arabs have got then is British autocracy, and the prospect of its continuance for an indefinite time. What is it that they want? Principally they want what any victim of imperialism wants – to be rid of imperialist control and of a policy directed in imperialist interests. But this desire has become complicated by the fact of Zionism, which, though in reality a British colonizing movement, tends to be seen by the Arabs as a separate act of aggression, separable from British policy generally, for which the Jews and not the British are responsible. Instead of seeing Zionism and British policy as a single enemy, Arabs tend to regard Zionism as their first enemy and British policy as their second; their resistance to both becomes more ineffective in consequence. Some simple-minded Arabs even think, or used to think before these disturbances, that British rule in Palestine would be unobjectionable if it could be purged of Zionism. Up to the present the struggle against Zionism has dominated and obscured the struggle against British rule.

The degrees of importance which the Arabs attach to these two aspects of the same struggle is manifest in the three demands for the satisfaction of which the present strike is being carried on. They are:—

    (i) the immediate stoppage of Jewish immigration;

    (ii) the introduction of legislation to prevent further sales of land by Arabs to Jews;

(iii) the setting up of a responsible national government.

The condition of calling off the strike is the satisfaction of the first of these demands only. The Arabs would then be prepared to negotiate in regard to the other two. The main point of the first two demands is that, unless they are granted, the Arabs will finally lose the power to struggle for the granting of the third. They are never likely to be able to achieve political independence if they are once dominated politically by the Jews. The effect of such domination would be to give the British an irresistible bulwark in Palestine which would be likely to block successfully all efforts of Palestine Arabs to obtain independence. Economically the Arabs are already dominated by the Jews who control the country's industries and share with the British control of its finance. Numerically the Arabs are in danger of becoming dominated: the present strengths of the two communities are roughly 900,000 Arabs to 375,000 Jews: the total Jewish immigration over the last three years (1933–35) has been about 150,000. As regards land, the prospect of Arab domination by Jews is more remote. At present Jews own only about 300,000 acres out of an officially estimated total of rather more than 3,000,000 acres of cultivable land in the country: but the area owned by Jews consists for the most part of plain land and is some of the most fertile in the country. The steady sale of lands is moreover turning a large number of Arab cultivators into proletarians, with the insecurity of livelihood which is bound to be the fate of proletarians under capitalism.

It is not difficult to see that if the Jews, who already control the economic life of Palestine and have a secure footing on the land, once become numerically in a majority they will become politically dominant. Then goodbye to any hopes of an independent Palestine.

It is not Jewish immigration *per se* or the sale of lands to Jews *per se* against which the Arabs are struggling but against immigration and the sale of lands controlled, or left uncontrolled, by the British Government in the interests not of the native population but partly of world Zionism, partly of Great Britain's trade and strategic interests in the Near East, to the frustration of Arab desires for independence.

The cause of the present disturbances is that the Arabs have now reached a point which almost all victims of imperialism are bound to reach sooner or later, when it becomes clear that it is impossible by methods of negotiation and petition to move a step further in the direction of independence, and that more effective measures must be used or the struggle abandoned. No sensible man likes violence. But equally no sensible man can pretend that imperialist governments, blindly pursuing their own interests, will not often give way on questions of colonial policy when violence is used and will not give way when peaceable methods are used. The present disturbances in Palestine are therefore unpleasant but reasonable.

Why it should have been meritorious in Lord Allenby to impose British rule upon Palestine by force in 1918 and wicked of the Arabs to use force now in order to take a step in the direction of getting rid of British rule is a question which only imperialists can answer. Those who now call the Arabs hooligans and bandits should remember the acts of hooligan Allenby and bandit Lawrence.

The following events, occurring shortly before the present disturbances, had influence in causing them to happen at the time at which they actually happened.

(1) After eighteen years of negotiation with the British and Palestine Governments the Arabs were at the end of last year as far as ever from obtaining any control over their own affairs. Instead the tendency had been for British control to become tighter. In November 1935, the titular leaders of the Arabs presented their three demands to the Palestine Government in the form of an ultimatum. It was generally understood that if the reply to these demands was unsatisfactory the Arabs would have recourse to other methods than negotiation. The reply was wholly unsatisfactory as regards the stopping of immigration, largely unsatisfactory as regards the checking of land sales, and instead of a responsible national government the Arabs were offered a castrated legislative council. It was clear that the Government would not budge from this attitude unless something drastic were done to budge it.

(2) Two recent examples, encouraging to the Palestine Arabs, of violence having been apparently effective in securing concessions from a colonial power which peaceful methods had failed to secure were the Cairo riots in December 1935, and the Syrian strike in January and February 1936. In both cases it was possible that the motives of the British or French Governments were simply to get order restored by the appearance of concessions which they were actually not prepared to grant: in that case the victories of the Egyptians and Syrians were apparent only and the struggle would have to start again. But at any rate the Egyptians and Syrians appeared to have gained something (at the date of writing it seems that the Syrians at least have really gained something) by violent methods, while the Palestine Arabs had obviously gained nothing by peaceful methods.

(3) Another event which moved the Arabs in the direction of

violence was the parliamentary debates on the legislative council proposals. They constituted an absolutely convincing piece of evidence of the Zionist strangle-hold on British policy in Palestine, in which the Arabs had always believed. In these debates, which were fully reported in the Arabic press and closely followed by the Arab public, die-hard imperialist and labour pro-Zionists united to condemn any movement in the direction of giving any measure of independence to the irresponsible Arabs. The subsequent offer of an Arab delegation to London was regarded by many as the Government's first step in a planned graceful retreat from its legislative council pledges.

II

As regards the second falsehood, the present strike is not the result of instigation, either by foreign agents or by local agitators. Doubtless Italian agents do subsidize the strike and local agitators do agitate. But they are no more the causes of the present resistance to the Government than a sheet of paper is the cause of what is written on it. The strike is a spontaneous movement which has the support of almost all sections of the Arab people, the natural response to the Government's continued frustration of all peaceful efforts of the Arabs towards independence. Its character is plain from its origin. It started as a movement from below not from above, and it has been kept alive by pressure from below. Attacks by Arabs on Jews (made as an act of counter-reprisals) and the shooting of Arabs by the police in Jaffa on April 19th led to the outbreak of a strike in that town on April 20th. No strike had been planned by the Arab leaders: the shutting of shops was a spontaneous act. Strike action followed in Nablus on the same day and shortly after in other towns. By April 23rd the Arab shops in all the main towns except Tiberias were shut. In each town local strike committees were appointed by the people of the town to organize and maintain the strike and to arrange relief for the strikers. The pressure of these local strike committees, brought to bear on the leaders of the five Arab political parties, compelled them to form a Higher Strike Committee, to co-ordinate the activities of the local committees and to negotiate with the Government. It would be foolish to pretend that the members of the Higher Strike Committee are disinterested angels. Several of them would probably be ready to sell the strike, betray their followers and compromise with the Government if they had the chance: the same is true of many of the local leaders. But they have no chance. They are now being carried on the backs of the exasperated Arab people, who are determined that this struggle shall go on until either the Arabs get satisfaction from the Government or are broken by the Government.

At the beginning only the towns and the villages in the immediate neighbourhood of towns were implicated in the strike: now, a good deal thanks to the repressive action taken by the Government against villages, the villagers throughout the country are solidly behind the strike and behind whatever line of resistance to the Government the towns may decide to take. So far their action has consisted in contributing generously to relief funds for the support of workers and shopkeepers whom the strike has rendered out of work; attacks on Jewish property; and attacks on Government communications. In the hill country of Samaria numbers of villagers have obtained arms and have left their villages for the hills where they carry on what almost amounts to guerilla war against any detachment of British troops that they come across. If it were not that they are now occupied with the harvest the villagers would probably be more active in their resistance to the Government than they are. In a month when the harvest is over, if the strike still continues, it is likely that the villagers will participate more actively.

The present resistance to the Government is not confined to men: women and schoolboys and schoolgirls have initiated demonstrations and presented protests in many of the towns. Most of the boys and girls attending Government schools in the towns have gone on strike and the schools have been closed down in consequence. Village schools have followed their lead. British teachers have written shocked letters to the newspapers deploring the fact that the children whom they have trained to be nice little Anglophiles should now show a cloven hoof. It is such a pity, they say, in the children's own best interests that they should spoil their chances in the forthcoming summer examinations.

The methods by which a subject people can put pressure on a great colonial power with almost unlimited military resources are restricted. The Palestine Arabs have hitherto had no training in these methods and have learned no technique. They are, moreover, naturally a peaceful-minded people. The villagers enjoy talking politics, but it goes against their grain to disturb the normal course of their lives in order to take violent action for a political end. Nothing but the blindly self-interested policy of British imperialism could have driven them to behave as they are now behaving. In spite, however, of their lack of training in methods of resistance and their natural unaggressiveness the Arabs have so far during these disturbances shown imagination and courage. In addition to the general strike, now in its sixty-first day, the Higher Strike Committee, under pressure from the people, has proclaimed civil disobedience. This has so far taken the form of a general refusal to pay the Government both the ordinary urban and rural taxes and the extraordinary fines and punitive exactions which the Government has imposed in the course of these disturbances. The value both of the strike and of civil disobedience is principally their protest value. They have a subsidiary value in that they put pressure on the Government by depriving it of a considerable amount of revenue. Arab Municipal Councils are already on strike, and, far more important, Arab Government officials and Arab police (who naturally resent being required to take part in repressive activities against other Arabs) have been considering joining the strike front. Among sections of both officials and police there is already strong feeling in favour of doing so. What chiefly deters them is: (1) that a strike, to be effective, would have to be unanimous or nearly so; (2) that for them to strike might well involve the permanent loss of their livelihoods; for shopkeepers and most town workers on the other hand the loss is likely to be only temporary; (3) that Government officials as members of the middle class, have a traditional dislike of taking part in strike action.

Should a strike of Arab officials and police actually take place the whole machinery of civil administration would break down and the Government would be paralysed. It would then presumably have no alternative but to yield to Arab demands or to govern the country by a complete, instead of as at present a partial, military dictatorship.

III

Finally there is the lie, possibly the biggest lie of all, that the Government has dealt gently with the disturbances. In the early stages the Government remained, comparatively speaking, on the defensive. When demonstrations took place and refused to disperse they were broken up with baton charges, and in some cases (in the towns of Jerusalem, Haifa, Acre, Nazareth and Jenin at least) with shooting. Several hundred Arabs were arrested for taking part in disturbances, for stone throwing and for picketing shopkeepers who kept their shops open. Savage sentences were inflicted by the courts: seven years for a man in a demonstration who wounded a British constable with a knife (how much lighter would the sentence have been if the constable had been an Arab); three years for throwing stones at the police; boys caught picketing were lashed. Numbers of people (including a large number of Communists) suspected by the police of being likely to be a danger to the peace if left at large, were kept in prison on remand without a trial. In some cases those arrested were beaten illegally. Heavy collective fines were imposed upon Arab villages and tribes believed to have been responsible for attacks on Jewish or Government property and, when they refused to pay the fines, their goods were seized.

In about the middle of May the High Commissioner decided that the measures so far taken were not severe enough to break Arab resistance. A Government offensive was therefore launched of which the two principal lines of action were: (a) the confining (without a trial) of political leaders to specified towns and villages, (b) the carrying out by the military or police or both of punitive raids against villages suspected of acts of damage or arson. The first of these measures hurt the Government more than it hurt the political leaders since the latter usually succeeded in intensifying anti-Government feeling in the towns and villages to which they were deported. The Government, realizing its mistake, has now changed its policy and has started a concentration camp with accommodation for a hundred Arab politicians at a place called Auja el Hafir in the Beersheba desert. A second concentration camp with accommodation for two hundred and fifty, is reported to be in course of construction at Sarafand, near Ramle. District authorities have power to order any person to be confined in a concentration camp, and if he escapes from the camp to be imprisoned, for any period up to one year – in both cases without a trial.

The Government has shown itself at its most brutal in the military raids against villages. These raids are described by the Government as 'searches', since their supposed purpose is to search for arms, which are actually almost never found: any villager who has arms has already left his village and gone into the hills. Although Martial Law has not been declared the troops (which have now been increased by reinforcements from the normal garrison of two battalions to eight battalions, in addition to units of the Air Force and tanks), are allowed a practically free hand in the carrying out of a raid, at which frequently no civil authority is present. In two cases raids have been accompanied by the shooting and killing of innocent people. Others have been beaten. Cupboards are broken open, flour and oil upset, clothes and mattresses slashed and destroyed: money and jewellery has been looted by the soldiers. In the case of one tribe tanks rode over their tents; all their personal property was destroyed, and their animals, on which they chiefly depended for a livelihood, killed. Up to the present not less than thirty of these raids must have been carried out in different parts of the country. Their effect on the villages in which they have taken place and in the neighbouring villages which have heard of them has been to intensify the villagers' hatred of the Government and to strengthen their will to resist.

When it was found that these measures were ineffectual to crush resistance the Government tightened the screw. The most recent measures of repression include certain 'Emergency Regulations': (1) empowering district authorities to force strikers to open their shops; (2) imposing the death penalty for shooting at a policeman or throwing a bomb (if it is done with the intention of assisting armed rebels), or for damaging or interfering with Government communications (if the act is one likely to endanger life), otherwise life imprisonment in both cases; (3) giving the Government power to confiscate and destroy any house 'situated in any town, quarter, village, or other area where the inhabitants have committed, aided or abetted any offence involving violence or intimidation, even though the actual offenders are unknown'. This last measure is so wide in its terms that it almost amounts to giving the Government *carte blanche* to pull down all the Arab villages in Palestine.

All the Arab daily newspapers which are published regularly were recently suspended for a fortnight. At the date of writing only one is allowed to appear and its comments on local events are strictly controlled. Every week fresh inroads are made on civil liberty. Over 1,300 Arabs have been imprisoned in the last two months for offences connected with the disturbances. With the fair excuse that 'order must be restored' the police and military are left free to bully the people almost without restraint. These are the gentle methods of the Palestine Government.

The contrast between England's attitude to Italy's treatment of Abyssinia and her own treatment of the Arabs of Palestine is one frequently pointed out by Arabs, with much justice. At a time when right-minded people in England are expressing their disgust at the successful conclusion of Mussolini's imperialist adventure in Abyssinia, and their contempt for the hypocrisy of Italy's gesture in 'liberating the Abyssinian slaves' they might spare some of these feelings for the events of their own democratic empire. Palestine, like Abyssinia, was conquered in the course of an imperialist war. The act of aggression by which Palestine was brought within the British Empire, like the act of aggression by which Abyssinia was brought within the Italian Empire, was represented as an act of liberation, and for some time the Arabs of Palestine were compelled to observe the day on which Allenby marched into Jerusalem and their country was formally occupied by the British as 'Liberation Day'. The British and Zionists claim that they have brought 'prosperity' to Palestine: the

Italians are going to bring 'prosperity' to Abyssinia.

You cannot have it both ways. Either it is just that Italy should annex Abyssinia by force in order that that country should serve the interests of Italian capital and Italian imperial strategy, and incidentally enjoy better roads and railways and a more efficient system of posts and telegraphs. Or it is unjust that England should have annexed Palestine by force, and should now be holding the Arabs down by force, to serve the interests of British and Zionist capital and British imperial strategy, and incidentally enjoy better roads and railways and a more efficient system of posts and telegraphs. You cannot eat your neighbour's cake and then look shocked when another fellow eats his neighbour's sugar biscuit.

TO TLH FROM RALPH POSTON   GOVERNMENT HOUSE
28 AUGUST [1936]   JERUSALEM

Thank you for your letter. It is good to know that you are still alive, and even more where you are.

I am not going to try to answer all the many points in your letter. Some of them made me very angry when I first read them, but I did not answer at once on purpose and now I have simmered down.

I quite realize your fury at being accused of doing nothing about your personal effects, when after 2 months you had just bestirred yourself. Now all seems to be well. Michail has got your good cheque, and now only seems to need 5/– or something of that sort for hire of donkeys for transport of your furniture, but is genuinely relieved to be rid of the books and clothes. I went out to Ain Karim to see if I could pack the books up properly to prevent their being damaged, but found that Michail had been there the day before, and could do nothing.

I can hardly give the money for your pony to the Strike Fund, and should feel in any case that by doing so *you* would be helping violence, a terrible thought. I shall send a cheque to your present address, or to any other you like to send me.

As for the political points you raise, I am not going to attempt to answer them. I read your article with interest, and yet with a great feeling of disappointment that you, with the brain you have and your knowledge of the situation, could have written quite such a one-sided effusion. Still, I have no doubt that that is the type of article required by the *Labour Monthly*.

In your letter you say of HE 'why doesn't he stop immigration and grant the country a reasonable measure of independence . . . If the CO won't let him do that why does he not resign?' He might have resigned, I or anyone as weak would have done, but it would not have done the country any good. He would have been replaced by a man with no knowledge of the country, who would be bound to obey the CO and almost certainly be subject to the military authorities here. When you accuse HE of harsh measures if you only knew how hard he has put the brake on, and how much he has been censured on all sides for doing so. You, knowing HE, might have guessed this. Then again 'Why this manoeuvre of the Royal Commission?' True, HE and the CO both know all about the Arab grievances, but how about a House of Commons that is well informed by the Jewish side only. Is it not worth getting a report of such weight that Parliament cannot turn it down? What about various proposals that have been turned down by Parliament? What about the Permanent Mandates Commission? How, in the face of Jewish outcry, could regulation of Immigration be changed from absorptive capacity? If you only knew the time HE went through with 'doubting Jim Thomas'. But who am I to defend HE to *you* who knew him better than I ever shall and have expressed an admiration for him that I never have. The thing that hurts me is that knowing the works as you do, you are not using your reason to its full extent to judge fairly. Personally I don't care a — who governs this country.